HENDRIX
ON HENDRIX

HENDRIX
ON HENDRIX

HENDRIX
ON HENDRIX
INTERVIEWS AND ENCOUNTERS
WITH JIMI HENDRIX

EDITED BY STEVEN ROBY

CHICAGO
REVIEW
PRESS

An A Cappella Book

Interior design: Jonathan Hahn

The Library of Congress has cataloged the hardcover edition as follows:
Hendrix on Hendrix : interviews and encounters with Jimi Hendrix / edited by Steven Roby. — 1st ed.
     p. cm.
 Includes index.
 ISBN 978-1-61374-322-5 (hardcover)
 1. Hendrix, Jimi—Interviews. 2. Rock musicians—United States—Interviews.
I. Roby, Steven. II. Title: Interviews and encounters with Jimi Hendrix.

 ML410.H476H55 2012
 787.87'166092—dc23
 [B]

                              2012019680

Printed in the United States of America

For Francine, a love supreme

CONTENTS

PREFACE

This book includes some of the most important Jimi Hendrix interviews that took place from 1966 to 1970—the peak of his career. They are arranged in chronological order by interview date (or the closest approximate date). Together, they represent Hendrix's story in his own words.

As editor, I excluded a few articles during the selection process. Originally I was going to include an interview that was done in 1967 at the club Speakeasy in London, with Eric Clapton chiming in with commentary. On the surface, this collaboration sounded like a historical event, but, after further review, I found it was more conversational. Furthermore, everyone at the table may have had just a bit too much of something. (A short, comical excerpt does appear in the "Quotable Hendrix" section in the back of this book.)

I would have liked to include more of Nancy Carter's interview from June 1969, when Hendrix was in a very philosophical mood. Carter was a student at the University of Southern California who wanted to ask Hendrix imaginative questions for her master's thesis. However Carter later revealed to me that she unintentionally cut off his responses due to her hearing loss. Listeners can hear some of Hendrix's frustrations on the recording.

Sue Cassidy Clark, a contributor to *Rolling Stone*, archived a transcript and audio recording of her late-December 1969 interview with Hendrix. However, I was only able to access Hendrix's responses, which I was told were reorganized and extensively edited, and Clark's questions do not appear on the transcript. Still, I felt Hendrix's answers were significant enough to include in this book.

I also felt it was important to conclude the book with an interview I conducted with the legendary Eric Burdon. Burdon crossed paths with Hendrix in 1965; during this time, Hendrix was playing with Little Richard and trying to make a name for himself. Over the next fours years, Hendrix and Burdon became good friends, and Hendrix's final jam was with Burdon and his band War. Burdon's reflections of their encounters are quite detailed.

Fans who followed Hendrix in various publications of the era witnessed a transformation start to take place in late 1967, when reporters began to ask better questions. Hendrix discussed his musical origins and occasionally revealed heartbreaking stories about his difficult childhood in Seattle.

Many years after Hendrix's death, his US Army personnel records became available and showed that his departure from the military wasn't as courageous as he depicted. During interviews, Hendrix also embellished the list of top performers he played with during his R&B years, which occurred from 1963 to 1966. On one occasion, he played in emcee Gorgeous George's backup band. He was seldom given the spotlight when he did perform with well-known acts.

Another inconsistency in Hendrix's story included his birth date. After Hendrix was "discovered" in 1966 at a tiny Greenwich Village coffeehouse, his managers repackaged his image for the record-buying public (think screaming teens with AM radios) and decided to knock a few years off his age. Teen readers were led to believe he joined the US Army at sixteen and performed for three to four years before going to England.

Hendrix interviews were mostly found in teen magazines, counterculture newspapers, and music publications. They were rarely found in the mainstream weeklies that many families had lying around the house. Europeans were lucky enough to see Hendrix on TV often, and BBC radio would have him on to chat and perform a few songs when his group was in town. In America, the opposite was true. Photographic evidence of only a few US radio interviews exists, but no audio tapes have surfaced. One short interview Hendrix did with DJ Harry Harrison on *The In Sound* quickly morphs into a recruitment pitch for young men to join the army.

Hendrix was more responsive in private interviews than he was during press conferences or occasions when the interviewers didn't push their own agendas. It was always a plus if the reporter was a woman and the interview took place in a hotel room or at his flat.

Interviews

For several interviews, I transcribed the exchange from the original recording and made a new transcription. These include the following:

- Interview by Klas Burling
- Interview by Nancy Carter
- Interview by Dick Cavett
- Interview by Gus Gossert
- Interview by Hans Carl Schmidt
- Interview by Flip Wilson
- United Block Association press conference

Other times I compared the original interview recording with a previous transcription and made corrections. These corrected transcriptions include the following:

- Interview by Chuck Wein and Pat Hartley
- Interview by Meatball Fulton
- Interview by Tony Glover
- Interview by Chris Romberg and Sergeant Keith Roberts
- Interview by Jay Ruby

I've transcribed the interviews as accurately as possible, editing for readability by excluding excessive occurrences of "you know," "uh," and "um." Ellipses in brackets indicate omitted material; ellipses without brackets indicate pauses. Most recorded interviews are presented in their entirety (or as much as survives); the main exception to this are interviews that discuss Hendrix's pre-fame career or his service in the army, which I felt had been covered in previous interviews with only minor variations.

I've presented the complete articles as well, but a few have been edited to eliminate redundant or nonrelevant material. Obvious spelling and punctuation errors have been corrected. Footnotes have been inserted for clarification, and I've corrected some of the previous English translations of European articles.

I edited and organized the transcription of Hendrix's 1968 pretrial examination testimony. In a deposition, responses are typically only a few words; in this case, several questions were asked in order to get a more coherent picture of Hendrix's train of thought. I linked Hendrix's answers to the basic question for flow and clarity. I also did this with his 1969 Canadian court transcriptions.

Some material that didn't make the final edit of this book can be found on my website, www.steveroby.com.

My introduction to Jimi Hendrix came in the spring of 1967. I was just twelve years old when I turned on my breadbox-sized one-speaker FM radio to KMPX, and the DJ announced he had a new record from an American guitar player who had just made it big in England. From that point forward—forty-plus years now—I researched, archived, lectured, and wrote about the guitarist's life, career, and music.

His music first drew me in, but I was even more fascinated hearing him speak on a variety of topics. I hope readers will find this collection of interviews and articles representative of what was on the man's mind and what he had to endure as one of the highest-paid rock acts of the late 1960s. I also hope this book proves to be a valuable reference for many years to come.

—STEVEN ROBY
Paia, Hawaii

ACKNOWLEDGMENTS

The book *Coltrane on Coltrane* was the inspiration for the one you are holding now. I'd like to thank its author, Chris DeVito, and John Coltrane historian Lewis Porter for their guidance on how to construct such an important historical document.

I'm very grateful for my editor, Yuval Taylor, who saw merit in this book from the start. And special thanks to project editor Kelly Wilson for her contributions.

I'd like to thank my fellow Hendrix archivists for their help in locating several key articles for this book: Ad Bastiaanssen, Greg Lapointe, Claus Rasmussen, Kingsley H. Smith, and especially Ken Voss.

Elizabeth Pope and Greg Plunges of the National Archives and Records Administration were extremely helpful in determining not only that Hendrix's 1968 court case was not sealed but that it was in the custody of the National Archives and Records Administration's New York City branch.

Acknowledgment is also due to the many editors of former underground newspapers who, without hesitation, allowed articles to be presented in this collection.

INTRODUCTION

Born in 1942 and raised on radio and records, James Marshall Hendrix left Seattle and joined the army at nineteen to avoid jail time for a second offense of joyriding. The high school dropout with very little musical training was filled with grand aspirations of becoming a famous guitar player. Little did he know that he'd become one of the world's greatest.

Army life was difficult. When commanding officers discovered that the misfit musician spent more time playing guitar than organizing his gear, he was summarily discharged from the service. Free at last, Hendrix pursued his passion for music.

After four years of struggling on America's unforgiving R&B circuit, Hendrix finally made it big—not in his homeland, but in England. The closest he'd come to any type of recognition from the US press was in 1963, when a Nashville newspaper billed him as "Jimmy Hendrix and His Magic Guitar." A second time, three years later, he was billed with bluesman John Hammond Jr. in a small *Village Voice* ad, but readers would've had to know that Hendrix went by the moniker "the Blue Flame."

Chas Chandler, the former Animals bassist who became a record producer and artist manager, lifted Hendrix out of Greenwich Village obscurity and brought him to swinging England. He was betting on the possibility that his wild club act would become a sensation in Europe and hit records would follow. Chandler couldn't have been more accurate.

The Jimi Hendrix Experience (JHE) was formed, and it featured Noel Redding on bass and Mitch Mitchell on drums. The group toured France in October 1966, but their first review had two major errors: "Tommy [sic] Hemdrix [sic], who, after having some trouble with his guitar strap, showed a fine style by juggling and playing his instrument with his teeth."[1]

A week later, English music fans were introduced to the new American guitarist in a *Record Mirror* article. But it too had its share of errors and even included a racist comment:

> Chas Chandler has signed and brought to this country a 20-year-old [sic] Negro called Jim Henrix [sic], who—among other things—plays the guitar with his teeth and is being hailed in some quarters as main contender for the title of "the next big thing."
>
> "He looks like Dylan, he's got all that hair sticking all over the place," Chas told me. "He's colored but he doesn't think like a colored person. He's got a very good idea of what he wants to do. . . . He's better than Eric Clapton," Chas claimed, getting to the main point about Jim. "He played with the Cream at a London college date and played Clapton off the stage. . . . Clapton admitted that Jim was a fantastic guitarist."[2]

Billboard may have been the first US publication to chart Hendrix's UK record positions, but the African American magazine *Jet* was the one to provide details of the guitarist's success in May 1967. "Folks up around Seattle will want to know that their little guitar-playing Jimi Hendrix is now 21 [sic], is living in London, and is at the top of the pop-record polls with his tune 'Hey Joe,' and is cleaning up with European tours."[3]

When Hendrix's American debut happened in June 1967, a crowd of young teens and peace-loving hippies at the Monterey Pop Festival were stunned by his music's deafening volume and his blazing guitar finale. Some of the media's reactions, on the other hand, were downright cruel. This excerpt from a June 1967 *Village Voice* article shows the venom some writers brought particularly well:

> Personally, I find his bejeweled transvestism vulgar, his grinding hips old-fashioned, his singing mediocre, and his guitar runs fancy but fickle. Any-

one who plays a stringed instrument with his teeth needs to know about Plus White, but that particular brand might put Jimi Hendrix out of business in England, since his major asset seems to be his hue. He comes on corrupt and debauched, like a drunk Rolling Stones song. Maybe England needs another mauve decade, but I think the kids here will forsake the big lie of exaggeration, after a short honeymoon.

Jimi's management team scrambled to keep the wave of popularity rolling despite these early dismissals in the US press. After they failed to pair the group with the Monkees on tour, the psychedelic-ballroom circuit proved the best route for the band.

The Experience's singles "Hey Joe" and "Purple Haze" were not as widely accepted as they had been in Europe. However record-buying habits were changing in America, and a market for stereo LPs—both in stores and on FM radio—was emerging. *Are You Experienced* held its ground with the Beatles' *Sgt. Pepper's Lonely Hearts Club Band*, and the Experience finished off 1967 with its second release, *Axis: Bold as Love*.

Then Hendrix failed to disclose a 1965 recording contract that he had signed before coming to England, and in 1968 the stack of legal papers grew along with his popularity. The mistake haunted him for years.

Management pressured Hendrix to record, tour, and interview. Bookings were added all the time to the Experience's grueling 1968 tour schedule. The group would crisscross the United States, often having to backtrack when new gigs were added. Hendrix showed signs of stress and grew bored of playing the same songs night after night.

In between tour dates, the group worked on their third record, *Electric Ladyland*, but tensions were developing within the group. Chandler eventually quit over frustrations with Hendrix's endless studio takes and hangers-on. Hendrix took over LP production, using the opportunity to experiment with jazz and augment his sound with additional musicians.

The Jimi Hendrix Experience's days were numbered. Robb Baker of the *Chicago Tribune* noted in his 1968 concert review, "The freshness and excitement were almost completely gone. Gimmicks looked like gimmicks. The sensualism now seemed crude, and (like many other things in the show) tacked on simply for effect. And, at the end of the show when Hendrix threw his guitar into the amplifiers you could see someone's hands behind the amps, holding them so they wouldn't topple, and (even worse) a shrug in Hendrix's shoulders that seemed to say 'What the hell. I've done this 1,000 times before and every little wimpy guitar player in suburbia has picked up on it by now.'"[4]

To complicate matters further, Hendrix was busted for drug possession when his entourage entered Canada in May 1969. By June, the JHE had called it quits. Hendrix resurfaced in August at the Woodstock festival, backed by a five-man group he called Gypsy Sun and Rainbows. He looked exhausted that summer and openly admitted to talk-show host Dick Cavett that he had experienced a nervous breakdown. Cavett looked awkwardly at his guest. "[You mean] a physical breakdown?" he asked, attempting to correct him. "Have you ever had a nervous breakdown?" Cavett inquired. Hendrix glared back, frowning in agreement, "Yeah, about three since I've been in this group, in this business." Cavett, still in shock, said, "Really?"

Hendrix struggled for creativity after Woodstock. His manager wanted him to reunite the original band, and the record company wanted a new product in 1969. Meanwhile, the FBI opened a file on him and kept close watch as his court date approached in December. After he was acquitted of all drug-related charges, Hendrix returned to his R&B/funk roots and formed the Band of Gypsys with his old army buddy Billy Cox and former Electric Flag drummer Buddy Miles. They rang in the new year at Bill Graham's Fillmore East with a series of four shows.

But this group didn't last long either. According to Miles, manager Michael Jeffery sabotaged the group in an effort to get Hendrix back on the path of successful record sales and concert performances. "We loved what we did, but business got in the way of the band," recalled Miles. "It was racial. . . . [He] made it very humanly understood he did not want three blacks playing together!"[5] The Jimi Hendrix Experience re-formed in April 1970, but Billy Cox replaced Noel Redding at Hendrix's request.

The JHE spent most of the spring and summer in concert halls and at rock festivals. After a brief break in Hawaii, Hendrix returned to New York in August for the opening of his new recording studio, Electric Lady.

To pay for his escalating debts, Hendrix was told he had to keep touring, and he returned to Europe. Over the course of a week, the JHE disbanded after Cox unknowingly drank some LSD-infused punch. He returned home to America to recuperate while Hendrix decided what his next move would be.

Hendrix settled back in London and spent time with Monika Dannemann, a former ice-skating champion he'd met in January 1969 while on tour in Germany. Plans were made to reunite with his mentor, Chas Chandler, and to finish production on a double LP, of which the working title was *First Rays of the New Rising Sun*.

However, on Friday, September 18, 1970, Hendrix died under mysterious circumstances after spending the evening in a flat rented by Dannemann. Ten days later, the coroner ruled that the cause of death was inhalation of vomit due to barbiturate intoxication; no evidence showing an intention to commit suicide was found. Hendrix's body was flown to Seattle, and his funeral was held on October 1, 1970.

1. *Républicain Lorraine*, October 17, 1966.

2. Richard Green, "EX Animal Adventures," *Record Mirror*, October 29, 1966.

3. Charles L. Sanders, "Paris Scratch Pad," *Jet*, May 4, 1967.

4. Robb Baker, "Hendrix: Surfeit of Alienation," *Chicago Tribune*, August 12, 1968.

5. Unpublished interview with Buddy Miles by Experience Music Project, April 20, 2000.

PART I

December 1966 to May 1967

Advertisement for "Hey Joe," the Jimi Hendrix Experience's first single. STEVEN ROBY/STRAIGHT AHEAD ARCHIVES COLLECTION

JIMI HENDRIX'S FIRST-CLASS FLIGHT landed at London's Heathrow Airport at 9:00 AM on September 24, 1966. His Stratocaster guitar in its case, a change of clothes, and acne cream were the only things he brought to conquer England. By the end of the day, he had a jam at the Scotch of St. James club lined up and a new girlfriend in his bed. Anything seemed possible.

Within days, Chas Chandler acquired a work permit and set up auditions for the new group, the Jimi Hendrix Experience. Guitarist Noel Redding, originally hoping to fill in the lead-guitarist position for the New Animals, was hired partly because of his willingness to learn bass—and because Hendrix liked his wild, bushy hair. By early October, the talented Mitch Mitchell was selected as the drummer.

Hendrix's sound quickly gained popularity. "Hey Joe," the debut single, received rave reviews and reached number twelve on the R&B chart and number thirty-eight in the national singles chart by year's end.

Hendrix was encouraged to write his own material, and the resulting album, *Are You Experienced*, became part of the psychedelic soundtrack for most of 1967. The next hurdle was Hendrix's homeland, America.

"MR. PHENOMENON!"

PETER JONES | From RECORD MIRROR, December 10, 1966.

On November 25, 1966, the newly formed Jimi Hendrix Experience held a press reception and concert at the Bag O' Nails Club in London. Hendrix arrived in England only two months prior, but he had already jammed with Cream, toured France and Germany, and recorded his first single, "Hey Joe." Within two days of this reception, he'd celebrate his twenty-fourth birthday.

RECORD MIRROR reporter Peter Jones had the honor of capturing Hendrix in his first interview with the English music press. The JHE played their first UK club date the following day.

Now hear this—and kindly hear it good! Are you one of the fans who think there's nothing much new happening on the pop scene? Right . . . then we want to bring your attention to a new artist, a new star-in-the-making, who we predict is going to whirl round the business like a tornado.

Name: Jimi Hendrix. Occupation: Guitarist-singer-composer–showman–dervish–original. His group, just three-strong: The Jimi Hendrix Experience.

Bill Harry and I dropped in at the Bag O' Nails Club in Kingley Street recently to hear the trio working out for the benefit of Press and bookers. An astonished Harry muttered: "Is that full, big, blasting, swinging sound really being created by only three people?" It was, with the aid of a mountain of amplification equipment.

Jimi was in full flight. Whirling like a demon, swirling his guitar every which way, this 20-year-old [sic] (looking rather like James Brown) was quite amazing. Visually he grabs the eyeballs with his techniques of playing the guitar with his teeth, his elbow, rubbing it across the stage . . . but he also pleasurably hammers the eardrums with his expert playing. An astonishing technique . . . especially considering he started playing only five or six years ago.

Sweatily exhausted, Jimi said afterwards: "I've only been in London three months—but Britain is really groovy. Just been working in Paris and Munich."

In the trio: drummer Mitch Mitchell, a jazz fan, and rock 'n' roll addict Noel Redding on bass. "We don't want to be classed in any category," said Jimi, "If it must have a tag, I'd like it to be called 'Free feeling.' It's a mixture of rock, freak-out, blues, and rave music."

Guiding Jimi's career here (discs have been cut; release information soon) are Chas Chandler, ex-Animal, and Mike Jeffery. Said Chas: "I first heard Jimi play in Greenwich Village, a friend of mine, an English girl,[1] suggested I called to see him. I was knocked out by his technique and his showmanship. He'd only just started singing, though he'd had a lot of experience with top American groups.

"Anyway, I suggested we get together—and he agreed. So we brought him over, auditioned to find the right musicians to follow his style—and gave the three of them the chance to find their feet on the Continent. Now we're waiting on a full work permit. . . .

"He really does play incredibly good guitar. You can watch him seven nights on the trot and he changes individual items each time. You just can't get bored with him. It's the first time I've seen such a brilliant musician who can put on such a good visual performance. He has this unique stage appeal. And this mastery of the instrument.

"We want to stick with just two musicians working with him. Noel and Mitch can follow his every mood—if we got even one more in, it could spoil the under-standing. Make it slower. Now we hope to get Jimi working the R and B clubs, building up a following."

Believe us, Jimi really is something positively new. We think he'll become a sensational success.

About that thing of playing the guitar with his teeth: he says it doesn't worry him. He doesn't feel anything. "But I do have to brush my teeth three times a day!"

---

1. Chas is referring to Linda Keith, then the girlfriend of Keith Richards of the Rolling Stones.

"JIMI HENDRIX TALKS TO STEVE BARKER"

STEVE BARKER | From UNIT, January 1967.

On October 1, 1966, Steve Barker, an eighteen-year-old journalism student, witnessed Jimi Hendrix sit in with Cream at London's Regent Street Polytechnic College. The amazing guitar duel between Hendrix and Clapton was motivation enough for Barker to contact Hendrix's management about scheduling an interview. They agreed, and an appointment was set up at Jimi's flat on Montague Square for early January 1967.

By the time the interview took place, the Jimi Hendrix Experience had recorded "Hey Joe" and made their British TV debut on READY, STEADY, GO!, and Hendrix had penned a draft of "Purple Haze."

Even though the interview was not for a major publication, Hendrix was generous with his time and open with his responses—especially about his true feelings for the Monkees.

Late last year the Cream appeared at the Poly, bringing a lost looking young Negro guitarist to appear for the first time in Britain. The guitarist with the medusan hair was Jimi Hendrix, who during the first few months of 1967 established his group, the Experience, in the avant-garde of the pop world.

I spoke to Jimi at his flat, where he apologized for keeping me from lectures by playing his collection of blues records and tracks from his new single and L.P. to be released in late March.

Modesty and thoughtfulness are not qualities normally possessed by a pop star, but then Jimi Hendrix was different.

Steve Barker: What are the main influences in your music?

Jimi Hendrix: Well, I don't have any right now. I used to like Elmore James and early Muddy Waters and stuff like that—Robert Johnson and all those old cats.

SB: Do you feel any heritage from the old bluesmen?

JH: No, 'cause I can't even sing! When I first started playing guitar it was way up in the Northwest, in Seattle, Washington. They don't have too many of the real blues singers up there. When I really learned to play was down South. Then I went into the Army for about nine months, but I found a way to get out of that. When I came out I went down South and all the cats down there were playing blues, and this is when I really began to get interested in the scene.

SB: What's the scene like now on the West Coast?

JH: Well, I haven't been on the West Coast for a long time. But when I was on the East Coast the scene was pretty groovy. I'd just lay around and play for about two dollars a night, and then I'd try and find a place to stay at night after I finished playing. You had to chat somebody up real quick before you had a place to stay.

SB: What do you think the scene is like over there, compared to Britain?

JH: Well, I never had a chance to get on the scene over there, but from what I've seen [in England] it's pretty good. I thought it could be a whole lot of cats who could play it but not really feel it. But I was surprised, especially when I heard Eric Clapton, man. It was ridiculous. I thought, "God!" And every time we get together, that's all we talk about—playing music. I used to like Spencer Davis, but I heard that old Stevie's [Winwood] left them, and I think it's official about two days ago, or it was yesterday.

SB: What about the Beatles and the things they're doing now?

JH: Oh, yes, I think it's good. They're one group that you can't really put down because they're just too much. And it's so embarrassing, man, when America is sending over the Monkees—oh, God, that kills me! I'm so embarrassed that America could be so stupid as to make somebody like that. They could have at least done it with a group that has something to offer. They got groups in the States starving to death trying to get breaks and then these fairies come up.

SB: Did you ever meet Bob Dylan in the States?

JH: I saw him one time, but both of us were stoned out of our minds. I remember it vaguely. It was at this place called The Kettle of Fish in the Village. We were both stoned there, and we just hung around laughing—yeah, we just laughed. People have always got to put him down. I really dig him, though. I like that *Highway 61 Revisited* album and especially "Just Like Tom Thumb's Blues"! He doesn't inspire me actually, because I could never write the kind of words he does. But he's helped me out in trying to write about two or three words 'cause I got a thousand songs that will never be finished. I just lie around and write about two or three words, but now I have a little more confidence in trying to finish one. When I was down in the Village, Dylan was starving down there. I hear he used to have a pad with him all the time to put down what he sees around him. But he doesn't have to be stoned when he writes, although he probably is a cat like that—he just doesn't have to be.

SB: How does the Experience get such fusion when you're basically a bluesman, Noel's a rock man, and Mitch a jazzman?

JH: I don't know! Actually, this is more like a free-style thing. We know what song we're gonna play and what key it's in and the chord sequences, and we just take it from there. And so far it hasn't bugged me in any way like saying, "Oh, no! There he goes playing that rock and roll bass pattern again." Everybody's doing pretty cool.

SB: Are you just experimenting in your music or moving towards an end?

JH: I guess it is experimenting just now. Maybe in about six or seven months, or when our next album comes out, we'll know more what we're doing. All the tracks on our first LP are going to be originals, but we might play Dylan's "Like a Rolling Stone" on it.

SB: What do you think of the auto-destruction and the things The Who are doing?

JH: We don't really break anything onstage—only a few strings. Actually, we do anything we feel like. If we wanted to break something up, we would do it. There's a lot of times in the past I have felt like that, too. But it isn't just for show, and I can't explain the feeling. It's just like you want to let loose and do exactly what you want if your parents weren't watching. I dig The Who. I like a lot of their songs! The Byrds are pretty good, too, though I know you don't dig them over here. They're on a different kick. I like them.

SB: How about free expression in jazz?

JH: I'd have to be in a certain mood if I could sit up and listen to it all day. I like Charles Mingus and this other cat who plays all the horns, Roland Kirk. I like very different jazz, not all this regular stuff. Most of it is blowing blues, and that's why I like freeform jazz—the groovy stuff instead of the old-time hits like they get up there and play "How High Is the Moon" for hours and hours. It gets to be a drag.

SB: How do you feel onstage?

JH: I get a kick out of playing. It's the best part of this whole thing, and recording, too. I wrote a song called "I Don't Live Today," and we got the music together in the studio. It's a freak-out tune. I might as well say that, 'cause everyone else is going to anyway. Do you want to know the real meaning of that? Now, all right, I'll tell you this—don't think anything bad, okay? This is what they used to say in California ages ago: "Guess what—I seen in a car down on Sunset Strip. I seen Gladys with Pete and they were freakin' out." That's what it means—sexual per-verting. Now they get freakin' off and out in all these songs, so it's got nothing at all to do with sex now, I guess. Anyway, that's what it used to mean—perversion, like you might see a beautiful girl and say she's a beautiful "freak," you know. [*Laughs.*] I'm being frank—that's all, so I guess I'll get deported soon.

SB: What about noses?

JH: Well, if you didn't have a nose you'd probably have to breathe out your ears, man. Then you'd have to clean your ears and blow them.

SB: Do you ever read the *International Times*?

JH: Oh, yeah! I think that's kind of groovy. They get almost too wrapped up with something, but it's really nice what they're doing. They have a paper like that in the Village, the *East Village Other*. The Village's Fugs are real crazy; they do things arranged from William Burroughs, songs about lesbians, and things like "Freakin' Out with a Barrel of Tomatoes," squashing them all between your armpits—euughh! You'd never believe it, man—those cats are downright vulgar. They tell these nasty, beautiful poems! The nastiest ones you could think of. Here's one thing I hate, man: When these cats say, "Look at the band—they're playing psychedelic music!" and all they're really doing is flashing lights on them and playing "Johnny B. Goode" with the wrong chords—it's terrible.

SB: What do you think of this psychedelic bit?

JH: There's this cat smashing a car when he might be singing a song about "I love you, baby." Now what does that have to do with it? Now, if he was saying the car is evil and the music is in the background and he's out there reading poetry with his little green and gold robe on that might have some meaning. Singing "Love Is Strange" while smashing an M.G. up is just stupid.[1]

SB: Have you seen Pink Floyd?

JH: I've heard they have beautiful lights but they don't sound like nothing.

SB: How's Donovan and his little scene?

JH: He's nice—kinda sweet! He's a nice little cat in his own groove, all about flowers and people wearing golden underwear. I like Donovan as a person, but nobody is going to listen to this "love" bit. I like Dylan's music better because it's more earthy and live. "Mellow Yellow" is slang in the States for really groovy. "Sunshine Superman" means he can get his girl—anyway, that's my interpretation. I'd like to play some sessions behind Dylan. His group ought to be a little more creative. These days everybody thinks everybody else has to have trips, and people are singing about trips. Like the Byrds when they made "Eight Miles High," it was just about a plane journey, and you do get a good feeling up there. They were even trying to ban "Green, Green Grass of Home"[2] back in the States.

---

1. Hendrix may have been referring to the psychedelic rock band the Move, who sometimes took an axe to a car during their show.
2. Singer Tom Jones covered this song in 1966, and some felt "grass" referenced marijuana.

"JIMI DOESN'T THINK HE'S A BIG NAME YET"

From RECORD MIRROR, February 25, 1967.

February was a busy month in the studio for the JHE as they readied tracks for their debut LP and performed a variety of club dates. An uncredited RECORD MIRROR reporter joined several other journalists at his Montague Square flat on February 15, 1967. Later in the evening, the Experience played the Dorothy Ballroom in Cambridge.

His appearance is striking. Heads turn as he passes. Tall, black military jacket with ornate braid, wild and shocking black hair, Dylan-like. A face hewn with character.

JIMI HENDRIX, guitar virtuoso, is modest. He doesn't regard himself as a big-name artiste yet. "We had one little record and I'm just wondering how people are going to take the next one, because it's so different from 'Hey Joe.' I think everyone will think we've used different instruments on it, but it's still two guitars and drums—at one point the guitar sounds like a flute. I recorded it exactly as we do it on stage. Everything we do on record we can do exactly on stage. If we had a disc with a violin on it, we'd hire a violin player to come on stage for that one number. Our third record will be even different. They'd picked out 'Loving [sic] Confusion' to be our next single, but I had this thing on my mind about walking on the sea. Then I wrote 'Purple Haze.'"

Songwriter Jimi has a fertile imagination that doesn't discount the existence of U.F.O.'s or life beyond death. An imagination weaned on Science-Fiction, poetry and painting.

"At school I used to write poetry a lot. Then I was really happy, like in school. My poems were mostly about flowers and nature and people wearing robes . . . and then I used to paint a picture of, say, a really pretty mountain, then write about four lines of poetry about it. I don't hardly get a chance to paint now. The girl in the office bought me a paint box—but I haven't had a chance to buy paper. I like to paint different things, but I don't like to paint people."

"Up to now I've written about 100 songs, but most of them are in these New York Hotels I got thrown out of. When I go back I'm going to collect them from these hotel rooms where I missed the rent—I'm not ashamed to say that. I can't write no happy songs. 'Fotsy [*sic*] Lady' is about the only happy song I've written. Don't feel very happy when I start writing."

The Jimi Hendrix Experience and Jeff Beck
on the cover of RECORD MIRROR, April 1967.
STEVEN ROBY/STRAIGHT AHEAD ARCHIVES COLLECTION

Jimi's first album will be released next month.[1] "The album will be different and all the songs will be mine except for 'Like a Rolling Stone' and maybe a MUDDY WATERS number. We like to have our own sound. I'm writing a number, 'I Don't Live Today,' it's really weird, man, I hope we can get it ready for the L.P."

The immediate future? "Britain is our station now and we'll stay here probably 'til around the end of June; then we'll see if we can get something going in America and then come back here. We'll be staying here off and on all the time."

---

1. The UK version of *Are You Experienced* was not released until May 1967.

"HENDRIX THE GEN ARTICLE"

KEVIN SWIFT | From BEAT INSTRUMENTAL, March 1, 1967.

Reporter Kevin Swift, from the United Kingdom's BEAT INSTRUMENTAL, was also present at the Montague Square flat when Hendrix gave a series of interviews on February 15. Swift, however, focused his questions on Hendrix's early musical roots and blues influences rather than his songwriting talents.

He was born in Seattle 20 [sic] years ago, he plays superb blues guitar, and what's more, he plays it from the heart, not from other artist's records. He is Jimi Hendrix, a very hot property in more than one sense, and he's come to Britain at just the right time. The scene was already set by the English bluesmen and visiting Americans, now we have the "gen" article, a young American blues star with a style that is born [sic] of deep "feel," hard work, and experience. If you belong to the school that believes you must suffer before you can play blues, this bloke qualifies with no trouble at all. He is a rolling stone in the true sense of the phrase, and his rolling has taken him all over the States.

Starting point, naturally enough, was his home town of Seattle. He learned to play little by little on a guitar, which belonged to one of his father's friends who came to play cards. While the two men played, Jimmy would creep out on to the porch with the friend's guitar and see what he could get out of it. "I didn't know that I would have to put the strings round the other way because I was left-handed, but it just didn't feel right," Jimi told me. "I can remember thinking to myself, 'There's something wrong here.' One night my dad's friend was stoned and he sold me his guitar for five dollars. I changed the strings round but it was way out of tune when I'd finished. I didn't know a thing about tuning so I went down to the store and ran my fingers across the strings on a guitar they had there. After that I was able to tune my own. Then I got tired of the guitar and put it aside. But when I heard Chuck Berry it revived my interest. I learned all the riffs I could. I formed this group with some other guys, but they drowned me out. I didn't know why at first, but after about three months I realized I'd have to get an electric guitar. My first was a Danelectro, which my dad bought for me; must have busted him for a long time.

"Then I went into the Army for a while, and I didn't play much guitar because the only guitars available were right-handed ones. After I came out I just moved around. I went to Clarksville where the group I was with worked for a set-up called W. & W. Man; they paid us so little that we decided that the two W's stood for Wicked and Wrong. Then we got in with a club owner, who seemed to like us a lot. He bought us some new gear. I had a Silvertone amp and the others got Fender Bandmasters. But this guy took our money and he was sort of holding us back: we moved about some more. Eventually I ended up on the big package tours."

I asked Jimi why he thought Chicago had the biggest reputation for blues men. "Most of the guitarists come from the South," he explained. "In Atlanta and Louisiana there are some great guys. There's Albert Collins. Albert King and Al King. You haven't heard of them here, but they are some of the best guitar-ists in the world. Most of the cats born in the South move North. They end up in Chicago because that is a sort of middle city and the competition isn't as fierce there as it is further north." And after hearing all these great guitarists, was Jimi at all influenced? "Well, I don't like to get hung up on any one guitarist," he said, "because I always feel kinda unfaithful when I move on to someone else. I should say that my influences were B. B. King and Elmore James."

One Bag

Many people have asked Jimi why he didn't complete the obvious image by engaging two blues-soaked men as drummer and bassist. Instead he has the extremely talented, but slightly pop-influenced, Noel Redding and Mitch Mitchell. Said Jimi: "If I'd had two blues men with me we would have gone straight into one bag, the blues. That's not for me. This way we can do anything and develop our own music. We might do our own arrangement of a Howlin' Wolf number followed straight away by 'Wild Thing,' or a Bobby Dylan number. We'll do things our own way and make our own sound." Let's hope that "our own sound" is one which the British public will take to and remain with. We can't afford to let this man roll off back to the States.

"JIMI HENDRIX SHOWS HIS TEETH"

JAN WALDROP | From HUMO, March 11, 1967.

The Jimi Hendrix Experience traveled from Paris to Belgium on March 6 to play "Hey Joe" on a TV show called VIBRATO. Their mimed performance was filmed on location in the Zoniënwoud Forest.

The big, quiet Zoniënwoud still rustles in the cold spring wind. A grey, hesitating sun sets the branches alight and an old man, old and warped as the branches of the weathered trees, gathers wood. A frayed cigarette-stump hangs out of his toothless mouth, a fact that is clearly in evidence as the mentioned mouth falls open at the arrival of Jimi Hendrix—"I have never seen anything like that before!" Thousands have said the same when they witnessed the new pop-phenomenon Jimi Hendrix. I had already read this in all the foreign music magazines, but one has to see it [firsthand] before one can endorse it. Short and sweet: it's true.

The "Black Bob Dylan," as some call him, is a curiosity on its own. Jimi has an overwhelming amount of dark hair, which semicarelessly waves around his head. He has a fantastic, almost picturesque, primitive head. His white-as-a-sheet teeth pierce as a battery of ready-to-fire field guns through his wide lips. Between his friendly dog eyes lies a nose like a trampled-down rubber hose. And if he feared in spite of all this he would remain unnoticed, Jimi wears cracking-red trousers and a fantastic military dress coat.

Jimi: This jacket dates from the Crimean War. From a Russian, I believe.

Jan: Any blood stains still?

Jimi: No, I had it cleaned.

In the meantime, producer Pierre Meyers and his camera crew are busy setting up the lights and cameras. An amount of sturdy walkers, many with dogs (every shape, size and colour) gather curiously around Jimi. But he only has attention for a signpost where with large letters it says that it is forbidden to wash your vehicle in the pond. At such preventive measures Jimi gives a chuckle and he spits in De Vijver van de Verdronken Kinderen [the Pond of Drowned Children]. A little further away an old person stirs patiently with a stick in the shallow pond.

"That one doesn't give up hope," ponders Jimi.

Jan: Have you played long?

Jimi: No, not all that long. About six years now.

Jan: How old are you?

Jimi: Twenty-two [*sic*]. I was born in 1945 [*sic*] in Seattle, state of Washington.

Jan: Did you live there all the time?

Jimi: Jesus, no! I couldn't stick it at home. I left school early. School wasn't for me. So according to my dad I thus had to work. So I did that for a couple of weeks . . . for my dad. He had a not-all-that-well-running contracting firm and in me he saw a cheap labourer. I didn't see it that way. I had to carry stones and cement all day and he pocketed the money. At the age of fifteen [*sic*] I ran away after a blazing row with my dad. He hit me on the face and I ran away. Because I didn't have a cent in my pocket, I walked into the first recruiting office I saw and went into the army.

Jan: What did you think of the army?

Jimi: Horrible! A mess. The only thing which I liked was parachute jumping but I wasn't all that good at it. After about half a year I made a terrible drop, broke my ankle and hurt my back. Just on time, because the army was really getting on my nerves.

Jan: Do you dislike a regular life?

Jimi: Enormously. As soon as I've done something a few times or I stayed somewhere a few weeks, I have enough of it! Then I *must* do something else or I walk with my head against the wall in misery.

Jan: What did you do when you left the army?

Jimi: Well, that took a while because I first had to be patched up. After that I went south. While in the army I had started to play guitar seriously and with that I was gonna try and make some money.

Jan: And? Was that successful?

Jimi: Not at all! For years I lived in misery and the biggest mess you could imagine. I slept wherever I could and stole my meals. I played in bars and on the streets and sometimes I made a few dollars. When things would become too boring I would go with some friends and we would beat up a policeman. Within half an hour we would have a smashing row. Sometimes you would end up in jail, but the food would be great, so it wasn't that bad. Most of the police guys were bastards, but there were also some good ones. They didn't hit that hard as some others and you could eat better. But even that got boring. One evening I had a gig in a club—something which happened rarely—and one of the Isley Brothers was in the audience. He asked me if I wanted to play in their backing group and I said "Yeah man, groovy." But it wasn't that groovy. I had to sleep in the clubs where they performed and [they were] full of cockroaches and rats. Those dingy beasts would walk at night on top of you and would eat your last bar of chocolate. Again I started to play on the streets. After a couple of months a complete soul package came to town, with Sam Cooke, Solomon Burke, Jackie Wilson, Hank Ballard, Ben E. King and Chuck Jackson. I got the job in the band and played backing for them. I learned a lot there. Not enough to get a job in the band of Little Richard. I had to do an audition for him in Atlanta and he thought I was OK. With him I went all over America. In Los Angeles I got enough of him and played behind Ike and Tina Turner. But even then I didn't make enough money.

Well, I made enough to buy bread, but not enough to put something between it . . .

Jan: What kind of music do you play nowadays?

Jimi: Blues, man. Blues. For me that's the only music there is. "Hey Joe" is the blues version of a one-hundred-year-old cowboy song. Strictly speaking it isn't such a commercial song and I was amazed the number ended up so high in the charts. Our next single, "Purple Haze," is commercially even worse.

Jan: So why do you release it then?

Jimi: Because we like it ourselves. I care less if the records sell or not. Making music is much more important.

Jan: And money?

Jimi: I don't give a shit about that. As long as I have enough money to eat and I can play what I want, I'm satisfied. I only hope to make enough money so that I can have a house built for my father.

Jan: I thought you had a row with him?

Jimi: Yes, I do. In the seven years I've been away from home I have never seen him. I phoned him once, when I had just arrived in England. I wanted to tell him what I had accomplished.

Jan: And what did he say?

Jimi: He asked me who I had stolen the money from to go over to England.

Jan: So why do you want to have a house built for him?

Jimi: To get back at him. Oh well, after all he did give me my first guitar. First I had to prove that I could play a couple of songs on a guitar of a friend, but I did get that thing still.

Jan: Why do you dress yourself so strikingly?

Jimi: I have an enormous dislike for ordinary things and ordinary people. Folks with "nice eyebrows" and things like that, those who dress so common.

Jan: What kind of guy are you yourself?

Jimi: Me? Well, I'm a quiet person. Usually I don't talk that much. What I have to say, I say with my guitar . . .

Jan: What do you think about these TV recordings for *Vibrato*?

Jimi: Oh, is that the name of the program? Well, it is bloody cold outside and it's a disaster that we can't play live. I can't mime. I can't play a song the same way twice. I feel it differently every time . . .

When the recordings start again and I plan to leave, I get a big, warm hand and Jimi says: "Now ya take it real easy, ya hear?" And this friendly American good-bye is a sincere one too.

"QUITE AN EXPERIENCE!"

ALAN FREEMAN | From RAVE, June 1967.

In this interview, Hendrix revealed important details of his early career in Nashville, life on the road with Little Richard, and the true origins of the military-style jacket that he wore everywhere.

I didn't recognize the elegant uniform. No wonder.

"Royal Army Veterinary Corps," said Jimi Hendrix, proudly flicking a bit of lint off his tunic sleeve. "Eighteen ninety-eight, I believe. Very good year for uniforms."

On Jimi it looked . . . well, interesting. Especially with a flowery shirt and a wispy scarf in his favorite red-purple.

As it happens, James Maurice [*sic*] Hendrix is one of the few younger people in pop who actually wore a uniform as a serving soldier—the jump kit of the famous Screaming Eagles airborne division in the U.S. Army.

"I was bored at sixteen after I left school, and there wasn't a lot doing in a town like Seattle, Washington. The legal age for joining was seventeen [*sic*], so I stuck a year on and got in the army! And you know what? It was even more boring than being outside.

"They tried to make us tough. So we had to sleep in mud."

I asked, "What for?"

Jimi shrugged. "To see if we could sleep in mud, I guess. We did push-ups in minus zero degrees. And we did jumping out of planes. That was about the best bit. But it scared me."

An Experience

He lit a cigarette and leaned back in the chair. It was a clear, sunny afternoon. Jimi stretched luxuriously, appreciating the leisurely atmosphere like a person who has tried living the hard way and knows which he prefers.

"The other night I was about half a block away from the Cromwellian Club, wearing this gear," he said. "Up comes this wagon with a blue light flashing and about five or six policemen jump out at me. They look into my face real close and severely and gather around. Then one of them points to my jacket and says, 'That's British, isn't it?'

"So I said, 'Yeah, I think it is.' And they frowned and all that bit and they said, 'You're not supposed to be wearing that. Men fought and died in that uniform.'

"The guy's eyes were so bad he couldn't read the little print on the badges. So I said, 'What, in the Veterinary Corps, 1898? Anyway, I *like* uniforms. I wore one long enough in the United States Army.'

"They said, 'What? What? You trying to get smart with us? Show us your passport.' So we did all that bit too. I had to convince them that my accent was really American. Then they asked what group I was with and I said the Experience. So they made fun of that as well and made cracks about roving minstrels. After they made a few more funnies, and when they'd finally got their kicks they said they didn't want to see me with the gear on any more, and they let me go.

"Just as I was walking away, one of them said, 'Hey, you said you're in the Experience. What are you experiencing?'

"I said, 'Harassment!' And took off as quick as I could."

Odd Gear

"While we're on the subject of clothes," I said. "Explain one thing. According to the wise-heads, the craze for uniforms is supposed to show a masculine reaction to the kind of feminine influence that's been getting into male gear. But here you are with a military jacket *and* a flowered shirt *and* a dolly scarf. I never saw one guy who could wreck everybody's theories with one lot of clothes, like you do!"

Jimi roared with laughter, throwing back his mound of hair. "I'll tell you, Alan. I guess I had to conform so long in what other people wanted me to wear that now I just please myself.

"Pretty soon I wanted to get out of the army. One day I got my ankle caught in the skyhook just as I was going to jump, and I broke it. I told them I'd hurt my back too. Every time they examined me I groaned, so they finally believed me and I got out."

He stroked the strings of his guitar, thinking back. "I messed about on guitar while I was in the service. Played occasional gigs out of town. Anyway, my discharge came through, and one morning I found myself standing outside the gate of Fort Campbell on the Tennessee-Kentucky border with my little duffel bag and three or four hundred dollars in my pocket.

"I was going to go back to Seattle, which was a long way away, but there was this girl there I was kinda hung up on. Then I thought I'd just look in at Clarksville, which was near; stay there that night and go home next morning. That's what I did—looked in at Clarksville.

"I went in this jazz joint and had a drink. I liked it and I stayed. People tell me I get foolish good-natured sometimes. Anyway, I guess I felt real benevolent that day. I must have been handing out bills to anyone who asked me!

"I came out of that place with sixteen dollars left! And it takes a lot more than that to get from Tennessee to Seattle! So no going home, 'cause it's like two thousand miles."

He chuckled again. "Two thousand miles. I thought first I'd call long-distance and ask my father to send me some money to get me out of there—he's a garden designer and he does all right. But I could guess what he'd say if I told him I lost nearly four hundred dollars in just one day. Nope. That was out.

"All I can do, I thought, is get a guitar and try to find work here. Nashville was only twenty miles away—you know, big music scene. There had to be something doing there.

"Then I remembered that just before I left the army I'd sold a guitar to a cat in my unit. So I went back to Fort Campbell and slept there on the sly that night. I found the guy and told him I just had to borrow the guitar back.

"I got in with this one-horse music agency. They used to come up on stage in the middle of a number, while we were playing, and slip the money for the gig into our pockets. They knew we couldn't knock off to count it just then. By the time the number was over and I got a chance to look in the envelope it'd be maybe two dollars. Used to have to sleep in a big housing estate they were building around there. No roofs and sometimes they hadn't put floors in yet. That was wild!"

Jimi put the guitar down and lit a cigarette.

In Nashville

"What were you doing besides the gigs?" I said. "Nashville used to be a pretty funny scene, with all those slick managers trying to sign up hillbilly singers who'd never been in a big town before."

He nodded. "Wasn't all that different when I was there. But when you learned the scene you knew it was like a game—you know, like one big put-on all the way. Everybody trying to take everyone else. Once you knew how to watch out for yourself it could be a lot of laughs.

"Every Sunday afternoon we used to go down town and watch the race riots. Take a picnic basket because they wouldn't serve us in the restaurants. One group would stand on one side of the street and the rest on the other side. They'd shout names and talk about each other's mothers. That'd go on for a couple of hours and then we'd all go home. Sometimes, if there was a good movie on that Sunday there wouldn't be any race riot."

He smoothed down his uniform jacket affectionately. "You were asking me about why I go for way-out gear, right? Well, it wasn't just the army. I had to conform when I was playing in groups too. The so-called grooming bit. You know, mohair suits. Alan, how I hate mohair suits! I was playing with the Isley Brothers and we had white mohair suits, patent leather shoes and patent leather hair-dos. We weren't allowed to go on stage looking casual. If our shoelaces were two different types we'd get fined five dollars. Oh, man, did I get tired of that!

Music Scene

"Well, I went on thinking, soon as I got a bit saved up I'd head off home to Seattle. But as time went on I got more interested in the music scene, and I thought less and less about going back. In the end I never did see home again. Five years or more now I've been away."

After playing here and there a while longer with the Isley group, Jimi found himself back in Nashville. A big tour came through, headed by Sam Cooke, Jackie Wilson and B. B. King. Jimi joined the show, travelled with them across the States, and learnt plenty about music.

"I'd have learnt more if they'd let Sam finish his act," he said. "But they were always on their feet and cheering at the end, and I never heard him do the last bit."

One day in Kansas City the misfortune that hits all touring musicians sooner or later descended on jumping Jimi Hendrix. He missed the tour coach and was stranded without a penny. A showgirl and her friend helped him, and soon he was able to make his way to the even deeper South—to the city of Atlanta, Georgia.

Hippy Gear

That dynamic pocket dictator of rock, Little Richard, made room in his show for Jimi. And once again he was living on wheels, two shows a night, pull out and head for the next town. But there too the Hendrix eye for hippy gear led to bother.

"Little Richard didn't want anybody to look better than him," he said. "I was the best of friends with Glen Willings, another guy in the band, and we used to buy the same kind of stuff, and wear it on stage.

"After the show one night Little Richard said, 'Brothers, we've got to have a meeting. I am Little Richard and I am the king of rock & rhythm and I am the one who's going to look pretty on stage. Glen and Jimi, will you please turn in those shirts or else you will have to suffer the consequences of a fine.'

"He had another meeting over my hairstyle. I said I wasn't going to cut my hair for anybody. Little Richard said, 'Uh, what is this loud outburst? That will be a five dollar fine for you.' Everybody on the whole tour was brainwashed."

But tours end, and spells of work alternated with weeks when Jimi and his friends nearly starved in New York. "We'd get a gig about once every twelfth of never," he said. "We even tried eating orange peel and tomato paste. Sleeping outside them tall tenements was hell. Rats running all across your chest, cockroaches stealing your last candy bar out of your pocket."

A Break

Then, one warm autumn evening last year, when Jimi had landed a solo job with a backing band in Greenwich Village, his chance came at last. Chas Chandler, late of the Animals, and manager Mike Jeffery met him. They said, "Why not come to England?"

Jimi flew to London with Chas—and ran into a six-hour argument with immigration officials. "They didn't want to let me in," he said. "They carried on like I was going to make all the money in England and take it back to the States."

Jimi's Publicist, who had come to the airport to meet the pair, got involved in the argument. He was amazed when the officials threatened to deport him too, seeing that he's British! Eventually, he managed to get Jimi admitted to our shores of dazzling opportunity on the grounds that Jimi, as the writer of several songs, had come to Britain, among other reasons, to collect royalties [owed] to him!

Success!

Another hundred Hendrix songs are lying around in various American hotels that Jimi was thrown out of when he couldn't find the money for his bill. He'd be glad to have them now. For, three days after London drummer Mitch Mitchell and Folkestone bass guitarist Noel Redding signed with Jimi to launch the Experience, the group were playing the Paris Olympia with Johnny Halliday. Never did a new group explode so fast into international acclaim—which was clinched in this country when Brian Epstein called them "the greatest talent to come along since the Rolling Stones."

Lost Songs

Top groups need top numbers, and Jimi has an uneasy feeling that there could be a few world winners among the papers left in those cheap, cramped little hotels—if they haven't been hurled in the dustbin.

Jimi crunched out his cigarette and stood up in the full glory of his Veterinary Corps regimentals. Tucking his guitar under his arm, he shook hands.

As long as there are guitars, I thought, there will always be other, better songs to be picked out and composed on them. And as long as Jimi has his guitar, there'll be no more sleeping in the mud!

Till next month, pop-pickers—stay bright!

"COME TO A SOUL REVIVAL WITH JIMI HENDRIX, A REBEL FROM MARS VIA CUBA"

KEITH KELLER | From BT, May 15, 1967. Original article title: "Kom til soul-møde med Jimi Hendrix, en troende oprører fra Mars via Cuba."

European reporters were often startled once they got a close look at Hendrix's wild appearance. The Swedish newspaper EXPRESSEN went as far as describing Hendrix as "a cross between a floor mop and an Australian bush Negro."[1] And even the photo caption for this article read, "Jimi Hendrix has good reason to look like this." The article was intended to promote a May 21 Copenhagen concert, but perhaps many had their doubts about the headliner's wild claims of planet origin.

"I look the way I do," said Jimi Hendrix, the concert attraction for next Sunday's soul revival in the Falkoner Centret, "to fulfill my dreams."

Hendrix's dream: "I was sent by Fidel Castro to infiltrate the confederate lines in 1864. I am a believer and a rebel."

The revolution of the soul-star has been an explosion on the pop-scene. The successful breakthrough is now evidenced on the charts with the Polydor singles, "Stone Free" and "Purple Haze."

Style: Adapted soul, not black, more white, as the audience in Europe prefers. Black inspiration, white stars on stage.

Jimi Hendrix's group delivers a deep screeching "Experience" sound, right on the guitar strings.

Lyrics, often by Hendrix himself, are psychedelic, man, what else. Although one of them, about Jimi walking on water, was changed to avoid provocation.[2]

It also has to be noted that Jimi Hendrix occasionally through his deafening and visually dynamic stage show plays the guitar with his teeth. Yes, the teeth.

Jimi Hendrix was born on November 27, 1942, in Seattle, USA. White or black? "I am Cuban, man," Jimi said, "I am from Mars."

---

1. *Expressen*, May 15, 1967.
2. Either Hendrix told Keller about the lyrics for his original draft of "Purple Haze, Jesus Saves," or he was confused with the line in "Are You Experienced?": "We'll hold hands and watch the sun rise from the bottom of the sea."

INTERVIEW WITH JIMI HENDRIX

HANS CARL SCHMIDT | From a broadcast heard on a Frankfurt radio station, May 17, 1967.

After two shows in Munich on May 16, the JHE traveled the next day to Frankfurt, Germany. In these excerpts from a radio interview conducted at the Hotel Intercontinental, Hendrix displays some insecurity in his talent, his thoughts on Motown, and a desire to show his father he's become successful.

Hans Carl Schmidt: Did you believe that when you got into the studio, first, let's say like [with] "Hey Joe," were you sure that this was gonna be a smash record?

Jimi Hendrix: Well, Chas was sure. For me, it was the first time I tried to sing on a record, actually.

HCS: People who've been watching you onstage say you put on a tremendous act. What do you feel? What is going on once you hear your music and once you sing? Are you putting on an act, as you say, or do you feel these emotions, [like] what you do with your hands or feet?

JH: We mostly feel it. If you see our show, for instance, once every night for about a week, it would probably be very different, because of a different mood you might be in, and the way the music might hit you, it's very emotional like.

[*Schmidt asks Hendrix what record he'd like him to play, and Hendrix selected "51st Anniversary." After the song, Schmidt interviewed Mitchell and Redding.*]

HCS: Why is it necessary to have long hair, or to be dressed up in a most peculiar way?

JH: Well, I don't consider it actually necessary, because there's a lot of groups around . . . pop stars like Englebert Humperdinck, Cat Stevens, and all of the beautiful people, they don't necessarily have to have long hair. I believe this goes for the other cats too. I dig it. I think it's very nice, especially in your own style. And as far as clothes go, anything I see that I like, regardless of what it looks like, and regardless of what it costs. If it cost only two shillings, I'll get it if I like it . . . if it would suit me.

HCS: I've been watching a live show of a beat band and the audience was going mad. How do you explain this feeling? What's going on in these kids at that particular minute? Is this some sexual involvement? What is it that they rave themselves nearly to . . . some of them shout . . . some of them have to be carried away . . .

JH: [*Laughs.*] That's beautiful, I think. It's good to see people enjoy themselves regardless of what it is. It might have something to do with sex. [Just] the idea of somebody being on stage playing or singing, and showing themselves, I mean bowing down and all this, and the people sitting knowing that they can't really touch him, but would like to. It's a frustrated feeling, but a good feeling. They probably don't get a chance to scream all year until this one time, and then they let everything out then.

HCS: What is Detroit sound?

JH: It might bring you down, but to me it's very commercial, very artificial . . . What is it? Synthetic soul sound. It isn't a sound like real Negro artists. It's put together so beautifully that I don't feel anything from it except the Isley Brothers and maybe the Four Tops. All they do is put a very, very hard beat to it, about a thousand people on tambourines, bells, a thousand horns, a thousand violins, and then a singer who overdubs his voice about a million times or sings in an echo chamber. To me it comes out so artificial. It's very commercial for the younger people.

HCS: What's your recipe for good interpretation?

JH: It's very primitive . . . a more freeform type of thing. It's what I hope we work up toward: a free style. Quite naturally it has to have a nice beat . . . where a person can almost feel in the music. [But] how can you feel in the beat when every single song comes out so synthetic? Synthetic soul is what I call Motown.

HCS: Do you have any feelings toward classic music?

JH: It's very beautiful, but I don't listen to it all the time, but I would like to at the most relaxing time. See, different music is supposed to be used different ways. You're supposed to appreciate music. During the bright day, and noise, I don't figure that's the best time to listen to classical. Anytime when it's quiet, and your mind is very relaxed, and you feel like daydreaming maybe or something, you can turn on the stereo.

HCS: Particularly for the younger generation, the kids always think it's easy to grab a guitar, and go on stage and make music. Could you tell them that it's not as easy at all?

JH: No. It was so very hard for me. At first I was so scared. I wouldn't dare go on stage. Like, I joined this band, and I knew about three songs, and when it was time for us to play on stage . . . I had to play behind the curtains. I couldn't get up in front. Plus you get so very discouraged. You hear different bands playing around you, and the guitar player seems like he's always so much better than you are. Most people give up at this point because they get very discouraged. But just keep on, keep on, [and] you can make it. That's the only way I tried to make it, is being very persistent.

HCS: There's this story in various magazines about Reprise, or the [Frank] Sinatra company buying you. What's true about this?

JH: It's just a contract, and they give advance royalties—in other words, they trust in us before we make any money for them.

HCS: Jimi, what would be your greatest wish? If I could fulfill a wish of yours, which wish would you take?

JH: I wish you could send me home so I could see my parents for about three days.

HCS: How long haven't you been home?

JH: About five and a half years. They don't know what's happening at all except I called them two times. Once when I came here to England about seven months ago, and once a few days ago when we was in London, and I told them we have three records out . . . and [my father] said, "Yeah?" He didn't know nothing about it. He didn't even know I was singing because I was too scared to sing. Chas made me sing, serious. Oh, by the way, would you care for a banana?

HCS: A banana?

[*After a break, Schmidt asks Hendrix to ad-lib a public-service announcement advising young listeners to stay in school.*]

JH: The best thing to do now is for you to finish schooling. It does seem like a drag because I used to be in school, and the flies used to fly all around me on a summer day, but it's best to stick with it. For instance, like drugs, and pills, well, just don't let nobody [*laughs*] sell you any bad stuff. [*Laughs.*] No, you better not do that. [*Laughs.*] Let's do it over again, man.

HCS: OK. I cut that.

[*Hendrix makes a second attempt.*]

JH: Well, just don't let nobody pull the leg on you because the people don't know what drugs is nowadays anyway. It's a very bad scene. Especially when you get caught with it.

[Hendrix was then asked to do a closing remark for the show.]

JH: It's been very, very groovy on the show . . . been nice eating bananas . . . so y'all take it easy out there in radio land. Good-bye. Auf Weidersehen. Jimi Hendrix.

[Hendrix made sure that Mitchell and Redding could make closing remarks as well.]

INTERVIEW WITH JIMI HENDRIX

KLAS BURLING | From an interview heard on the Swedish radio show POP '67 SPECIAL, broadcast May 28, 1967.

The JHE broke all box-office records at Stockholm's Tivoli Gardens on May 24, 1967, drawing a crowd of eighteen thousand. The following day Hendrix gave this interview for Swedish radio; he talked about ARE YOU EXPERIENCED and how he achieved a special effect with his guitar.

Klas Burling: Welcome to Sweden, Jimi Hendrix.

Jimi Hendrix: Hello.

KB: And congratulations to your great success out here in Stockholm.

JH: Thank you very much.

KB: [What are] your plans for the future? You are going, for example, to the States; you are planning a big international publicity thing.

JH: Yeah, we're going to the States around . . . I think we're gonna leave about the tenth or twelfth of June and we're gonna play at the Monterey Pop Festival and then we have about four days at the Fillmore Auditorium. Well, we have this TV and all this other stuff in between.

KB: I suppose before you really recorded "Hey Joe" you did a lot of club jobs in London?

JH: No we don't. We didn't do too much. We, ah, I couldn't work too much 'cause I didn't have a work permit, so what they had to do was line up a lot of gigs. So when we did the first, one of the first jobs we ever did was, we had about four hours' practice, and Johnny Halliday asked whether we'd like to come play at the Paris Olympia with him, and we did after being together only about four days and after having about four hours of practice and so . . .

KB: And you went there and . . .

JH: Yes, so we came back [to] record "Hey Joe" around December. Well, we couldn't work too much because . . . I had to get enough jobs to have a long work permit so I could stay in England longer.

KN: And then things really started to happen and really you found another song. You didn't find it 'cause you wrote it.

JH: Yeah, I realized on the new LP, and the last two records I wrote myself. We write all our own stuff now.

KB: How do you get the ideas of songs? For example, like "Purple Haze"?

JH: I don't know. I don't know. [*Laughs.*]

KB: Some people say there is a bit of Dylan in some of your lyrics.

JH: Well.

KB: Well, if you think of "[The Wind Cries] Mary," with the traffic lights turning blue . . .

JH: Um.

KB: That's right to compare you with Dylan in that way?

JH: Well, whatever they want to do, 'cause they don't, I don't know who I seem like, 'cause I been livin' with myself for about twenty-one years, so I don't know really, so, there's nothin' . . . I don't care who they compare me with, actually.

KB: But when you write a line like that for example . . .

JH: Oh, I don't think . . .

KB: You got the deep meaning behind it or is it just . . .

JH: Oh yeah. Well, like "The traffic lights turn out blue tomorrow"—that means like tomorrow everything's gonna be blue. Blue means feelin' bad. In other words, like for instance if you do your everyday things like go across the street or somethin' like that, instead of the traffic lights bein' red and green, well, they're blue 'cause, in your mind, yeah, 'cause it's nothin' but a story 'bout a breakup. Just a girl and boy breakin' up, that's all. And even when you just say one thing, you say somethin' like that; did you mean what, this means something else. There's no hidden meanings, it's just the way you say it, express the words.

KB: What do you call it yourself?

JH: I don't know. Just a slow song. That's what I call it.

KB: A slow song. And uh . . .

JH: Slow, quiet.

KB: You got an LP for release in Sweden in about a week's time.

JH: Yeah, I hope so. It's named *Are You Experienced*, and it has about three or four different moods. It has a little rock 'n' roll. It has about two rock 'n' roll songs, which you can call rock 'n' roll, and then it has a blues, and it has a few freak-out tunes.

KB: You're not playing your psychedelic music in there?

JH: Yeah, there's one or two in there. There's the one named "Are You Experienced?" is one. Well, that's the name of the last track on the LP. It's like, an imaginary freeform song, where you just use your mind, where you just imagine with your mind. And this other song named "Third Stone from the Sun." It's completely imaginable. It's just about these cats comin' down and takin' over the earth, but then they find out they don't really see anything here that's worth takin', except for chickens.

KB: And this thing about Transylvania, and, er . . .

JH: Oh, but . . . oh. Oh, what do you mean, like vampires and all that?

KB: Oh, yeah.

JH: Oh, that isn't nothing like that. It's just like, "Third Stone from the Sun," it lasts about seven minutes and it's an instrumental—these guys comin' from another planet. And the third stone from the sun is Earth, that's where it is. They have Mercury, Venus, and then Earth. And they observe Earth for a while and they think that the smartest animal on the whole earth is chickens, hens. And so there's nothin' else here to offer. They don't like the people so much so they just blow it up at the end. So we have all these different sounds, all of them made from just nothin' but a guitar, bass, and drums, and then our slowed-down voices.

KB: Tell us one thing: after watching you, for example, the sound for the introduction of "Wild Thing." The plane crash, and all of [that], what you can describe it like? How do you really get that sound?

JH: Well, I guess I just turn the amp up very loud and it's mostly feedback and the way you control the knobs. And the back, see, I play a Fender Stratocaster guitar, and you can take the back off. A little small plate and you can tap the springs. There's little springs back there. And it makes these weird little sounds sometimes.

KB: Got some other tricks as well of course. . . . Aren't you a bit fed up [with] playing, like picking with your teeth and . . .

JH: Well, I do it just when I feel like it. I don't consider myself that I have to do it, 'cause sometimes we don't do it at all. It's just when I feel like doin' it.

KB: Because the audience might expect it from you, really.

JH: Yeah, but that's what I try to get straight to them now, that it's best not to expect anything from us. That it's best just to go on stage, 'cause if you expect something then you might not see it, then quite naturally you're gonna be disappointed.

KB: Some people say for example, playing with your teeth that you are also helping with your hands. [Using] your fingers at the same time . . .

JH: Oh no. No, no, no. It's like playing with your hands, like this. You have to move this finger in order to make the notes. So instead of pickin' it with my left hand, I just pick it with my teeth. That's all.

KB: And also the guitar—it really seems like it was playing by itself at times. You just keep your . . .

JH: Well, that's when you play with the one hand.

KB: Yeah. Only one hand.

PART II

June 1967 to December 1967

BEATLE PAUL MCCARTNEY CAUGHT HENDRIX'S first gig in London and remained a devoted fan thereafter. Had it not been for McCartney's influence, Hendrix may not have played the Monterey Pop Festival.

The admiration was mutual. *Sgt. Pepper's Lonely Hearts Club Band* was released on Friday, June 4—two weeks prior to Monterey Pop—and Hendrix learned the title track in time to play it at the Saville Theatre concert on Sunday, June 6. The Beatles attended and were blown away by Hendrix's blazing, psychedelic guitar rendition of their tune.

Reprise Records signed the JHE and released *Are You Experienced* in America in August 1967. As "Purple Haze" broke in the States, the JHE got an offer to headline a tour.

The group returned to England with more than 180 live shows under their belts and entered Olympic Studios with fresh ideas. Hendrix used guitar-gadget inventor Roger Mayer and engineer Eddie Kramer to express the unique sounds he had in his head, such as the effect of a guitar floating on a flying saucer—it panned from speaker to speaker and then "disappeared" into space. Many such aural illusions were found on *Axis: Bold as Love*, the band's second LP. Finished on October 30, 1967, it went into the top ten on both sides of the Atlantic.

"WILD, MAN!"

DAWN JAMES | From RAVE, August 1967.

The JHE spent June I, 1967, rehearsing at the Saville Theatre in London. Later Hendrix was interviewed for RAVE magazine at his Upper Berkeley Street flat. The tagline to the article read, "Wild—that's Jimi Hendrix, but Dawn James finds he's not as wild as he sometimes makes out!"

Jimi Hendrix, way-out pop star. Is there anything he knows is wrong and never does?

"I play it by ear, man. There's one thing I never do, clean my teeth with hair spray!"

Laughter filled the flat in Upper Berkeley Street as Mr. Hendrix's road manager, his drummer, and a friend appreciated his wit. Here was something of the Proby[1] pageantry, the followers who stand a little behind and laugh and admire. But Jimi Hendrix claims he doesn't need people.

"I guess I could do without them. In fact, sometimes I'd rather be alone. I like to think. Yes, gee man, I'm a thinker. I can really get lost thinking about my music. But then I think so much I have to get out among people again. I hear music in my head all the time. Sometimes it makes my brain throb and the room starts to turn. I feel I'm going mad. So I go to the clubs and get plastered. Man, I get real paralytic, but it saves me."

His is rather a twilight world. Music is life to him, but because of music he adopts strange values and unorthodox escapes. He gets up when the sun is setting, and breathes in the smoke-caked air of basement beat bistros. His friends are musicians. His hopes are married to music.

Hendrix on the cover of RAVE maga-zine, July 1967. The article appeared in the August issue. STEVEN ROBY/ STRAIGHT AHEAD ARCHIVES COLLECTION

"It's all I really care for. My ambitions are tied up with it. Even my girlfriends are part of it because I meet them where there is music, and they are part of the scene I associate with music." He doesn't have a steady girl.

"I don't meet any girls I could be serious about," he said, and rolled his eyes, and shrugged.

"Sure I'd like to meet a real nice girl, one I could talk to like she was a fellow. But I've had so many girls and they're all the same. The ones I meet look good and make you feel like a man, but you can't talk to them. I get cross with them because they just talk gossip. I get sad about all the girls I see walking on the street when I'm in a taxi-cab, because I'll never meet them, and perhaps one of them is the right girl for me."

He has had three hit records. What does he think he has to offer pop and what has pop to offer him back?

"I've got a lot to offer pop," he said. "I care so much about my work. I record stuff I believe is great. Pop has less to offer me back because it is run by people who only talk about what is commercial."

Jimi talks freely but he isn't easy to reach. A shutter comes down and a facade puts you off just as you close in. He has lived a hard, full life. His parents were separated and his mother died when he was a small child. He went to live with an uncle and aunt.

"So? Lots of kids have it tough," he said, casually, but added, "I ran away from home a couple of times because I was so miserable. When my dad found out I'd gone he went pretty mad with worry. But then I don't really care about other people's feelings."

When did Jimi return home?

"When I realized my dad was upset. Not that I cared, but well, he is my dad."

Jimi has super manners. When he asks you out he says, "Would you do me the honour of dating me tonight?" When he leaves a room you are in, he says, "Excuse me for a moment please." When he meets you he shakes hands and says, "Nice seeing you."

Somewhere deep down beneath the raving recording star there is a lot of old-world charm.

He says he doesn't know himself well. "I can't say what makes me happy or sad. It has to happen before I know. It doesn't happen the same each time either. I must say that people being rude about me doesn't ever bother me now. The only time I get uneasy is when I know that pop critics and writers are waiting for me to fail so they can jump all over me. This is how pop is. You have a hit record and, gee, they love you! But you have one failure and they kill you. It's like a tight rope.

"I get kinda tense before a show. I like to be left alone to think. My road manager tries to keep the dressing room free from people then. If people come in I find a corner somewhere else. I have to think myself into my act. I can't just turn on."

How is he affected by other people's music?

"Again I can't define it. A blues or a sad melody can make me real happy. I am affected by sounds though. They can change my mood."

He has no religion.

"Religion is all the same—Catholic, Protestant, Jewish, it's just a lot of reasonable commercial quotes that sell because they're somewhere between very good and very bad, and people can easily hang on to that. It gives them something to believe in."

I asked him if he likes his looks.

"I've learnt to live with them. The hair is rather wild, but it grows that way, and I look awful with it short and neat. The clothes aren't deliberate. I pick up what I feel like wearing when I dress. They represent my mood."

I looked at the scarlet and purple and orange. Was he in a gay mood? He shook his head. "Gee no, I'm quite melancholy today," he said. It would be hard on the eye balls if one caught him when he was wild with joy!

---

1. Dawn James was referring to American singer P. J. Proby.

"OUR EXPERIENCE WITH JIMI"

BOB GARCIA | From OPEN CITY, August 24–30, 1967.

Before returning to England, the JHE spent three days in Los Angeles. On August 18, 1967, Hendrix was interviewed at the Hollywood Bowl during afternoon concert rehearsals.

HENDRIX—The sullen, sneering, wild-haired John Cage of Cock Rock?

HENDRIX—X marking the spot where pants bulge meets guitar cunt?

HENDRIX—The searching, violent, sloe-eyed voyager through shrieking glades of puffed-up electronics?

HENDRIX—The tri-decibel masturbator of phallic amps?

HENDRIX—The black Nero who burned the amplified vox of Rome?

HENDRIX—All these things on stage. But off—HENDRIX is a beautiful cat.

Open City interviewed the Jimi Hendrix Experience during the hectic three hours preceding their sell-out appearance with the Mamas and the Papas at the Hollywood Bowl last Friday evening (Aug. 18).

We arrived at Hendrix's hotel for a 3:30 PM interview, only to receive a frantic call from Hendrix's English PR man. "The Bowl's fucked us with the amp system. Jimi has to have everything right, don't you know? Join us here, won't you?"

At the Bowl, the controversial Hendrix is on stage, looking traditionally PR-sullen, up-tight, yet incredibly small and young facing the thousands of Bowl seats. Says PR man, looking like a Jr. Ustinov, "It's almost right, don't you know. How do you like this bird?" inserting his chubby leg between those of a Vampira-eyed "bird" lolled out beside him. She smiles. "There are lots more birds that will call us later at the hotel."

We roar back to the hotel and first talk with Mitch Mitchell, the Experience's drummer; Noel Redding, second guitarist, all with the unction of English PR. Finally Hendrix arrives, looking dazed, and bewildered by the whole afternoon. We sit by the hotel pool with him as screams of swimming teenies punctuate his statements.

ON [SEX] AND VIOLENCE SHOWS ON STAGE: Everybody thinks we do it every single time we perform. So we do it about three times in 300 different times we've played. That's a very lopsided average. Like we don't depend on this, you know. Like I've burned the guitar three times¹ out of 300 gigs we've performed. That's a small percentage.

A lot of people think that what I do with my guitar is vulgar. I don't think it's vulgar sex. I don't consider it anything like that. It's a spontaneous action on my part and a fluid thing. It's not an act, but a state of being at the time I'm doing it. My music, my instrument, my sound, my body—are all one action with my mind. What people get from what I do is their scene. It's in the eye of the beholder. You know if you lick girls' bicycle seats every morning before they go to school—then you should really think that what I do is masturbation of the instrument or something like that about sex or love.

(On destruction: Drummer Mitchell stated that "We don't break it up every night. For instance, once I couldn't get the right sound out of my drums while performing. I was hitting them so hard my hands began bleeding. I got so mad that I destroyed them right there on stage. It was just like destroying a piece of writing that was bad. It was my own creation and I wasn't satisfied with it. I got a new set of drums that sounded just fine. They worked for me like a good woman. I worked out all my frustrations and emotions on those drums, and they responded.")

It might be sex or love to certain people in the audience when I'm playing, but to me—it just gets me stoned out of my mind when I'm playing. It's like a contact high, between the music and me. The actual music is like a fast-lingering high.

ON DESTROYING THE OLD POP SCENE WITH NEW SOUNDS: I'm not here to destroy anything. Don't forget, there are other people still around making those nice, sweet sounds. You've still got the Beach Boys and the Four Seasons to hang on to. And dig, we're not trying to destroy the Pop Scene or anything like that. I think we're just going into another vein of it. You know, we're not necessarily destroying it, just translating it into our own image. You'll always have cats to stand up there and sing you pretty songs.

WANDERINGS THROUGH THE PADDED JUNGLES OF ELECTRONICS: We're using amps just like anybody else. All the sounds we produce are strictly from guitar, bass and drums. On records we might overdub, but here—again—the sound is still guitar, bass and drums, basically. The feedback you hear is from a straight amp—and a little fuzz thing I had built. We don't even use an oscillator. That could really blow a lot of minds, but it just doesn't interest me that much right now. We improvise an awful lot. Like, we don't really rehearse a thing. It's a spontaneous performance. For instance, one of us is in a rock bag, another in just jazz, while I'm in blues. We are all doing our separate things together. Rehearsals are only to see how the amps sound or something technical like that. Otherwise we just let it happen. "Spontaneity" is what I could best term it. We are constantly growing in this spontaneity. We have other sounds to make, other singles and LPs to cut.

Critics are already classifying us on the basis of ten months (the length of time the Experience has been playing together), one album, and perhaps one or two concerts they've heard. I think it's fine for these people to understand that we are not always in the same bag with each performance. How can you be when you are constantly reaching, improvising, experimenting? It's impossible. It just is going to take time to reach those labelers with our sounds. It's like cowboys and Indians; all Indians are bad because they've got the clap—so nowadays something different like the Experience comes along, and a lot of the labelers are frightened by it. It's not easily classifiable, but they sure as hell are going to try. So quite naturally, they're going to start little rumors about people they don't understand like "Jimi Hendrix is sullen, he's always stoned, he drinks watermelon juice with his coffee, he uses shower curtains for toilet paper."

ON GOING TO ENGLAND: I didn't feel I had to go to England. I started out in Seattle originally about seven years ago. I should say that I really started out playing all over the States seven years ago. I played at that time behind at least 40 top R&B artists.

I eventually got tired of this, so I went on and formed my own group in Greenwich Village, New York. I played at the Cafe Wha? and Cafe Au Go Go. Eventually two agents from England saw me there and asked me to come to England. So I did, and I formed the Experience.

You must remember that Jimi Hendrix, US, didn't really have a chance to do anything because he was playing behind people, man. People say that I had to go to England to make it—that's not true. Like, I had enough respect for a performer to know that I would have to simmer down with what I wanted to do before I went on stage to back him. Like, what would have happened if Little Richard started doing his thing, and I got all fired up and started doing mine in front of him—playing the guitar with my teeth, or start burning up the amp? I was bored to death really as a backup man, but I had respect for the people I was playing for—so I got out and did my own thing.

IS HENDRIX'S MUSIC PSYCHEDELIC?: There are only two songs in my album that would give anybody the horrors if they were on a trip: "Are You Experienced," and "May This Be Love." But they are actually peace-of-mind songs, whether you are stoned or not. They are just relaxing things, like meditational shades. As long as you can get your mind together while you are listening to them—they've made it with you, man.

TEENYBOPPERS: They're good, groovy, I guess. All their screaming and sexy moving and squirming doesn't really bother me at all. I feel it just slightly. But sometimes they scream in the wrong parts. Like when I cough, or something—and they scream—well, I feel funny then. It's like, "Oh, oh, here they go."

Like sometimes while you're into your music, you might hear little teenie-weenies—or little piglets—squealing out there. You know it's a good feeling, but it's a little hard to explain what really bugs you about that scene. So you don't let the squeals get you uptight. You can't work by screams, I mean you don't perform according to how they scream.

HENDRIX ON SOUL: A Spanish dancer has soul and grace. Everybody has soul. I really don't like that word in connection with the Experience. I like the words "feeling" and "vibration." Like playing together. We play together in free form—yet everybody has a chance to do his thing, to express his own feeling. I get very hung up in this feeling bag. The sounds of a funky guitar just thrill me, go all through me. It's something I can put my own mind onto to rest. I can get inside it, almost. I'm not saying that I play that good, but I'm just explaining my feeling towards it and the feelings toward the sound it produces.

HENDRIX ON DETROIT AND WATTS: Well, quite naturally I don't like to see houses being burnt. But I don't have too much feeling for either side right now, because my bag is completely different. Quite naturally, a lot of things have happened to me. But don't forget every human being on this earth is different. So how are you going to classify races by what they do? Sure, I get mad when I hear about people dying in wars or ghettos. Maybe I'll have more to say later when I get more political.

WHERE THE HENDRIX EXPERIENCE IS HEADED: When I was a little boy I wanted to be a cowboy or a movie star. Quite naturally they didn't have many colored cowboys around, so I decided on the movie star role. I used to have these dreams then. It sounds a little silly, but it's the honest-to-God's truth. I used to dream in Technicolor that 1966 was the year something would happen to me. So I would get scared then. Scared that my dad was going to die or something. So eventually it's come true. 1966 is my year—in Technicolor.

Right now I'm scared. Like, soon I'll be going into another bag with a new sound, a new record, a new experience. We'll go exactly the way we feel. I don't know which way that'll be. Nothing will be intentional. It'll just happen. We won't do anything with gimmicks, music-wise. We're not going to try and keep up with trends, because we've got a chance to be our own trend.

---

1. Hendrix officially burned his guitar twice while he performed with the Experience: March 31, 1967, and June 18, 1967. According to guitarist Bobby Womack, Hendrix also burned his guitar on the 1964 Sam Cooke tour.

"SPANISH GALLEONS OFF JERSEY COAST OR 'WE LIVE OFF EXCESS VOLUME'"

BILL KERBY AND DAVID THOMPSON | From the LOS ANGELES FREE PRESS, August 25, 1967.

In addition to the interview given to Bob Garcia for OPEN CITY, Hendrix gave several more interviews on August 18, 1967, while in Los Angeles. In this interview with Bill Kerby and David Thompson, he gives more details about his early career and the recently aborted tour with the Monkees.

In the avant-garde of pop music, one of the most fruitful thrusts is being led by a 22-year-old [sic] black high school drop-out named Jimi (spelling was never his long suit) Hendrix.

On a good night, he can sound like the best of Lightning Hopkins and Karlheinz Stockhausen. Hendrix, on the threshold of a meteoric career, was greeted at the Monterey Pop Festival by the normally coolly laconic Stone, Brian Jones, who ripped his glasses off trying to scramble over the press picket fence to get closer to him. In England, Hendrix's home for the last 9 months, the Beatles, M.B.E.s and all, sit at his feet in the front row of clubs and watch him whip an endless procession of miracles out of his guitar.

He is normally joined by Mitch Mitchell on drums and Noel Redding (who Hendrix thinks looks suspiciously like Bob Dylan's grandmother) on bass, and together these three musicians produce a sound so wide and thick that it may well serve as more than just a figurative base for the Pop music of the future.

"If you can get your mind together

come across to me . . .

Are you experienced?"

. . . Jimi asks the musical question. He is experienced and he is an experience. Hendrix doesn't just play a guitar, he rapes it, abuses it, violates it, eats it, and masturbates it. Out of this chaos comes a beautifully absurd electronic sound, a dirty sound as opposed to a group like the Paupers whose electronic sound is clean. Not in value, but in style, like the difference between the Beatles' sound and the Stones' sound.

Hendrix and the Who, both show stoppers at Monterey, along with "unknown" English groups like the Pink Floyd, the Move, the Action, and the Soft Machine are involved in not just playing music but in acting it out; performing theatrical and environmental pieces that involve the audience as participants, not just spectators. They are adding experience to experience in their music, going far beyond just a light show. The theatrics of Hendrix's stage performance is not merely a cover for mediocre playing ability, it is a part of a whole, an idea from a total concept.

FP: How long have you been playing and how long has it taken you to develop your playing and performing style?

JH: I've been playing six or seven years, constantly developing a playing style. Most of it started about four years ago. When I first started, some cat tried to get me to play behind my head, because I never would move too much, y'know. I said, 'Oh man, who wants to do all that junk,' and then all of a sudden you start getting bored with yourself.

FP: You played around Nashville and the South for a while before going to England. What was it like?

JH: In the bars I used to play in, we'd get up on the platform where the fan was in one of them nice, hot, greasy, funky clubs. We'd play up there, and it was really hot, and the fan is makin' love to you. And you really had to play, cause those people were really hard to please. It was one of the hardest audiences in the South . . . they hear it all the time. Everybody knows how to play git-tar. You walk down the street and people are sitting on their porch playing more guitar . . . That's where I learned to play, really, in Nashville.

FP: What kind of equipment—guitars and amps—do you use?

JH: I use a Fender Stratocaster. Everyone's screaming about the seven-year-old Telecaster, and the 13-year-old Gibson, and the 92-year-old Les Paul. They've gone into an age bag right now, but it's nothing but a fad. The guitars now days play just as good. Y'know the salesman is always telling you that Chuck Berry took this one to the bathroom with him and he didn't have no toilet paper, so watch out for the pick guard . . .

The Stratocaster is the best all around guitar for the stuff we're doing. You can get the very bright trebles and the deep bass sound.

I tried Telecaster and it only has two sounds, good and bad, and a very weak tone variation.

A Guild guitar is very delicate, but it has one of the best sounds. I tried one of the new Gibsons, but I literally couldn't play it at all, so I'll stick with Fender. I really like my old Marshall tube amps, because when it's working properly there's nothing can beat it, nothing in the whole world. It looks like two refrigerators hooked together.

FP: You played on the recent Monkees tour. What was that like?

JH: We played seven performances on that tour. The personal part was beautiful—they're such good cats—but we weren't getting any advertising. The people didn't even know we were there until we hit the stage. Us and the Monkees? Different audiences. But it wasn't their fault. They knew what they wanted to see. They came to see the Monkees.

FP: Were you influenced at all by the Yardbirds, especially the electronic stuff they did with Jeff Beck?

JH: I wasn't really influenced by Beck. I only heard one record by him, "The Shape of Things," and I really dug it. I just listened to it and I liked it. You've got to dig everything and then get your own ideas. Too much digging and not enough doing will set you spinning. I mean other musicians are doing so much in their own way. There's one cat I'm still trying to get across to people. His name is Albert Collins. He's buried in a road band somewhere. He's good, really good. But he's a family cat, and doesn't want to go too far from home. Ain't that always the way?

FP: What American groups that you've heard do you like?

JH: Well, I really, really like Bloomfield's Electric Flag, and on the East Coast there's a group called the Mushroom. Big Brother. Moby Grape. Vanilla Fudge has a good record, but I've never seen them so I can't really say. East Coast Clear Light will be good. I picked up a whole lot of albums here one time and it turned out to be a whole lot of mess. Now I'm scared to buy anymore until I get to hear them.

FP: What do you think of the trend in Pop music, especially in England, toward the performance of theatrical pieces on stage, a total environment, utilizing a light show and such?

JH: It's good in one way, but it's kind of bad in another, because groups like the Procol Harum are overlooked because they don't move around. Then the people read a review and say, "Oh, this proves it, they bore the people," But the Harum's got words to say, they just don't jump around. It's not their fault. It's the fans who want only whatever's in fashion. A light show should work for you, not you for it. The Jefferson Airplane's nothing but shadows; nothing but voices to the light patterns. It's sloppy now, they'll throw any kind of light behind them. Like in the Roundhouse the strobes were on for four hours straight. I don't dig that . . . that's just pure nonsense.

But theatre pieces is really a different scene. Can you imagine taking *Othello* and putting it on in your own way? You'd write up some real groovy songs, you wouldn't necessarily have to say the exact lines . . . Great!

The Who is doing theatre pieces like, "A Quick One, While He's Away," but golly man, they just stand there when they sing it. They should jump into it . . . like we're going to do in October. I can't say any more [than] that. We got a little something in the skillet and I hope the grease don't burn away. Heh heh.

FP: Have you worked with the Beatles?

JH: Yeah, we work with them. Not musically though. Heh heh. They're beautiful cats. The Beatles and the Stones are all such beautiful cats off record, but it's a family thing. Such a family thing that sometimes it all begins to sound alike. Sometimes you just don't want to be part of the family.

I believe soon all the English records will sound alike, just like Motown all sounds alike. That's nice in a way, but what happens if you have your own thing going?

FP: What's happening with the Hippie Movement in England?

JH: It's not as organized over there, they've just got weird-looking cats. It's a small thing, not like it is here. I think the police are very groovy over there. They don't bother you very much. As a matter of fact, I was walking down the street in London completely out of my mind, completely and utterly, and a Police wagon came and they said, "Hi, Jimi, how are you doing?" and I replied, "Is it tomorrow . . . or just the end of time . . ."

"JIMI HENDRIX TALKS TO STEVE BARKER"[1]

STEVE BARKER | From UNIT, February 1968.

The JHE concluded their American tour and returned to England in late August 1967. In September, MELODY MAKER awarded Hendrix the title "World's Top Musician," and session work continued in October for the band's second LP. On November 8, the JHE played a gig at Manchester University, and Steve Barker was there to interview Hendrix for a second time.

In November 1967, whilst at Keele University, I was involved in the student magazine *Unit*—edited by Tony Elliott, who was to go on to found *Time Out*. I suggested a Hendrix piece, as the Jimi Hendrix Experience was due to play at Manchester University Students Union. In the period since the first interview, Jimi had become a megastar and was packing in audiences up and down the country and into Europe. I travelled to Manchester with some friends and we made our way to the gig.

On arriving I found the dressing room packed with people, including Mitch and Noel—but no Jimi. I asked where he was and someone said, "Check next door." I entered the room to find Jimi alone, leaning on a radiator next to a window about fifteen or twenty feet across the room. He looked up and said, "Hello, Steve. How are you?" I didn't think much about it at the time, but soon after, on reflection, I appreciated this as the mark of the man. Since I'd met him nine months previously, Jimi had experienced incredible success, fan adulation, and had accrued all the trappings of what was to become "the rock-star lifestyle"—hangers-on, sycophancy, pressure, freely available narcotics, etc. But he still remembered my name and behaved like a perfect gentleman, which is the way I always remember him.

—STEVE BARKER

2011

Hendrix on the cover of UNIT, February 1968. COURTESY OF STEVE BARKER

Steve Barker: [*Into microphone*] Testing 8, 12, 0.

Jimi Hendrix: [*Sings line from Bob Dylan's "Just Like Tom Thumb's Blues"*] "When you're lost in Juarez and it's Easter time too."

SB: The blurb on your first LP says you are trying to "create create create." Are you satisfied with what you're creating?

JH: We like to have our own sound, but we're not satisfied, not yet. You might be pleased with what you're doing once in a while, but never really satisfied. We're pleased with the LP we've just finished [*Axis: Bold as Love*], for instance, but the ideas we got out of it could go on to our next one.

SB: How far can you go with the music you're playing now?

JH: I don't know. You can go on until you bore yourself to death, I guess. You got to try something else.

SB: What will it be?

JH: I think I'll start all over again and come back as a king bee. [*Laughs.*]

SB: You write all of your own material. Where does it come from?

JH: Just from me. It's like . . . er, where does it come from? I'm not sure. Like, we go to clubs a lot and all around, riding in taxis, and you happen to see a lot of things. You see everything, experience everything, as you live. Even if you're living in a little room, you see a lot of things if you have imagination. The songs just come.

SB: [*Steve quotes a line from Jimi's "Burning of the Midnight Lamp."*] "Loneliness is such a drag?"

JH: That's what it is. It really is sometimes. That was the song I liked best of all we did. I'm glad it didn't make it big and get thrown around.

SB: Does this mean you're an introvert?

JH: Well, sometimes. Right then when I wrote "Midnight Lamp" I was, but really I have to catch myself and find out. I was feeling kind of down like that. So you go on into different moods, and when you write your mood comes through. So you can go back and listen to your own records and know how you were feeling then and how your moods change at different times.

SB: "Loneliness is such a drag" is a kind of whispery, quiet thing. How come you put these words in among powerful, extroverted music?

JH: I like to play loud. I always did like to play loud. The words of the song just come. They mean a lot, but I don't know how they come out. It starts off very quiet until we get into it.

SB: How much do you owe to a blues background?

JH: Not necessarily anything! I went down South and just listened to the way the people played, and I dug it. But then I like a lot of other things too—that's why we try to do our own stuff, make something new.

SB: There's been a lot of controversy over the responsibilities of pop stars. Do you yourself feel any?

JH: That's silly. Whatever a cat does in his private life should be his own business. Everybody knows this. But you can say it a million times, and it still won't get through to some people. I really don't feel responsible too much to myself— maybe that's all. There are so much other things inside that you feel you can do. There are so many things on my mind. I could start again now—a year of creative work for us is like nothing to a lot of other groups.

SB: Do you ever feel like going away and sorting yourself out, like Bob Dylan did?

JH: I think that's going to have to happen soon anyway, because everyone's getting so tired. You work so hard sometimes, and it gets to be really frustrating. . . . Just around now it's coming up to winter, and you've got to give everything a chance to work up in the spring. It's natural. That's when everything happens anyway—you know this—so everyone's going to have a heart attack just 'cause the flowers are lowering their heads for a second or two.

SB: What's happening to you in the spring?

JH: If I don't get hit by a car or a train, I'll be around.

SB: How come you got caught up in the hippie scene?

JH: What do you mean? [*Writhes and says in a deep voice, "I'm a hippie, I'm a hippie, baby."*] No, it just happened to come about that we were around at the time of psychedelia and all the in clothes. I dug that scene, but not necessarily what you call the "hippie scene." 'Cause I don't like classification anyway, regardless of the scene. We just happened to be playing freak-out and psychedelic things, but it does bother us because "psychedelic" only means mind-expansion anyway. I can't hear one single word the Pink Floyd are saying. It happens to us, but that's just anybody's opinion. There's so many other types of music—we just happened to be in that groove, that bag, right then.

SB: Do you try to communicate by words or sound when you're onstage, or both?

JH: Most of the songs we're doing now, people know the words, I think, but it probably doesn't mean much to them. They just want somebody to break their neck onstage.

SB: Does this mean you write primarily for yourself?

JH: Oh, definitely. One song we did called "I Don't Live Today" was dedicated to the American Indian and all minority depression groups. All I did was just use a few words, and they said, "What does that mean? That doesn't mean anything." Eeurggh! 'Cause it was only three or four lines in there anyway.

SB: How about straight piss-talking, like the Mothers of Invention?

JH: I like to listen to them, but we do our own thing. You know, we had a chance to go into that bag 'cause everybody's mind is still open, but we decided we didn't want to go that way completely towards strict freak-out. I hit the harp on our next LP [*laughs*]. The words are very, very important on this next one.

SB: Do you still dig Donovan and his golden underwear?

JH: We go over to his house, but he's in the States now. We have a lot of fun together.

SB: You said the love bit wouldn't last—looks like you're going to be right.

JH: This scene's like bells and everything and all those little pseudo-hippies running around flashing their little "Love, Not War" badges. Those kind won't last because they're going to hop on the next train, any train, that comes close to them and is easy to hop. But you don't really know anymore what a hippie is supposed to be.

SB: Is stage work still the most important part of your scene?

JH: Well, tonight I was so frustrated, man. We just couldn't get it together because we haven't been playing in so long. We've been working on the LP. If we did those songs now, they'd miss half the words because the P.A. went out, and we were playing so loud. So it wouldn't mean nothing to them if we did our new songs. Now we got to wait till the LP comes out—then we can interpret them so much better. It's so frustrating now—we're playing the same old songs, and they expect you to do this and do that, and then your guitar gets out of tune and you don't get a chance to play well. I don't like laying around. I like to play all the time.

SB: You once wanted to do the old Bukka White song "Fixin' to Die" as a single, but it never came out. Are there any pressures on you as to what material you record?

JH: No, not at all. We're just writing and playing what we want, but our moods change. Like once we wanted a Dylan song as one of our singles, then we wanted this and that. But we always wind up doing our own—regardless of whether they flop or not, at least we're doing our own thing. If you do someone else's song every fifth single, it shows something's missing. But you don't throw just anything out on record.

SB: What do you do it all for anyway?

JH: I like to be involved, and I like music. The same old story—all that goody-goody stuff. Music is a love to me. I love it, and the people are so nice. [*In a strained, sarcastic voice*] The money's great too.

SB: I heard you were in a group in New York with Tim Rose and Mama Cass.

JH: That's not true. It was another Jimmy. We just happen to have liked "Hey Joe." I seen Tim Rose about one time in the Village, for about half a second, and this is after we went back to the States. He tapped me on the shoulder and said [*imitates a stoned-sounding voice*], "Hi. I'm Tim Rose." And then he disappears. All this happened within a third of a second. I like his songs, but that's all I've ever seen of him.

SB: What are you trying to do with your new LP?

JH: I really can't say. It's very hard to explain your own type of music to some-body. Unless you have a very definite idea of where you're going, it doesn't really make any difference which direction you choose, as long as you're really honest about the songs you write.

SB: What do you think about the commercial pop scene right now?

JH: [*Simulates a confused stutter*] Well, have you heard the Marmalade and their record "I See the Rain"? I don't understand why that wasn't a hit.

SB: Because they have no name and no publicity?

JH: We didn't have a name when we first started.

SB: But you had the publicity.

JH: But we earned it, though, didn't we? I think we did. My hair is breaking off now from the hard English water. I'm almost going bald. I guess I used to have it cut much longer.

SB: What level are you aiming for when you make a record—the kids?

JH: No, not necessarily. We quite naturally want people to like it—that's the reason for putting the record out. You see, I have no taste. I couldn't say what's a good record and what's a bad one, really. We play records at the flat sometimes and say, "This is great," and then somebody will say, "Oh, yeah, but it's something else." Then they say, "That's terrible," and I'd say, "That's great—the tremolos, for instance." [*Laughs*.] So I don't have no feeling about commercial records. I don't know what a commercial record really is. So what we do is write and try to get it together as best as possible for anybody who'd really dig it. It doesn't make any difference who.

SB: How big a part do visuals play in your stage work?

JH: You just do it when you feel like it sometimes. I didn't feel like leaping about tonight too much. I used to feel I had to do it, but not anymore. Man, you'd have a heart attack if you were doing it every night like we were doing it two or three months ago. We'd be dead by this time. Anyway, you can't do it right unless you feel it. Half of the things I do I don't even know it, because I just felt like it at the time. If you have everything planned out and one little thing goes wrong, you think, "Oh, no! What am I supposed to be doing now? Oh, yeah, I'm supposed to be going like this—do do do de do. 'Hi, everybody. I'm doing it.'" So you'd really be in a world of trouble if one little thing goes wrong.

SB: Do you think you're a changed person since you came to England?

JH: I didn't used to talk so much before.

SB: To people like me.

JH: No, that's alright. [*Laughs*.] Ho hum. I'm as good as bunnies—and you know how good bunnies are.

Noel Redding: Talk to Mitch. He's got a very good voice.

SB: What would you think if people went off on you like they do with Dylan?

JH: I don't think about it. Ever since he's been around, people have been kicking him around, saying, "Oh, man, he sings like a broken-leg dog."

[*At this point, Jill Nicholls from the* Manchester Independent *asked Jimi the following question*] Mr. Hendrix, is there anything you want materially?

[*Noel and other men in the room burst into laughter.*]

JH: Eh?

JN: Is there anything left?

JH: There's a whole lot of things left—thousands of them. I see them downtown every day. Millions of 'em. Ohh! Marvelous!

SB: Do you ever think about going back to the States?

JH: I think about it every single day. I really miss it—like the West Coast, because nothing has happened for me. I just like to be out there. I like the weather, the scenery, and some of the people. You can buy a chocolate milkshake in a drugstore, chewing gum in a gas station, and soup from little machines on the road. It's great, it's beautiful. It's all screwed up and nasty and prejudiced, and it's great and beautiful. It has everything. The same things we hear from there now about the troubles is the same things we hear from Russia—it's just propaganda, just like Radio Free Europe tells the Russians. [*At this point the road manager asks Jimi if he will do a photo shoot, but Jimi continues.*] In the States I was playing behind other groups. And for only the first two months before I left the States, we was playing in the Village. I had my own group and we had offers from record companies all over the place, but I don't think we was ready then. So finally I came over here [to England] with Chas Chandler, with the main ambition to get a group and try to make with something new, whereas in the States I'd been playing behind people like Joey Dee.

SB: What did you think of it?

JH: I don't dig playing in Top-40 R&B groups. They get feedback in "[In the] Midnight Hour." You can't do nothing free—everything is completely precise. We came over here with one purpose, and that was to make it. That's the whole scene. As soon as we start getting behind the times, that'll be the time to give up. That might be tomorrow evening about 5:45, but we'll try for as long as possible to keep our own sound, regardless of how it might change. [*Jimi notices Steve's microphone.*] What a pretty microphone!

SB: Yeah, it's cute, isn't it?

JH: Yeah. Thank you!

1. "Jimi Hendrix: An Unpublished November 1967 Interview with Steve Barker," by Steve Barker, Jas Obrecht Music Archive, March 30, 2011, http://jasobrecht.com/jimi-hendrix-unpublished-november-1967-interview-steve-barker/.

"AN EXPERIENCE WITH HENDRIX"

LIAM AND ROISIN MCAULEY | From THE GOWN, December 7, 1967.

On November 27, two Queens University reporters from the independent student newspaper THE GOWN interviewed Hendrix and reviewed the evening concerts at Whitla Hall in Belfast. This date also marked Hendrix's twenty-fifth birthday. The JHE's third American single, "Foxey Lady" (backed with "Hey Joe"), was released in the United States as well.

It is now an acknowledged fact that a Pop Concert should be ear-splitting and kaleidoscopic. Last week's Jimi Hendrix concert fulfilled both criteria. On stage, amplifiers dwarfed and deafened the performers; in the gallery frenzied amateurs feverishly juggled with six squares of colored cellophane and two spotlights. Fifteen hundred people sat in the "Whitla" and waited for their minds to be blown . . .

It was Hendrix' s birthday. The audience sang "Happy Birthday" in a feeble and slightly embarrassed fashion. The compére hurriedly initiated a cry of "We want Jim." The lights dimmed and weaved; Hendrix exploded onto the stage; "Plug your ears, it's gonna be LOUD."

The ensuing welter of noise, confusion and flashing lights could not obscure the fact that Jimi Hendrix is a guitarist of considerable talent, though it is at times difficult to separate sheer gimmickness from genuine musical expression. He played the guitar in fifty different positions from the Kama Sutra, made an indecent assault upon the amplifier, and in a final frenetic gesture smashed a Fender

71

Stratacaster [sic] against the wall (having first displayed method in his madness by unplugging it). It was as though he had finally succeeded in identifying the instrument with his own arrogant virility and subsequently frustrated with the latter had involved it in the final act of destruction. It is now as important to smash a guitar as it is to play it. Hendrix did both with admirable expertise.

Offstage, Hendrix is incongruously mild, affable, and unassuming. He sat in the dressing room, temporarily detached from the bevy of road-managers, and munched birthday cake. He constantly strummed a guitar covered in psychedelic patterns, "Just something I painted on in half an hour."

"The comments on my dress don't worry me, it's good publicity. My hairstyle? I got it from watching a lot of old Tony Curtis movies." Playing for anything from £750 to £1,000 for a single performance, Hendrix claims that the money is not so important now, although his original motive in coming to Britain was that he "needed the bread." "I don't mind about the money so long as the atmosphere is good."

"Influences? I'm influenced by Dylan; I'm influenced by the whole world. My songs are usually personal. I was glad, for instance, that 'The Wind Cries Mary' which meant a lot to me, wasn't a big hit. I wouldn't like it kicked around like any old Dave Dee number.

"Drugs? If they do something for people then it's up to them. Take the Beatles for example. People are like sheep, they have to follow somebody. If this Maharishi cat turns them on, I suppose that's OK. But I think that a human being should believe in himself a little more.

"I have no views on Vietnam because it doesn't affect me personally. If something doesn't directly affect my life, then I'm not interested.

"The press depict me as some kind of monster."

Hendrix is indeed widely known as "the wild man of British Pop," but whatever one may make of his performance on the stage, offstage he is polite (he deftly prevented me from sitting in a puddle of cold coffee), approachable, and articulate. A monster? Hardly.

"POP MAN JIMI TO SUE DISC FIRM"

PETER OAKES | From THE PEOPLE, December 17, 1967.

In September, MELODY MAKER reported news of producer Ed Chalpin's lawsuit against Hendrix for breach of a 1965 contract. To complicate matters further, while the JHE were on tour in the States, Hendrix visited Chalpin's New York studio, where several songs were recorded. When Decca Records released the single "Hush Now" from that 1967 session, Hendrix filed suit. Ironically, Decca had turned down Hendrix's "Hey Joe" the year before when he was looking for a UK record deal.

Not for nothing is Jimi Hendrix called The Wild Man of Pop.

He has a way-out hairstyle, a raving stage act . . . and now a hit-size grievance against a giant British disc firm.

In fact, he is to sue the company—Decca Records.

The fuss is revolving around a record called "Hush Now," which Decca have recently issued on their London label. The record, says the 22-year-old [sic] coloured guitarist and leader of the Jimi Hendrix Experience, was out without his consent.

He is claiming high-court damages against Decca.

Jimi, who has had four hit records since coming to Britain a year ago, said: "I walked into a record store and saw this record of mine. When I played it, I discovered that it had been recorded with a jam session I did in New York. We had only been practicing in the studio. I had no idea it was being recorded."

Jimi Hendrix mocking the Curtis Knight single "Hush Now," December 16, 1967. MIRRORPIX

Independent

Jimi went on: "On one side of the disc is 'Hush Now.' I only play the guitar, the singer's voice has been superimposed. On the other—'Flashing'—all I do is play a couple of notes. Man, I was shocked when I heard it!"

Jimi—his record called "Purple Haze" reached No. 3 in the charts earlier this year—is being represented by solicitor David Jacobs.

His previous hits have been issued by Polydor, an independent label. So far the disc in dispute made little impact on the record-buying public. On the record credits for both the numbers are given to Jimi Hendrix and Curtis Knight, who is an American soul singer. A spokesman for Decca said: "We recently released a single recording of Jimi Hendrix over which there is some dispute. We acquired the material from an American producer who said it had been recorded in New York. We cannot make any further comment as the matter is in the hands of our solicitors."

Five months ago Jimi was reported[1] to have been banned by the Daughters of the American Revolution, the American women's organization. They felt he was too erotic for his audiences of predominantly seven to 12-year-olds.

---

1. A press release was concocted to explain Hendrix's abrupt departure from the Monkees tour. Many publications printed it as a news story, but in fact all on the tour agreed it was time for the JHE to make it on their own.

INTERVIEW WITH JIMI HENDRIX

MEATBALL FULTON | From an interview conducted by Meatball Fulton on December 9, 1967, for ZBS Radio.

Journalist Meatball Fulton, aka Tom Lopez, interviewed Hendrix in London on December 9, shortly after the JHE's second album was released in the UK. Fulton approached the interview freestyle, without any predetermined questions. This allowed Hendrix to talk openly about whatever was on his mind. During the interview, Fulton sensed Hendrix's recurring frustrations with recording techniques and management issues, but he kept recording. Fulton later commented, "It's a very weird thing to hear. I had the impression that he had few friends if any that could see him as person, not as a pop star or a thing, and if that's true, it's really sad" (HENDRIX SPEAKS: THE JIMI HENDRIX INTERVIEWS, Rhino Records, 1990).

Meatball Fulton: Did you start to flow with it when you started to get this image [with women]?

Jimi Hendrix: Oh, it was worse before. I used to be on the block starving, and girls used to help me . . . really help me, too. Ever since then, that's why I say to myself, "Wow. Any girl I meet now, I want to show her my appreciation for what they did for me before." No, serious though. [*Laughs.*] I don't know. It's just nature . . .

I really don't care what my record does as far as chart-wise. We had this one that only made number eleven, which everyone around here hated. They said it was the worst record, you know. But I think that was the best one we ever made . . . "The Burning of the Midnight Lamp." Not as far as recording, because the recording techniques are really bad, you know. You couldn't hear the words so good. Probably that's what it was.

MF: How are you satisfied with the recording techniques generally?

JH: Not at all.

MF: What about the LPs?

JH: Not at all. Even worse on the LPs. It makes me so mad. 'Cause, you see, that's a part of us. See, we record it and everything and then all of a sudden something happens and it just comes out all screwed, and you just get so mad, you just don't want to know about it anymore. Our next LP, every track is gonna have to be just right or else I'm just gonna forget about it. I mean, not forget about it . . . you say that but you know you're not. But that's the way I feel.

MF: Do you think they're better in the States as far as recording? It really depends on the engineer, though.

JH: It all depends on what you want really. It all depends on where you go, too. It really depends on so many things, the cutting of it—that's a whole scene, the cutting of it. You can mix and mix and mix and get such a beautiful sound, and when they cut it, they can just screw it up so bad.

MF: I don't understand.

JH: I wouldn't understand that either 'cause we, you know—ooooh, it comes out so bad. 'Cause they go by levels and all that. Some people don't have any imagination. See, when you cut a record, right before it's being printed, you know, when you cut the master, if you want a song where you have really deep sound, where you have depth and all this, you must . . . almost remix it again right there at the cutting place. And 99 percent don't even do this. They just say, "Oh, turn it up," so their mixture doesn't go over or their mixture doesn't go under. And there it is, you know. It's nothing but one-dimensional.

MF: Do you get the time you need? I mean, because it's so costly anyway.

JH: The money doesn't make any difference to me because that's what I make it for—to make better things happen. I don't have no value on money at all. That's my only fault. I just get things that I see and want. And try to put it into music. I want to have stereo where it goes . . . up—the sounds goes up, and behind and underneath. But all you can get now is just across and across. Our new LP was made in sixteen days, which I'm very sad about.

MF: That one that's just out recently?

JH: Yeah. No use even talking about or discussing why. 'Cause it's really a bad scene. But it just makes me mad. It could have been so much better.

MF: It's mainly the sound quality?

JH: Well, the songs could have been better too. You know, that's what I think though. As soon as you're finished you got a hundred completely new ideas.

MF: Well, it's good in a sense, because your mind's purring along, moving along nicely.

JH: It's not necessarily getting any better, but like you might move to different things, you know?

MF: Do you feel that the groups are free to change as they want to?

JH: No. Half of them aren't. They're all thinking about their career, about their future so much. I really don't give a damn about my future or my career. I just want to make sure I can get out what I want. That's why I say we're very lucky. Because we didn't have to, you know, make it. I said it'd be great but I really didn't care. Just as long as we could be happy with what we're doing, with what we're recording and stuff like that. With doing what we want to do, we're still— we're not really doing what we want.

MF: What about the new LP? You've been thinking about this.

JH: Yeah. Well, I wanted to make it a double LP, you know? Which will be almost impossible.

MF: Because of the cost, you mean?

JH: Yeah. Well, it's a big hassle. Nobody wants to do that. The record producers don't want to do it and companies don't want to do it. I'm willing to spend every single penny on it if I thought it was good enough. But there you go, you know? I do that and then they leave me out there.

MF: What about the length of the songs too? Would you like them to be much longer?

JH: It all depends on what kind of song it is. If it's a song with three or four movements, well, yeah. Now there's this one song I wrote named "Eyes and Imagination"—that's the name of it. And it's about fourteen minutes long, but every sentence or every two sentences tell a completely different story. It's nothing but imagination. It starts off with this baby crying, a brand-new day is being born, and then you hear these bullets, you know [*laughs*], in the background . . . But it goes on about four major movements, and it always goes back to this one little thing. You must have that one little thing through it. But I don't know. There're so many songs I wrote that we haven't even done yet and we'll probably never do. It's because—oooh, I don't know—there are a lot of things around here. It's a really bad scene. You know, we must be Elvis Presleys and rock 'n' rolls and Troggs. We must be that. [*Laughs.*] And there'll be no smoking in the gas chamber.

MF: Do you think people will be doing longer numbers, or trying to? Moving towards symphonies . . .

JH: Well, I think they should if they have something to offer really. If the number really has to be long. If they say "I have this number and it's really . . . but I just can't get it together unless I have more time, I just need more time on it." Well, then they should. They really should. They should never hold time like that because of a number. You know the song we had named "Purple Haze"? That . . . had about a thousand, thousand words and oooh, oooh; it just gets me so mad 'cause that isn't even the "Purple Haze," you know.

MF: What do you mean that it isn't—

JH: I don't know, man. I'm just a frustrated little hen. That's all. That's what I feel like. You should have heard it, man. I had it written out. It was about going through, through this land. This mythical . . . because that's what I like to do is write a lot of mythical scenes. You know, like the history of the wars on Neptune. And all this mess, you know, and the reason why the rings are there. They got the Greek gods and all that mythology. Well, you can have your own mythology scene. Or write fiction. Complete fiction. I mean anybody can say, "I was walking down the street, and I seen an elephant floating through the sky." But it has no meaning at all, there's nothing except the elephant there, you know. And if you don't watch out you might break your neck!

MF: Do you think you'll be able to make more demands as you continue?

JH: Yeah. This whole thing is gonna blow wide open . . . Can you remember when you was a little baby? I think your memory comes through. When you think now, it's blank before that. I think that's the way you come about other scenes, too. 'Cause human beings die too easily, you know.

MF: What about the animal? You were talking about an animal?

JH: Like you might see an animal or something like that. And also you might have a very funny feeling go through you for a second.

MF: Do you mean like looking into its eyes? Or not necessarily . . . or just the animal itself?

JH: Okay. One time I seen this deer, you know—'cause you know I see a lot of deers around where I used to be from. And I said, "Wait," and something went through me for a second, like I'd seen him before . . . like I had some real close connection with that deer for one split second and then it just went away like that, you know? A lot of friends of mine told me about that happening to them, you know?

Have you ever laid in bed and you was in this complete state where you couldn't move? And you feel like you're going deeper and deeper into something, but not sleep, but it's something else. And every time I go into that I say, "Ah hell, I'm scared as hell," and you get all scared and stuff and so you try to say, "Help, help." You can't move, you can't scream, and you say, "Help, help." You can't move and you can't speak but you say, "Help, help," and you finally get out of it, you know? You just can't move. It's a very funny feeling. But one time that feeling was coming through me and I say, "Aha, here we go. This time I'm just gonna let it happen and see where I go to." I just wanted to see what happens and it was really getting scary, man, it was going *whoosh* like that, you know? And I said, "I'm not even asleep, this is really strange." And then somebody knocked on the door. I said, "Oh," because I wanted to find out.

MF: Can you remember some things really far back? Like when you were a baby?

JH: Yeah, I can remember the nurse putting the diaper . . .

MF: Can you really?

JH: Yeah. When the nurse . . . I don't know what I was there for, but I remember when I used to wear diapers. And then she was talking to me. She took me out of this crib, or something like that. And then she held me up to this window—this was in Seattle—and she was showing me something up against the sky. It was fireworks or something like that. It must have been the Fourth of July, you know. I remember her putting the diaper on me and almost sticking me. I remember I didn't feel so good, you know. I musta been in the hospital sick about something, and I had a bottle and all that kinda stuff and then she held me up to the window and she was saying something about . . . I was looking, and the sky was all [*makes strange noises*] . . .

MF: Almost an acid thing.

JH: That's right. That's what it was. Only beforehand. [*Laughing*] My first trip there. That nurse turns me on. Being high off the penicillin she probably gave me.

MF: Can you remember any other things?

JH: I remember when I was small enough to fit in a clothesbasket. You know those straw clothesbaskets they have in America, that they put all the dirty clothes in? It's only about like that [*gestures*].

MF: They call them hampers or something.

JH: Yeah. Hampers. I remember when my cousin and I was playing around. I must have been about three or something. Sometimes when you're sitting around and you start remembering things. Those are the first two that come to my mind. And some dreams that I had when I was real little, you know. Like my mother was being carried away on this camel. And there was a big caravan and she was saying, "Well, I'm gonna see you now," and she was going under these trees, and you could see the shade—you know, the leaf patterns—across her face. You know how the sun shines through a tree, and if you go under the shadow of the tree the shadows go across your face. Well, these were in green and yellow shadows. And she was saying, "Well, I won't be seeing you too much anymore, you know." And then about two years after that she died. And I said, "Where you going?" I remember that, I always will remember that one.

There are dreams you never forget. There's this one dream where you go down like that, you go down this real big hill, but it has this real long grass and there are a whole lot of bananas on the floor, on the floor of this hill, but they're all growing from the ground, each one separate. I remember that, and we was skating across that. I don't know how we were, but what we did was we poured out this stuff that we made up. You know, these big bags. We poured it out across the bananas. And it fills up all the gaps between the bananas and then you skate across it. I remember those things.

MF: You must have been dreaming in color when you were very young.

JH: Oh yeah. I was. I don't remember too many. The closest thing to a black-and-white dream I ever had was in pastel shades like . . . maroon and ah . . . dark, you know, then very light maroon. And then there's this big gold clip—out of nowhere. It was great. And that was the closest I ever got to black and white.

[*Because Fulton did not ask a question to prompt these next comments from Jimi, he narrated, postinterview, "This final section is only a few words about reincarnation and death."*]

JH: Everybody shouldn't get hung up when it's time for you to die, because all you're doing is just getting rid of that old body, you know. The same old body you've been having for about—what is it?—about seven years. People really believe that every single person born here is completely different, you know, I mean that's true but, through the times, can you imagine all these. But what if we all was supposed to go to heaven and all that. Can you imagine all these people who died beforehand, and all of us, all up in heaven? All living on top of each other, "Hey, man, move over man, I don't have no room up here! 'Cause oh hell, you had no business dying, did you?" So oh, well, God! So can you imagine that?! Wow!

PART III

January 1968 to June 1968

THE JHE'S GROWING POPULARITY caused management to keep a full schedule of recording, touring, and interviews for the group in 1968. Hendrix began showing signs of stress and grew bored with playing the same songs night after night.

On January 4, police in Gothenburg, Sweden, arrested Hendrix for smashing up his hotel room. He admitted to consuming three beers and two whiskeys but felt someone may have spiked his drinks. The authorities enacted an immediate travel ban until he appeared for a court hearing. Hendrix was eventually fined 3,200 Swedish crowns for his flare-up and had to pay for damages to the hotel. A brief mention of the incident turned up in the song "My Friend."

In between tour dates, the group worked on a new double album, but tensions simmered. On January 21, Redding walked out of a session, frustrated with Hendrix's endless takes. Comanager Chandler quit work on the sessions in May and parted ways with the group. Hendrix took over production and used the opportunity to experiment with other musicians and studio effects. The result was *Electric Ladyland*, which would be the group's highest-charting album yet. It featured "All Along the Watchtower," the group's only top-forty hit in America.

Hendrix was voted "Best Musician in the World" by Britain's *Disc and Music Echo*'s reader poll, and *Rolling Stone* later bestowed on him the title "Performer of the Year" for 1968.

On May 3, ABC-TV started sixteen days of filming for a documentary titled *Jimi Hendrix Experience*. The crew captured the JHE in concert, in the recording studio, and in casual moments in their hotel rooms. During one of the interviews, Hendrix mentioned he was working on a new type of music that would give pop more respect.

INTERVIEW WITH JIMI HENDRIX

JAY RUBY | From the original press-conference recording, January 31, 1968, and JAZZ & POP, July 1968.

The JHE returned to America on January 30, 1968, and a press conference was set up the following day in Manhattan. Several journalists were there to interview the group, including Jay Ruby, who was an assistant professor of anthropology at Philadelphia's Temple University.

On January 31, 1968, *Jazz & Pop* interviewed Jimi Hendrix together with other members of the Experience, Noel Redding and Mitch Mitchell, at the Copter Lounge atop the Pan Am Building in New York. The occasion was a press conference given for Jimi and four other British groups, Eric Burdon and the Animals, Soft Machine, the Alan Price Set, and Nova Express. Amid the usual noise and confusion provided by the press, TV cameras, agents and assorted other freaks and a fistfight, we managed to corner Jimi long enough to tape this interview. If parts of it seem somewhat disjointed, it's because we were interrupted several times, and on one occasion another interviewer started his own interview in the middle of ours. Jimi appeared to weather the event much better than we did. It was truly a mixed-media environment.

Jay Ruby: What's the musical scene like in England? Is it different from here?

Jimi Hendrix: Well, yes, it is. It's a little more together as far as the musicians are concerned. They all know each other and they get a small place and everybody congregates around London. It's not that much different really. They have their own scene and we've got our own scene over here.

JR: Do you like it better over there as a musician?

JH: Not necessarily. I like to jam a lot and they don't do that much over there. I like to play with other cats, but you just can't do that over there sometimes.

JR: For what you are trying to do with your music, do you feel that the trio form is best?

JH: We just happen to be a trio; that's the reason we are like this. We tried the organ for about fifteen minutes and it didn't work out. It made us sound like just anybody. But it isn't ideal that it's a trio. It just happened like that. But we might offer a [completely] different presentation. I can't really say more about that part . . . say around summer or late fall for instance . . . we'll offer a [completely] different presentation to it.

JR: Are you really into this [destruction] thing?

JH: Not basically. There are times when we do it; but we play millions and millions of gigs, and when we do this [destruction] thing maybe three or four times, it's because we feel like it. It might have been because we had some personal problems.

JR: So when you do it, you're doin' it because . . .

JH: Because I'm mad, or worked up or something, you know.

JR: How does it feel?

JH: Oh, it's a feeling like . . . you feel very frustrated and the music gets louder and louder and you start thinking about different things, and all of a sudden, *crash, bang*. The next thing you know, everything's up in smoke.

JR: Do you think about it ahead of time?

JH: No. You couldn't get that together. We did it once before and somebody said, "That's great, why don't you plan it out?" Plan what out? It just happens, that's all.

JR: Whom do you admire most as a guitarist? Who's doing things that you like now?

JH: Well, it's very hard to say. But as far as the blues scene goes, some of the things that Albert King or Eric Clapton do are very good. I don't have any favorites. It's very hard because there are so many different styles and it's so bad to put everybody in the same bag.

JR: Whom do you listen to?

JH: I like to listen to anybody as long as they don't bore me. I tend towards the blues as far as guitar players are concerned. The music itself . . . I like things from Roland Kirk and the Mothers [of Invention].

JR: A lot of people compare you to Clapton.

JH: That's one thing I don't like at all. First of all they do that, and then they say, "Okay now, blues first of all," and we just say, "We don't want to play blues all the time." We just don't feel like it all the time. We want to do other things, do nice songs or different things. But, like, the blues is what we're supposed to dig. But, you see, there are other things we can play, too. And we just don't think alike . . . Sometimes the notes might sound like it, but it's a completely different scene between those notes.

Mitch Mitchell: When we first started, Jimi was very much influenced by people like Dylan, and I wasn't into that scene at all. Now Jimi's gotten turned on to people like Mingus and Roland Kirk. We just learn from each other, balance each other. It's a lot better.

JR: And enjoy each other, right, and have the whole thing happen.

JH: Right. You should hear him really get together on drums; that's another thing that makes me mad too. All three of us, we all have our own little scene as far as

The Jimi Hendrix Experience on the cover of BEAT INSTRU-
MENTAL, April 1968. STEVEN ROBY/STRAIGHT AHEAD ARCHIVES COLLECTION

music goes. Noel likes nice gutsy rock, and he plays guitar. He's been playing bass only since he's been with us. And Mitch plays a whole lot of drums and yet people get stuck on one thing.

JR: Working with three people is so beautiful. You can integrate yourself tightly and together. And the new sound seems to be so big.

JH: On the first LP we were emphasizing sustained notes and the really free scene. On this new LP we have now, it's quieter as far as the guitar goes, and it might seem dull to some people, but we're emphasizing the words and the drums. On the next one we're getting together, it's going to be completely out of sight.

JR: Yeah, I've heard on the new album that hasn't been distributed yet here, but the integration of the sounds of the street and the happenings outside . . . the sound of people's feet in the studio . . .

JH: [*Laughs.*] Yeah, Roger Mayer's big feet.[1]

JR: Some people have difficulty making the transition from concerts to records. You have not. Do you see yourselves as primarily a live or a studio group?

JH: Either you can dig it as a record or in person. Like some want to hear one thing—when you make a record you put a certain sound in the record or a certain little freaky thing—like the sound of raindrops reversed and echoed and phased and all that. It's because you are trying to emphasize a certain point in the record. So people already have this in their minds when they go to see you, and they expect to hear that. But the main thing is the words, and they can feel the other thing and not necessarily hear it. We improvise so much on stage that a two-minute song might come out to be twenty minutes.

[*At this point in the interview, Ruby is interrupted by another reporter who is upset and feels he's doing this for his own magazine, which was not the case.*]

JR: I'm celebrating a new magazine, baby. Jimi Hendrix and I have just incorporated a new magazine called . . .

JH: Captain Curry's Coffin.[2]

[*Confusion in the room continues before the interview resumes.*]

JR: Let's get back to the blues for a minute. How do you define it?

JH: You can have your own blues. It doesn't necessarily mean that folk blues is the only type of blues in the world. I heard some Irish folk songs that were so funky—the words were so together and the feel. That was a great scene. We do this blues one on the last track of the LP [*Axis: Bold as Love*] on the first side. It's called "If 6 Were [*sic*] 9." That's what you call a great feeling of blues. We don't even try to give it a name. Everybody has some kind of blues to offer, you know.

JR: What about the white/black scene? Is white blues really the blues?

JH: Well, I'll tell you. The Bloomfield band is ridiculously out of sight and you can feel what they're doing no matter what color the eyes or armpits might be, because I can really feel it. One time I said, "Okay, Paul Butterfield, they've got this white cat down in the Village playing harmonica, really funky." So we all go down to the Village and then, wow, he turned me on so much, I said, "Look at that!" He was really deep into it and nobody could touch him there because he was in his own little scene. He was really so happy. I don't care, like I said before, it all depends on how your ears are together and how your mind is and where your ears are.

JR: They say that in England, it's a whole different thing. They don't make a distinction. It's a sound—and it doesn't matter what color you are—you're playing. We've still got that hang-up here.

JH: It isn't really a hang-up because that's human beings—deep down inside anyway, you know. That's natural, just like being in a fight, nobody can go out on the street with this little boy. America is a little boy. Countries to me are just like little kids, playing with different toys. But all these countries will soon grow up. It's no problem. Humans just compete with each other.

JR: Do you play different to an American audience?

JH: I couldn't even compare it. They're quieter over there. They listen very, very close, and then they show their appreciation at the end.

JR: Let's talk a little bit about jazz.

JH: Well, Roland Kirk and Charlie Mingus, and he [Noel Redding] can take care of the rest.

JR: That's it for you?

JH: Oh, no. Those are just the main people I think about.

JR: How about Coltrane?

JH: Oh yes, he's great. There are so many cats, they've got their own little scenes. Mitch digs Elvin Jones a lot.

JR: Who are some of the groovy people in jazz that you like?

MM: There's Tony Williams, and the structure of Richard Davis. I like Coltrane, as well. But Kirk is nearer to what I actually like. It's very comparable with Jimi. A lot of people call Jimi like a joker for using electronic effects. Well, I call Kirk a joker when he plays two horns, but he's no joker to me, man. There are only two kinds of music—good and bad— regardless of what you play or what sort of bag you might be in.

JH: [Kirk] hasn't even started yet. We haven't even started yet either. When you hear [his music], you can hear so much for the future. You can hear some of the things he's going into—not necessarily about notes, but you can hear the feelings.

MM: It's people like Kirk who are cutting down snobbery, because in every kind of music, even in rock 'n' roll, it exists. Where people just can't see anything outside. It's like certain jazz musicians I met in London recently who just don't want to know anything else apart from maybe Sun Ra, and it's a bad scene. If you can't sit outside your music—outside one particular scene, man, you need something done to your head.

JH: There's so much happening, especially if you have an open mind for music, because, as we all know, music is an art.

JR: The thing that turns me on to the scene today is the way everything changes so fast. For instance, what you did on your first album is different from what you did on the second.

JH: Yes, we noticed that after we listened to it. We were really deep into making our second LP.

JR: This is not conscious, you're not aware of the fact?

JH: No, not at all. We try to make a change. You fix your life and say, "Well, we're going to do this next time." We get ideas—groovy ideas, you know.

MM: Everything's a very natural progression. I don't know—I might not be here tomorrow, so I'm doing what I'm doing now.

JR: This is very different from what music has been before. No music has ever changed as fast as this has.

JH: Well, I know what you mean, like the Chuck Berry scene. I'd feel guilty if we did something like that—using the same background with every single song and only different words. That shows that you're going in the word scene. It's like anybody who's hungry—that's young and wants to get into music—anybody like that has got to go into so many different bags. They have got so much to be influenced by, so many different things in the world.

JR: Is it just being young?

JH: Not necessarily, no. I mean "young" being ideas, being hungry . . . not necessarily being hungry for food.

JR: So maybe it's always going to change?

JH: Well, maybe. Maybe we'll settle down. There are some things . . . but some things are just too personal. They might catch up to us later. Everyone starts talking about that—they have to pick on something, and they say, "Instead of using guitar, bass, and drums, they're getting tiresome." Blah, blah, woff, woff. Dig Bob Dylan. He's been in this business for ages and he's really out of sight because there's a lot of personal things. You just don't want to put a lot of junk on top of it, like violins for certain numbers, unless it calls for it.

JR: When you record, who does what you call the gimmicks?

JH: All those things are our own mind . . . all those things are coming out of us. We do a lot of things. Like, on the last track of the last LP ["Bold as Love"], it's called phasing. It makes it sound like planes going through your membranes and chromosomes. A cat got that together accidentally and he turned us on to it.[3] That's the sound we wanted, it was a special sound, and we didn't want to use tapes of airplanes, we wanted to have the music itself warped.

JR: When you put a song together for a recording session, what do you do? Do you play first and then put the sounds in or do you put them together at the same time?

JH: Well, it depends. Sometimes we play through Leslie speakers and then some-times we might put it on afterward as we play. A lot of times we record the three of us as one instrument and then build around that.

JR: You don't do an arrangement ahead of time?

JH: Oh yes. We have ideas in our minds and then we'll add to them.

---

1. On the track "If 6 Was 9," a wooden platform was constructed to capture foot stomps.
2. The odd phrase stuck with Hendrix—on April 20, 1968, "Little Miss Strange" was first recorded under the title "Lilacs for Captain Curry's Coffin."
3. Hendrix was referring to engineer Eddie Kramer. Roger Mayer also had a lot to do with the special foot-pedal devices he made for Hendrix's guitar.

"THE PERSECUTION & ASSASSINATION OF ROCK AND ROLL, AS PERFORMED BY THE JIMI HENDRIX EXPERIENCE . . . UNDER THE DIRECTION OF JUMPING JIMI HIMSELF, THE CASSIUS CLAY OF POP"

MICHAEL THOMAS | From EYE, July 1968.

The JHE performed two shows on March 2 at New York's Hunter College, where EYE magazine's Michael Thomas interviewed Hendrix. The reporter touched on a variety of topics, including what happened on Hendrix's first visit home after becoming an international superstar.

Jimi (Jimmy?) Hendrix dropped out of the toughest school in town, Garfield High School in Seattle, Washington, six years ago [sic],[1] and didn't go home till this spring. They say the mayor was all set to give him the keys to the city, but it was Lincoln's birthday and City Hall was closed. So old Garfield High School said they'd give him an honorary diploma to make up. Somehow, though, that didn't work out either. Even then they would have liked to have him perform before

97

Tuesday-morning school assembly. The trouble was, all his equipment was on its way to Los Angeles, but he went on over anyway and said hello and he was glad to be back, and split after ten minutes. All of which just goes to show that you can't go home again, even if you are the best guitar-picker in the world and the ranking psychedelic superspade heavyweight of pop.

That is, people *say* he's the best guitarist in the world—people who know how to play the guitar; and even those who don't, like me, can tell that it takes a soul man to wrestle with one, and produce, in the heat of battle, such a thrilling, and at the same time unsettling, assembly of down-home blues and orgiastic electronics. It's one thing to play the guitar, but it's something else to violate it. And Jimi Hendrix, be forewarned, has only just begun.

Each of us has his own special gift, and it's no easy thing, for example, to smash up a pile of quarters with a nine-pound hammer (and end up with more money than you started with), which is quite often the experience that the Jimi Hendrix Experience reminds me of. What's odd about that is that I've never heard the sound of smashing quarters, in the same way that I've never heard anything like Jimi Hendrix, but I *have* heard the sound of a handful of quarters (old ones) being shaken in the hand—it's pretty, and it seems a shame to smash them up, just as it seems a shame for Hendrix to smash up his own music in order to demonstrate a special gift. He is a truly gifted guitarist. He can play blues riffs, snatches of folksy melody, all night long, and more than likely never repeat himself, and he can do it with one hand behind his back. His rhythms evolve with all the twists and turns, unexpected deaths and suspended explanations of a murder mystery, and he leaps from key to key like an acrobat, and rarely, if ever, loses his footing. He has, too, an intuitive understanding and mastery of electronic melodrama, and he's got all the amplification he needs to try it out. The trouble is, he doesn't know when to stop. His whole performance assumes that nothing succeeds like excess. He's always got a little something up his sleeve, or over his shoulder, or between his legs to add, and then a little something else, and zing go the strings, fun goes the box, and wah-wah goes the pedal, in a kind of relentless, nihilist destruction of the elements. To give him his due, it's done with awesome panache. "I'm gonna wave my freak flag high," he sings, and he not only waves it at least, say, eight miles high, he envelops you in it, batters you with it until you submit, all the time wishing he'd leave it at half-mast just now and again.

Hendrix constructs vicious circles of feedback and distortion. He stomps on the fuzz-tone pedal on the floor and his six speakers and two two-hundred-watt amps threaten to explode. He has only to tap the body of his guitar with his ring and it sounds as though Big Ben itself is tumbling down. He blows across the strings and you can hear a minor hurricane approaching. He pulls a lever and you'd swear someone was playing the bagpipes. He turns a dial and it quacks like a duck. All that, and he's not even *playing*. When he strikes the strings, the sound is so loud you get the feeling General Hershey is telling the truth: Today's rock 'n' roll may well be destroying the hearing of the generation. The song, meanwhile, is forgotten. It's been buried in the rubble. And spare a thought for young Mitch Mitchell flailing at his drums, trying in vain to be heard.

"We're not playing as loud as we can," says Hendrix. "And we don't play all the songs loud. Do you hear a whole lot of feedback in 'The Wind Cries Mary'?"

It's true, there are gentler moments in the Experience experience when he plays tasty, delicate chords and sweet dynamics, but even then he's just as likely to use the wah-wah pedal just to shake things up. (The wah-wah pedal, if you're not familiar with, it is simply a pedal that makes the music go wah-wah.)

But Muhammad Ali, when he was Cassius Clay, did not have very good manners either, and that was why he became the first champion of the world in a long while to have as much charisma as courage. He was a good fighter because he could hit hard and step lightly. He was an outasight champion because he was a ham. He went boogalooing down Broadway with Marianne Moore, he made up all those outasight poems, and he was sexy. Jimi Hendrix, though, might make him blush. Jimi's got muscle, he's just as mean and a lot more provocative. The reason I could've asked twenty-five dollars for my five-dollar seats at one of his recent New York concerts, and gotten it (as one enterprising young man in the queue behind me did), is not because he plays the guitar so well, but because he plays it so absurdly. And, Mamma, you know, he looks so fine.

Hendrix is a master of ceremonies. He saunters onstage, looking like a buccaneer Othello come to Camelot in velvet and lace and boots of Spanish leather, a Mexican bandit's hat on his head with a feather in the gold chain-band, his silk blouse open to the navel, a shiny gold medallion sparkling on his chest his crotch grimly outlined. He's the black sheep all wrapped up in the golden fleece. I once saw Liberace, but it's not the same. Hendrix doesn't have ten-thousand-dollar diamond cuff links in the shape of his Fender Stratocaster guitar; he doesn't grin and sing, "Hey, look me over." Liberace's the victim of his own glamour. Hendrix is, simply, beautiful. And supercool. There's a cigarette dangling from the corner of his mouth. Noel Redding, the bass player, has got red boots, and Mitch Mitchell, the drummer, has a purple hat but they're just pretty. They're Hendrix's elves. From the moment he takes his cigarette out of his mouth and impales it on the loose end of a string up near the pegs, the Jimi Hendrix Experience is psychedelic vaudeville. It is a series of gestures and effects, shameless theatrics, peppered with just an odd evil grin, as if to say, "Did you dig *that*? Well, now dig *this*." He starts out easy, he rubs the strings along the microphone stand to hear them crackle, and he whips off little licks with just his right hand fretting the strings. (Hendrix plays left-handed.) As the songs go by, he gets more and more outlandish: He plays the guitar behind his back, on top of his head, between his legs, he leaps into a crouch and plays with it. He plays a couple of solos with his teeth, then throws out his crotch and whispers, "C'mon and s-s-s-s-sock it to me," and laughs, wickedly.

At the finish, he switches to a dispensable guitar, announces "the international anthem," that raunchy little number "Wild Thing," and, after thirty minutes' foreplay, he rushes the Experience headlong into climax.

Wild thing, I think I love you, he sings, threatens, pointing at a hapless little blonde in the front row.

But I wanna know for sure . . .

And he flicks his tongue at her, grins, falls to his knees and begins ripping the strings off the guitar. Still, the game goes, he's not satisfied. He runs at the amplifier and begins to smash and batter it with his guitar, and, finally, in the supreme ejaculatory moment of rock 'n' roll hype, he tears it from his neck and hurls it at the wall.

And all the time Mitch Mitchell's nailing away at his drums, unheard.

The whole thing seems to put Noel Redding a little bit uptight. He winces now and then, and even stops to pick his teeth. Once, in London, Hendrix got so excited he leaped on Redding and wrestled him to the floor. That was once, like once at the Monterey Pop Festival he actually set his guitar aflame in a kind of ritual sacrifice, at the end. He is, after all, the Great Pretender of rock 'n' roll burlesque. He is, unchallenged, the Cassius Clay of pop.

Aw, shucks, if my daddy could see me now ("Up from the Skies").

The Experience experience is harrowing. But it's fabulous spectacle. It relies entirely on Hendrix's virtuosity, his erotic athletics and exotic pyrotechnics. It may be a bunch of good tricks, but good tricks done well are what magic is all about, and Hendrix pulls them off, if you'll forgive the phrase, like a true magician, or, more accurately, like a witch doctor. Theater should be a show, and Hendrix is a fabulous showman.

And, don't forget: Musicians, who know, say he's the best guitarist in the world.

At a college concert on Long Island, I saw kids mob the stage at the end in the kind of frenzy I've only seen before at a Stones concert, and they were college kids, not teenies. At a concert at UCLA, grown men cried, the audience crawled onto the stage and tried to kiss his boots. Not a hip audience either—they were history students and science majors who give each other Aqua Velva for Christmas. In San Francisco, the week after Hendrix broke all records at the Fillmore, the whole town was in a kind of breathless, anticlimactic lethargy. In Stockholm, just recently, seventeen thousand people came to see him in one night. He's toured Scandinavia three times and each time broken his own house records in every hall they've got. He's never had a No. 1 record, but he's had three or four singles get to No. 2 in England. Both his albums have sold a million copies here. And the Jimi Hendrix Experience has been together just over a year.

In 1966 he was just Jimmy (Jimi?) James, playing guitar at the poky little Cafe Wha? in Greenwich Village.

The whole thing, happily, has a lot to do with a transatlantic lovely named Linda. It was she who happened to run into her old friend Chas Chandler at a New York discothèque called Ondine, and took him down to MacDougal Street to hear Jimmy James play. Chandler was feeling fed up after twelve years of playing bass behind Eric Burdon and four years of running round the world with the Animals. ("I'd gone about as far as I could go. My playing hadn't improved a note in four years.") He didn't dig the Cafe Wha? band, the Blue Flames, but he dug Jimmy James. He dug the way he played the guitar between his legs. He dug him so much he took him home to London. Says James, born Hendrix:

"I knew there was somethin' I wanted to do like that but I was gonna wait in the Village until my mind was ready for it. Then Chas came down every night and we talked and so forth and so on. And, I mean, the rest . . . Oh, please . . . We took a little plane ride to England."

Hendrix didn't sing much then. Even now he's a lazy kind of singer—often he just talks and chuckles his way through. In those days, too, it was almost always someone else's gig. Hendrix, before he became an Experience, spent five or six years in back-up groups behind rhythm 'n' blues singers like the Isley Brothers, Jackie Wilson, Little Richard, Wilson Pickett, in package tours all over the country, "paying dues," hopping from one funky Broadway to the next. The soul circuit is tough. There are lots of great guitar players who never got past the end of the block. On the soul circuit there's no faking it.

"Jimmy James, Maurice James, millions of names, I can't remember now. I don't know, man, it's really strange, I don't know too much about it . . . I was playing in this top-40 r 'n' b soul hit-parade package, with patent-leather shoes and hairdo combined, and I got tired of feeding back on 'Midnight Hour.'"

Here and there and now and then, he'd stop and put together a group of his own for a while, like the band at the Cafe Wha? It wasn't exactly what he had in mind when he picked up his ax and left Seattle for two months some five years before. ("I didn't want to go back until I had something to show for it, you know.") In between, he'd played a lot of rock 'n' roll and rhythm 'n' blues, listened to a lot of other people play more rock 'n' roll and rhythm 'n' blues, and he'd also done fourteen months in the 101st Airborne Division. That's parachutists.

"I just signed up for the Army, that's all. I just signed up for the Army. I wanted to get everything over with before I tried to get into music as a career, so's they wouldn't call me up in the middle of somethin' that might be happening. I was sixteen [*sic*]. I got sent to Kentucky."

("No one else'd have him," says Noel Redding, the way an Englishman can; and Hendrix, being a patient man with a studied cool, laughs politely.)

"I was thinking about playing then . . . I was *slightly* playing. I knew about four songs on the guitar, you know, the usual rumble. I listened to everything. Everything from Eddie Cochran to Elvin James, Chet Atkins, everything. Chuck Berry, Jimmy Reed, B. B. King, Albert King. . . . The first guitarist I was ever aware of was Muddy Waters. I heard one of his records when I was a little boy and it scared me to death, because I heard all those sounds. Wow, what was *that* all about? It was great."

The soul circuit ends at the Apollo Theater in Harlem. Apollo audiences are the aficionados of black music. They're merciless and they're impatient. If they catch the least whiff of jive they're not shy of showing a performer the door before he's finished his first song. It's the soul bullring. If they like you at the Apollo, they adore you; if they dislike you, they are quite capable of destroying you forevermore. The response is honest, violent, partisan. They play fair, but they don't suffer fools gladly, they don't suffer them a moment longer than it takes to realize somebody let a fool in. A bummer at the Apollo is like an invitation to a beheading. And on Wednesday nights, amateur nights, the burden of proof rests heavy, on those ambitious or brave or foolhardy enough to enter the ring, and it can get bloody if they don't have a lot more to offer than their good intentions. If an act is bad the audience doesn't stop at booing and hissing. They throw things. When he was eighteen, Jimi Hendrix came up from Atlanta, played in the Wednesday-night amateur contest, and won first prize. And if the soul circuit ends at the Apollo, it begins there as well.

While he was in New York, he sat in at clubs around the city. He played for a while in Curtis Knight's band at the old Lighthouse on 76th and Broadway. The Lighthouse is closed now, which is a pity, because there are few places in New York quite so far from heaven and so close to Desolation Row. The losers, the Broadway hookers and junkies, held their heads as high as they ever may in the Lighthouse. Anyway, Curtis Knight is, no doubt, good to his friends, but he's the kind of singer who doesn't even sound good in the shower. There was a truly shameful record out this year called "Get That Feeling," a Curtis Knight record, except that it said at the top, "File Under: Jimi Hendrix." I suppose you could wear the cover on your head as a Jimi Hendrix party hat, but you'd be lucky to hear much playing. Once Knight hollers, "Play a thing, Jimi (Jimmy?)," and there's a few bars of neatly edited rhythm thing, but it's all a bit like releasing some rehearsal tapes of the Lincoln, Nebraska, Symphony Orchestra, and saying "File Under: Second Violinist in the Fourth Row, Third from the Left." He's there, but that's all.

Hendrix and Chandler have since had the record withdrawn. Chandler has worked hard to get Hendrix out of the fourth row and right up front, and both of them are understandably piqued at Capitol's opportunism.

Dimly remembered concept from Camus: The quality of an experience is deduced from the quantity of an experience.

A proud and gaudy bucko eating his guitar is a sight to see, but each time you see it, it reminds you of the time before, and it doesn't seem as much fun, and wasn't it better the time before that? Like any experience, you never forget the first time. It may be, though, that I'm getting tired, because the rest of the world can't seem to get enough of the Experience. Ever since their first gig in Paris and their fiery histrionics at Monterey, they've barely stopped to change strings. Hendrix has made it plain that the only wilder thing than Elvis Presley is a black Elvis Presley.

When he first arrived in England he was skeptical about the kind of musicians he'd be able to find, despite Chandler's assurances. But five days later, with five songs down, the chaste Experience, bold as love, played the biggest theater in Europe—the Olympia in Paris—and nobody had any further doubts. In fact the two anemic, skinny Englishmen in their Chelsea pretties and electric bouffants— though they don't look strong enough to squash a strawberry between them— provide their tough, resilient and sometimes flashy two-thirds with all the fury of the Big Bad Wolf himself. Guitarist Redding had never played dirty bass before he joined Hendrix (he'd arrived to audition for Eric Burdon's new Animals, met Chandler and switched), and Mitchell came out of Georgie Fame's Blue Flames. He's a drummer with a sharp, military style, one of the best rock drummers there is. Says Redding:

"When we went to Paris, we'd hardly even met. Mitch was a big jazzer, I loved rock 'n' roll, and Jimi was playing blues. Oh, it was funny. But we only had to do three numbers, so we were all right. We did 'Everyone Needs Someone to Love,' 'Have Mercy,' and 'Hey Joe,' I think."

Since then they've been playing for eighteen months solid . . . they haven't even had time for a haircut if they wanted one.

"I've always been a believer in grabbing the big money while you can," says Chandler. He's a big, humorous man, with a twinkle in his eye.

"We don't know where we are sometimes," says Hendrix.

He needn't worry. Chas Chandler knows. He's a rock 'n' roll professional. He's played nearly every auditorium and ballroom and high school gymnasium in the world, and he's got a pretty good idea of what it takes to fill them up with paying customers. He knew that America wasn't ready to fall at the feet of the Jimi Hendrix Experience until it had a reputation. And he knew that England and Europe were the places to find it. When he first saw Hendrix in the Village, Jimi was already pretty intimate with his guitar; he was already a bit of a show-off. Chandler made him a showman.

"We were all sitting round backstage, it was a British tour, monoliths like Engelbert Humperdinck were on the bill, and we were wondering what Jimi could do to take the starch out of the show-business people. And somebody said, 'Why don't you burn your guitar?' So somebody went out for lighter fuel . . .'"

England is the country where they voted Otis Redding the best singer in the world last year; it's where the Cream learned to play the blues; it's where they call a spade a spade. When they saw Jimi Hendrix, they couldn't believe their luck. He was Real, he was soulful, and he was theirs. Madmen walk the streets in London. It's an odd place, where oddity is not only respected, it's adored, and nowhere more enthusiastically than in the odd Modish underworld of pop. English bands, gifted ones like the Who, and ten-cents-a-freak ones like the Crazy World of Arthur Brown, have been fooling with the theatrics of pop performance for years (Arthur Brown has a nifty trick of arriving onstage in a flaming headdress), but Jimi Hendrix's crotch-rock is no mean joke. What is more, it's what everybody had had in mind all along. Nobody had had the impertinence. He brought a little well-groomed black power to the plush, members-only supper clubs where the ladies and gentlemen of pop go to dance. He arrived with an open invitation to naked lunch. England and Europe ate it up, like it was a barbecue.

Six months later, Hendrix arrived home at Monterey with the best wishes of the Beatles and the Stones. I wasn't there, but I've seen the movie a couple of times and the Experience really do a number. It comes right after the smoke of "My Generation" has cleared and the Who have gone off to lick their wounds. It was Hendrix's first gig in America, and he was out for blood.

"It was a daft carry-on to see who could outdo the other," says Chandler. "Jimi and the Who dared each other. But I knew that if Jimi burned his guitar again, we couldn't pretend it was another accident. It had to be cool, like a sacrifice."

"Cool" might not be the word. It struck me as fetishism. Hendrix really had his heart in it. I've never seen him so eager to please. He huffed and puffed and jumped and pumped and moaned and groaned his way through a couple of verses of "Wild Thing," all the time threatening to burst. He somersaulted across the stage, fell to his knees, hoisted his hand-painted guitar into its now familiar (and ever so apt) position, made a couple of passes over it with his hands, and then he squirted lighter fluid from a can held between his legs and dropped a single match. He never stopped chewing gum. Not even when he swung the flaming guitar around his head and smashed it to pieces on the floor. It was cruel, but it was all in good, kinky fun.

"That burning thing, we don't do very much. Let's see, yeah, I've done it a couple more times, just for kicks, 'cause the guitar might have been broken anyway. It would have only lasted about five or six more performances, so I might as well burn it up, as long as it's still working, so no one will think it's a fake," says Hendrix, smiling.

The Experience experience is showy and excessive, but it ain't no fake.

"I can't do nothing I don't feel like. When we got together in England, we didn't say, 'All right, now, we're going to play this song, I think I'll go down on my knees, and Mitch, you twirl your sticks there, and Noel, you put the bass on top of your head.' We didn't do nothing like that. We just got thrown together, we didn't know each other from Adam, and all these things just started happening. Like, I get boiled at myself sometimes, and I like to entertain myself, too."

After Monterey, the Experience toured with the Monkees. It may have seemed like an unlikely coupling, like Little Red Riding Hood giving the Big Bad Wolf a piggyback ride, but Chandler doesn't make that kind of faux pas. After a week, the Experience walked out, complaining of poor promotion. Everybody heard about it, the way Chandler knew they would. There were rumors that indignant mums covered their babies' eyes during the Experience. Others left the audience in horror, said the rumors, the kind of rumors that come from public-relations offices.

"I don't remember the Monkees tour, it was about a thousand years ago, I can't remember it. Hey, I like the Monkees; themselves, they're great. We had a lot of fun with them. I don't know anything about their music, I haven't had a chance to really get *into* it." He smiles his sly smile.

For all the extravagance and camp of the Experience, for all Hendrix's strung-out chat, he's a bitch on the guitar, and there are few things he enjoys more than to play it. In New York and California, he and whoever else is in town, frequently a couple of musicians from his favorite American music band, the Electric Flag, get together and jam until dawn. That's when he really plays music. Like Cassius Clay, he can hit.

"They got millions of beautiful solo guitarists in the world now. Like it's really greasy, beautiful solos, but some of them are forgetting their rhythm section. They don't have creative rhythms anymore, and it's really getting monotonous to hear—especially three-piece groups that don't have no kind of rhythms. Dig it, anybody can make regular chords, but it's nice to get into some kind of creative background; you can make background a thing in itself. Three-piece bands should get off it and start playing beautiful chords. I was jamming with Eric once, you know, Eric Clapton, he's pretty nice. But I wanted to hear him bring out some chords. . . . There's a band that's happening now that's the best band in the whole world that you don't know about. It's a jam band. It's spread out all over the States. Any chance we have, we jam. That's what playing is about . . . that's when you're playing, when you're creating music with other musicians. That's what you live for. You can't express yourself by jabbering and talking all the time. And half the people don't know how to jam nowadays. They don't play together. They don't really think they can be beautiful musicians, but they don't really think about the other person. That's what jamming is about, it's playing *with* everybody. Like, we have Buddy Miles and Harvey Brooks (of the Electric Flag) and Steve Stills (of the Buffalo Springfield) and the bass player from the McCoys. We have a certain little crowd, which is great. We'd like to bring in other jammers, but then, after playing a while you feel the flow that goes through the music and you can follow each other, and finally you get to where, jamming, you can be more together than on a record you might have worked on for two weeks. Like, changes of key and timings and breaks and, like licks, it can be one of the most beautiful things if you have time to hit it. That's what Ravi Shankar is doing. He's up there jamming. He's creating as he goes along. Quite naturally, he knows the regular technical figures here and there and the technical flow and beats and bounces, but he's jamming in his own professional little way."

Hendrix doesn't play "Midnight Hour" these days. He writes almost all his own songs, blues like "If 6 Was 9," hard-rock like "Foxey Lady," and, lately, more wistful things like "Little Wing."

The lyrics are quirky, bits of meat-and-potatoes, I-like-it-like-that blues from the old days, clumsy metaphoric bathos left over from Bob Dylan. And, more often, dank open-ended fables like "Castles Made of Sand," in which the girl in the wheelchair walks again at the sight of a golden-winged ship, but not before a little Indian brave is slain in his sleep. Or like "Wait Until Tomorrow," in which Dolly Mae's father shoots her would-be lover dead while you watch. He's not my favorite poet but once in a while he turns a phrase, isolates an image uncluttered by bland adjectival psychedelics:

"*Somewhere a queen is weeping,*
Somewhere a king has no wife,
And the wind cries Mary . . ."

"I'm very inconsistent, you know. It just all depends on how I feel. Sometimes I write in a rush, but the things I'm writing now take a little longer to say. I really wouldn't know what I'm doing, I really wouldn't know. It might be more primitive, I don't know. Maybe I'm going to write a big thing, maybe not. I'd have to look around and see what's around the house."

Hopefully he's through with all his hallucino-sexual patter, like "Are You Experienced" (*Not necessarily stoned/Just beautiful*).

Meanwhile, Noel Redding's written one little song; it's called "She's So Fine." and he should quit while behind.

Both Experience albums are untidy, often pretentious (there's a little comedy routine at the beginning of *Axis: Bold as Love* involving a Mr. Paul [Caruso] that'll make you shudder) and, most important they allow themselves too little room to move. But Hendrix has plans to change all that.

"I'm going to take Buddy Miles and Paul [Caruso] into the studio, and Noel's going to take some people in by himself, too, and get all our little rough ideas together. I plan to have more instrumentals and longer tracks on the next album, 'cause you just can't express yourself in two minutes in every song, you know."

Not only will the new Jimi Hendrix music be freer and, no doubt all the more bewitching, bothering and probably bewildering; the entire Experience experience will become more spectacular. The performance itself will no longer be limited to a thirty-minute concert but promises to develop (or degenerate) into, quite naturally, an environmental orgy.

"We're working on a really different presentation to what we're doing. Like, we'll have about a two-and-a-half-hour show, and maybe use another group. But see, nobody will be the star, everybody will be working together. In other words, every single song will have a completely different stage arrangement and setup. And we're using films and stereo speakers in the back of the auditorium, all over the place . . . Oh, it's hard to explain . . . If any song calls for augmentation, we'll have it there too, only the setting and the musicians will be part of the background. This'll be at theaters, curtain theaters, Broadway, wherever they have theaters. It'll be so natural, in a rehearsed way."

Natural, in a rehearsed way, is the Jimi Hendrix kind of rock 'n' roll theater.

There is a theater up in Harlem, the Apollo, where Hendrix won first prize in the Wednesday-night amateur contest four years ago, but the Jimi Hendrix Experience hasn't played there. They've played colleges and ballrooms all over the country. Hendrix does for white audiences what James Brown does for black audiences. He makes their juices run. But he hasn't been to Harlem. At his concerts there are few Negroes.

"I want us to play up there once, yeah. They were supposed to set up a gig there, but I think somebody got scared. I don't know why." [. . .]

He does dedicate a song to the American Indian ("I Don't Live Today").

Said one young lady to another, standing in the queue outside Hunter College, slipping a flask of Seagram's to keep out the chilly winds:

"I just came to see him burn his guitar . . . eat it, burn it, doesn't he do that?"

The Jimi Hendrix Experience is the most notorious legal entertainment in rock 'n' roll, but Hendrix ain't got his satisfaction yet.

Who needs a diploma from Garfield High School, who needs the keys to Seattle?

---

1. Hendrix dropped out of Garfield High School on October 31, 1960, at age seventeen.

JIMI HENDRIX'S 1968 PRETRIAL EXAMINATION

In October 1965, Hendrix met singer Curtis Knight, who loaned him a guitar and introduced him to New York record producer Ed Chalpin. Nine days after Hendrix's first recording session with Knight, Chalpin signed Hendrix to an exclusive three-year recording contract.

In 1967, after Hendrix had become famous, Chalpin released two singles that Hendrix recorded with Knight through Capitol Records. He issued writs against Track Records, Polydor Records, and Warner Brothers, and he attempted to enforce Hendrix's 1965 contract.

On March 7, 1968, Hendrix gave a pretrial deposition in New York City. This "interview" was conducted in the middle of the JHE's second US tour. In fact, the night before, Hendrix jammed with the Hollies at the Scene Club, and he returned to the club the next day for an informal jam with a very intoxicated Jim Morrison of the Doors.

A transcript of the examination was prepared for the United States District Court, Southern District of New York, by David M. Horn, a notary public of the state of New York. It was held at the offices of Halperin, Morris, Granett & Cowan, 1350 Avenue of the Americas, New York, New York, and started at 10:15 AM. Hendrix was obviously coached by his attorney beforehand; he used the expression "I'm not sure" 27 times, "I can't remember" 65 times, and "I don't know" 101 times.

Jimi Hendrix, also known as Jimmy Hendrix, and Yameta Co., Ltd., were the plaintiffs. Capitol Records, Inc.; PPX Enterprises, Inc.; Edward Chalpin; and Curtis Knight were the defendants. The following are excerpts from this deposition.

Jimi Hendrix, a plaintiff appearing herein, having been first duly sworn by the notary public, was examined and testified as follows:

　　Examination by Mr. [Elliott] Hoffman [counsel for PPX Enterprises]:

HOFFMAN: Mr. Hendrix, what is your full legal name?

HENDRIX: James Marshall Hendrix.

HOFFMAN: What is your address?

HENDRIX: My address is in London. 43 Upper Barkley [*sic*] Street, London, W1, flat no. 9 . . . I [also] stayed at the Hyde Park Towers Hotel in London. . . . Before that I was living in the Village.

HOFFMAN: What was your address there?

HENDRIX: Well if you wanted to get in touch with me then it was the Cafe Wha?, which was, I think, located on MacDougal Street.

HOFFMAN: Are you a member of the American Federation of Musicians?

HENDRIX: Yes.

HOFFMAN: Would that be Local 802?

HENDRIX: Yes.

HOFFMAN: Do you have a union card that you carry with you?

HENDRIX: No, not that I carry with me because I always lose wallets; and I never carry hardly anything except my passport.

HOFFMAN: When did you start playing music professionally?

HENDRIX: It must have been when I was about seventeen, sixteen or seventeen; semi-professionally, but for pennies . . . my main instrument [is] guitar . . . drums; a little bit organ, piano [also].

HOFFMAN: Have you ever had any formal training on any of those instruments?

HENDRIX: No.

HOFFMAN: Do you read music?

HENDRIX: No.

HOFFMAN: How do you compose music if you don't read it?

HENDRIX: It's mostly by memory; and if something is in your mind good enough and strong enough you remember. . . . I write down the words and keep the music in my mind, that's all.

HOFFMAN: Who publishes your music?

HENDRIX: It's a company that is connected with Chas Chandler and Mike Jeffery.

HOFFMAN: When did you sign the contract for management [with Mike Jeffery]?

HENDRIX: I haven't signed it. It's a verbal contract; a verbal agreement.

HOFFMAN: At the time you made this deal with Jeffery, did you have a lawyer present of your own?

HENDRIX: No.

HOFFMAN: What was the compensation that he was to take?

HENDRIX: I don't remember numbers at all . . . whatever it came to, like. I was interested in—like I wanted to see what England was like, you know. And plus the things that he told me, I really believed, like they would spend money on me—the promotion plus the expenses, plus equipment. And I had a salary a week. It was like hotels bills were paid, clothes, you know. And this indicated to me that I had a very good thing, a good chance. And it gave me belief in them, like . . . they bought so much equipment. . . . I had some personal debts that he paid . . . amounting to a few hundred dollars. . . . Anytime I asked for money they gave it to me because I would say I want something, and they gave it to me.

HOFFMAN: When was it that you met Mike Jeffery?

HENDRIX: I was playing at the Cafe Wha? in the Village. . . . He said, "I like the group very much." He came back several times. . . . He was telling me he liked the act and he would like to talk to me further about it. . . . He asked me like did I have any contracts or did I sign any contracts or anything. I told him I was managed by a company that works with Sue . . . I believe it was [called] Copa.

1965 Contracts

HOFFMAN: Then the Sue Records contract, which was dated July 27, 1965, was the first contract that you ever signed in your entire life?

HENDRIX: Yes.

HOFFMAN: What [were you told] about the contract?

HENDRIX: Juggy Murray, [who] runs Sue Records, explained to me [that] I would be a regular artist in my own right as Jimi Hendrix—like he would manage me, you know. And he said—and he explained the money situation to me, which I can't remember now; I'm sorry. And he explained the term[s] of the contract. He said—I believe it was something like two years—yes, I think it was two years' option, with three options of one year apiece. In other words, it came to September 1970. I don't know too much about the options and all that, but it came up to 1970 . . . I tried to write my songs so I could present them to him, you know, sing them to him, [and brought him] a demo. It's like you make a little rough thing, and I did.

HOFFMAN: Did he give you a copy of the contract at the time?

HENDRIX: No, because I'm very bad at keeping things.

HOFFMAN: Did you read it? . . . Did you go back the next day to look at it again?

HENDRIX: I didn't. It was my fault, you know. I must have slept too late or something.

HOFFMAN: What other contracts had you ever signed in your life, at any time in your life?

HENDRIX: I signed agreements with PPX [in October 1965] . . . a group contract with RSVP in June of 1966.

HOFFMAN: When did you first meet Ed Chalpin?

HOFFMAN: I met him by way of Curtis Knight.

HOFFMAN: How long had you known Curtis Knight at the time he introduced you to Ed Chalpin?

HENDRIX: I believe it was the next morning after I met Curtis Knight that we went to the studio.

HOFFMAN: Did you do any singing of any sort on any of the PPX tracks?

HENDRIX: There was one on "How Would You Feel." I sang the background with about three other guys or two other guys, or one or two; I can't remember.[1]

HOFFMAN: Is it possible that there were any others that you sang on the PPX tracks?

HENDRIX: There might have [been] . . . because I didn't have the confidence to sing, you know.

July 17, 1967, PPX Sessions

HOFFMAN: While you were here in New York, did you see Ed Chalpin?

HENDRIX: . . . It was during the time when I went up to the studio.[2]

HOFFMAN: You went up to the PPX Studios . . .

HENDRIX: Yes . . . We banged on the door. There was like playing so we waited until it softened down before somebody let us in. . . . I sat down on the couch, and we started talking. And I believe I started talking to Ed Chalpin. We was talking over old times, and all that, you know. And during this time like they were taking a break, or something, but Bugs was still in the studios, messing around with his bass. So I went in there; and plus I had my—I happened to carry this eight-string [Hagstrom] bass along that I had with me that was a completely new type of guitar, you see, a new type of bass guitar. And I was going to go around in his house, because he had some stuff around that we can plug it into. And I wanted him to hear what it sounds like. So there wasn't opportunity for me to try it there in the studios. So we was messing around on the instruments. So then it turned into a jam, like free-playing musicians, you know.

HOFFMAN: Were there any microphones around?

HENDRIX: Oh, yes . . . microphones all over the place. . . . Like we was playing and I got—you know, I started thinking after awhile that we was being recorded. But I didn't think nothing of it because—you know what I mean, it was a jam session . . .

HOFFMAN: How did you know you were being recorded?

HENDRIX: I can't remember. Like I think Rosalind came in and told me—she says, "You know, you're being recorded." And that's all. But I didn't really get scared, because like I was feeling very nice. And you do this all over the country, you know, any place and time you get a chance, you just play with other musicians.

HOFFMAN: Did you play along with the tapes as they were being played back to you?

HENDRIX: Maybe in the thing of jamming. But as far as, you know, actually playing them back, playing over on top of them, no. I don't remember doing that intentionally, no.

HOFFMAN: You did no singing on that day at all?

HENDRIX: They tried to make me sing, but I just couldn't make it because I didn't feel like singing.

HOFFMAN: How long did you stay at PPX that day?

HENDRIX: Approximately two, two and a half hours.

HOFFMAN: Then where did you go?

HENDRIX: Let's see. I think—I'm not sure if it's the same day, but I think that they invited us for breakfast, or something. . . . [Chalpin] was asking me different questions. He said, first of all, like he said, "You want to do very good over in England," saying like we were doing very good over in England. I said, "Yes, we're doing all right, you know." And then he said—wait a minute, there's one more thing. Oh, yes, I asked him—I said, "What is all this—" I thought about the letter. There was a certain letter I got a long time ago, and I never did give it any thought. I said, "What's this thing about," you know, because I was hearing about things, you know. They were trying to get the record played in England, you know, the record "How Would You Feel." I believe it was, I think, a record named "How Would You Feel."

HOFFMAN: What was the letter that you were talking about, that you asked him about?

HENDRIX: [...] When I came back from a tour sometime I found a letter from [...] I think it was from PPX [...] I think it was sent to me. [...] I thought this is something to give to my manager. And right away I gave it to him.

HOFFMAN: Did you know that you were involved in some kind of fight over the recording contract?

HENDRIX: I don't know about the recording contract. I thought it was over a record named "How Would You Feel"; the release of it, you know.

August 8, 1967, PPX Session

[*Hoffman asks Hendrix about the second time he returned to PPX studios in 1967.*]

HENDRIX: It was very late, because we played at this club.[3] And as soon as we got out of the cab to go to the place that we was playing at, you know, Curtis—I think it was Curtis or somebody—approached me, kept asking me, you know, to come up to this session and, "We'll give $200." He said something about making $200. "Would you like to make $200?" I said. "Doing what?" He said, "Like recording." So I didn't want no $200, to get paid $200 for no reason at all; plus I had other things to do. I was very busy, and I wanted to do other things, because we was going to leave the next morning, and I would be very tired[4] [. . .] during the session, you know, at the end of it I said, "All right, yes," you know, it was recorded, had been recorded. But it was in a jam session, and I really don't care, because a jam session, you know, you don't really take it serious. You're just playing along with friends. And I just said, "Since it's like that, you know, I don't want my name to be mentioned anywhere on these tapes." First of all I said I don't want them to use the tapes, you know. And then later on, I said, "Yes, you can use it if you want but you know, without my name" [. . .] everybody heard it I said it about ten times; I kept saying it over and over again.[5]

HOFFMAN: Did you know you were being recorded?

HENDRIX: Let me think. Yes. I think—you know, I'm getting these two [summer of 1967 PPX sessions] mixed up. I think this was the time when Rosalind came up, and somebody came in and told me, you know. . . . First of all, I said, "Whatever you do, don't use these tapes regarding my name." I said, "You can use them, but don't use my name with these things."

HOFFMAN: Did Ed Chalpin give you any money that night?

HENDRIX: No, they tried. I don't know if it was that night or the other night. . . . They even had a check and everything, and they tried. As a matter of fact, the next day or soon after that, I was across the street, you know, buying some records in a store. And like Curtis and Ed was there and they was trying to give me a check. And I said, "Man, I don't want it."

HOFFMAN: Why didn't you want the check?

HENDRIX: Because I had fun in doing what I did, like playing and all that. Like I said before, The Beatles—like for instance The Beatles don't ask The Stones for money when they're jamming around like that.

HOFFMAN: When you were present at the August session at PPX did you know that Ed Chalpin was suing you?

HENDRIX: I didn't exactly know what was happening. Like I said before, I thought he was trying to—the way he explained it to me, I thought that he was trying to just get a release on a certain record, you know, in England, but with a strange billing, you know . . . with a billing of Jimi Hendrix and Curtis Knight.[6]

---

1. A photo from this 1965 session shows Hendrix, Knight, and Johnny Star singing what appears to be a background vocal track.
2. The date in question is July 17, 1967—the day after the final show with the Monkees in New York City.
3. The JHE played the Salvation Club in New York City on August 8.
4. The JHE played in Washington, DC, from August 9 to 13, 1967.
5. A recording of the July 1967 session for "Gloomy Monday" surfaced in the 1980s that backs up Hendrix's claim. He clearly says to Ed Chalpin in the recording booth: "Edward, can you hear me? [. . .] You can't use my name for any of that stuff . . . right?"
6. Hendrix's testimony concluded at 1:45 PM. Then, on July 24, 1968, *Variety* announced that the suit brought against Hendrix by PPX was settled: "Under the terms of the settlement, made before Judge Dudley Bonsai in New York Federal Court last week, rights under PPX's original three-year deal with Hendrix, signed in 1965, have all been sold to WB–Seven Arts. Chalpin will participate financially until 1972 in all of Hendrix's recording ventures, past and future. . . . As part of the settlement, Capitol's current Hendrix–Curtis Knight album will be followed with a second release. There will also be a third Jimi Hendrix Experience album on the Capitol label."

PART IV

July 1968 to December 1968

ON JULY 25, 1968, THE JHE RETURNED to New York after a brief tour of Europe and began an American tour five days later. Even though the tour schedule was hectic, Hendrix found time for club jams with Eric Burdon, Larry Coryell, and others.

Look magazine sent a reporter out to California in September to get Hendrix's perspectives on race. Hendrix spoke about a white schoolteacher who pressured him into leaving school because of a fling he had with a white girl. On the drive to the show at the Oakland Coliseum, Hendrix mentioned that race wasn't a problem in his world, yet *Look* pointed out that concert attendance dropped dramatically after news of Black Panther leader Huey Newton's conviction hit the streets.

The JHE returned to the studio in October to record a follow-up to *Electric Ladyland*. Musicians Jack Casady, Lee Michaels, Robert Wyatt, Buddy Miles, and Andy Summers all had a chance to join in.

Toward the end of the year, the group talked about forming side bands but continued to keep the Experience alive. Mitchell came up with Mind Octopus for his band name, while Redding was more serious with his outfit, Fat Mattress. Hendrix told *Melody Maker* in November that the group would probably break up by the new year.

"I FELT WE WERE IN DANGER OF BECOMING THE U.S. DAVE DEE"

ALAN WALSH | From MELODY MAKER, July 20, 1968.

The JHE spent most of the first half of 1968 touring and recording in America. On July 4, the group returned to England to play the upcoming MELODY MAKER–sponsored Woburn Festival of Music. Two days after the festival, he was interviewed by the paper.

The electrified hair has been shortened somewhat, but it was unmistakably still Jimi Hendrix. He loped into his manager's Gerrard Street office, grinned slyly, shook hands all round, fastened onto the latest copy of MM, accepted a stick of chewing gum, and settled comfortably into an office armchair.

Magical Jimi, purveyor of excitement and mind-expanding music, was back in town, if only briefly. "I'm flying back to New York tonight," he said, "I left some recordings there that will make our next single and an album—no, a double album—and I've got to listen to them again and remix some of them."

Hendrix flew back to Britain from the States especially for the MM's Woburn Festival of Music ("It was really only a jam, we hadn't played for so long," he said) and was also due to visit Majorca ("It'd better be a gig or I'm not going") but we managed to pin him down long enough to catch up with the world of the man of Experience.

And the immediate world, as far as Jimi, one of the most ferocious-looking yet benign of men, was the group's next single.

He hopes to have it ready for release within the next two weeks—a welcome bit of news for Experience fans who've had to wait a long time since their last album, *Axis: Bold as Love*.

But the delay has been deliberate. They felt the group was becoming too pop-oriented. "People were starting to take us for granted, abuse us. It was what-cornflakes-for-breakfast scene. Pop slavery, really."

Tired

"I felt we were in danger of becoming the American version of Dave Dee—nothing wrong with that, but it's just not our scene.

"We decided to end that scene and get into our own thing. I was tired of the attitude of fans that they've bought you a house and a car and now expect you to work the way they want you to for the rest of your life.

"But we couldn't just say 'Screw them,' because they have their rights, too, so we decided the best way was to just cool the recording scene until we were ready with something that we wanted everyone to hear. I want people to hear us, what we're doin' now and try to appreciate what we're at."

What Jimi, Mitch and Noel want everyone to hear are the tracks they have recorded at a New York studio. "It's the 12 Track Record Plant, a new studio. It's new, and we're all learning at the same time."

The tracks include three from which the new single will be chosen. One is titled "Crosstown Traffic," another is "House Burning Down," either of which could be the single.

The Experience have also recorded enough material for a double album. It will probably be called *The Electric Ladyland* which will have a total of about 17 pieces, rather than numbers, on two albums. "All the tracks are very personal . . . they're us."

Picture

"That's why we want to get them out as soon as possible, because this is how we are . . . now! I want them to be heard before we change." The album will kick off with a 90-second "sound painting," which Jimi said is an attempt to give a sound picture of the heavens.

"It's different from what we've ever done before. I know it's the thing people will jump on to criticize so we're putting it right at the beginning to get it over with."

The track is called "And the Gods Make Love"—it's typifying [*sic*] of what happens when the gods make love "or whatever they spend their time on," said Jimi.

"The album is so personal because apart from some help from a few people like Stevie Winwood and Buddy Miles of the Electric Flag, it's all done by us. We wrote the songs, recorded and produced it.

"I don't say it's great, but it's the Experience. It has a rough, hard feel on some of the tracks. Some of the things on it are hungry."

It's a source of discontent among certain Experience fans that the group spends so much time these days in America. But Jimi doesn't agree.

"I'm American," he says simply. "I want people there to see me. I also wanted to see whether we could make it back in the States. I dig Britain, but I haven't really got a home anywhere.

"The earth's my home. I've never had a house here. I don't want to put down roots in case I get restless and want to move on. I'll only get into the house thing when I'm certain I won't want to move again.

"The other reason for working in the States is that we make 20 times more money there. And there's no harm in that . . . we have to eat like everyone else. America is so large, too; when you work regularly in Britain, you end up going back to the same places. That doesn't happen in America."

He doesn't feel it is ironic that he had to come to England to get success in America. He says that England was first because that's where his managers Chas Chandler and Mike [Jeffery] thought it would be best to start. "I want to be known everywhere," he said.

Lucky

Jimi is, however, a native-born American, though he doesn't, he says, identify closely with that country's problems. "I just want to do what I'm doing without getting involved in racial or political matters. I know I'm lucky that I can do that . . . lots of people can't."

He does, however, have an awareness of the problems and wish to help.

He sent a cheque for 5,000 dollars to the Martin Luther King memorial fund because he thought that this was the best way he could help. He was busy working and thought vaguely that active participation could do the cause harm rather than good in an inverted way, because of his pop music connection.[1]

He expressed regret at the news that the Cream had decided to break up at the end of the year. But he expressed no fears about his own group doing the same.

"We were lucky. When we started, we were thrown together, but we managed to create a personal scene, as well as a musical appreciation.

"But if someone did leave, there'd be no hang-ups, it would be amicable, because it's like a family. If Noel or Mitch quit I'd wish him well because it'd be like a brother going on to better things. I'd be pleased for him. The only hard feelings would be in the minds of the selfish fans.

"I'd like to see Mitch and Noel getting into the things that make them happy. Noel is on the English pop and hard rock scene and is writing some good songs these days. Mitch is becoming a little monster on the drums. He's involved in his Elvin Jones thing.

"*He's the one I'd worry losing. He's becoming so heavy behind me that he frightens me!*"

1. On June 28, Hendrix attended the Soul Together memorial concert for Martin Luther King Jr. at Madison Square Garden. He received a long round of applause when his contribution was announced.

"JIMI HENDRIX: AN EXPERIENCE, AN IMAGE, A GREAT TALENT"

MARGARET ROBIN | From BLACK MUSIC REVIEW, January 1969.

On July 22, 1968, journalist Margaret Robin interviewed Hendrix in London for an article that eventually appeared in the short-lived **BLACK MUSIC REVIEW** magazine.

In his opening comments in the magazine's debut issue, editor Richard Robinson argued that Hendrix's music had no color boundaries: "Hendrix has managed to do what no other black performer before him considered possible: meet the white audience on their own ground and introduce them to the black musical heritage of this country. Certainly Jimi has his own style, his own unique method of presenting his lifestyle through music, but underneath it all is a solid foundation of the music that made rock what it is today: a firm basis for a world in change."

Many times when you hear groups like the Jimi Hendrix Experience you wonder what they're all about. What kinds of individuals make up the group and what's happening with Jimi Hendrix himself. The Experience has rocked the English pop-scene and everybody seems to dig the group.

The last time I was in England I had a chance to talk to Jimi himself to try to find out "what makes him tick." Many times when you're going to interview an artist you have definite questions in your mind that you want to know, sort of a format. But at the same time, there are many artists that just turn you off into the other direction by their personalities. I must admit, after all I had heard about Jimi and I had heard a few of his recordings and even seen him at a few concerts, I really wasn't prepared for the personality I found myself confronted with.

QUESTION: Jimi, had you considered forming a trio or group before you came to England?

JIMI: No. I was thinking of the smallest pieces possible with the hardest impact. If it had taken two or twenty or ten, you know. But it came out a trio, which is great.

QUESTION: Jimi, can you tell us a little about your songwriting? I mean, the words and lyrics seem so way out. Do you just plan it that way for effect or is that what happens when you sit down to write?

JIMI: Well, a lot of times you get an idea from something you might have seen . . . you know. And then you can write it down the way you might have wanted it to happen or the way it could have happened, you know. For instance, you know, like . . . I can't think of one song I wrote. [*Laughs.*]

QUESTION: How about "Bold as Love," you put a great deal of feeling across in that one.

JIMI: Like some feelings make you think of different colors. Jealousy is purple— I'm purple with rage or purple with anger—and green is envy, all this. This is like you explain your different emotions in color towards this certain girl who has all the colors in the world, you know. In other words you don't think you have to part with these emotions. But you're willing to try.

QUESTION: What prompted "If 6 Was 9"?

JIMI: That's just how you feel at the time. You know, straightforward.

Jimmy [*sic*] has a way about him, especially when you question him about his talent and the talent of others. He never really will put anyone down.

QUESTION: What do you think of Bo Diddley? Jimi, I heard you dig him a lot.

JIMI: I like Bo Diddley a lot and think he made a great contribution to rock.

QUESTION: How about the other musicians in your group, Noel and Mitch? How do they compare to you, and do you dig their personal style?

JIMI: Look at Noel and Mitch, my guitar work is there and everybody talks about it but Noel and Mitch are providing just as much of musical value as I am.

Hendrix seems to recognize the fact that he is capable of going on as a solo artist but says "Sure different people could be in the Experience, but only because Noel and Mitch are talented to be doing what they've got a desire to do."

QUESTION: Jimi, let's talk a little about your stage concerts: How does the audience make you feel up there and how do you think they feel about your "act"? Some people have even called you obscene.

JIMI: Well first, I love making music for people and I figure people come because they dig music, you know. I feel great about audiences, especially when they get involved with you.

As for the obscenity, well man, I don't think there's anything vulgar about it all. I've been using the same act since I've been in Britain. I just don't know where these people get the idea that it's an obscene act.

Hendrix is indeed a spectacle in himself. But musically or verbally, he is capable of expressing whatever he wants to, and he's not going to shoot his mouth off—wild man or not—because it's not in his nature. He's been playing the guitar for eight years. He does most of his work on a Fender Stratocaster and occasionally switches to a Gibson. He's left-handed, which narrows the field.

Hendrix is actually quiet in manner and soft-spoken. He never stops moving. If he sits down it's only for a moment. Then he's up again, lighting a cigarette or putting on a record. He uses his hands when talking and listening, and he's obviously never more at ease than when playing a guitar.

"EXPERIENCE"

DON SPEICHER | From GREAT SPECKLED BIRD, August 30–September 12, 1968.

The JHE had just flown into Atlanta, Georgia, from Columbia, Maryland, and was exhausted. Two shows were scheduled at the Municipal Auditorium on August 17, and this concert was the first to have Vanilla Fudge added to the bill. For the first performance, fans sat through four bands before the JHE played. GREAT SPECKLED BIRD, Atlanta's underground counterculture newspaper, later visited Hendrix at his hotel for an interview.

There is a concert—a rock concert with several serious new music groups, and advertising that promoted only the top-40 dribble that some of the groups produce: WQXI control prevails! Five groups play the afternoon show—the Heir Apparent[1] [sic] introduce the show; the Soft Machine do a long and powerful riff with drummer stealing the show; the Amboy Dukes really get into it and steal the entire concert; Vanilla Fudge come on as showmen and do some fine music and gain support of many critics; the Jimi Hendrix Experience leaves most of the audience cold, the audience leaves Hendrix cold, he finishes the show.

The evening show is much the same except the Amboy Dukes does not appear, we are told because of time considerations. Rumors fly, Hendrix was outperformed earlier in the day so he gets insurance against that for the evening: no Amboy Dukes. Hendrix plays again, and again many people are disappointed, not without cause. He didn't really try; man, it's only Atlanta, Ga.; where's that, what is it? However, he plays his ass off on "Red House," a blues thing unlike the head tunes that made him famous. Nothing freaky, just great music. He gets polite Atlanta applause. He does "Purple Haze" and the crowd is pleased; he plays "Wild Thing," "The Star-Spangled Banner," etc., smashes his guitar and amp and leaves the stage with the audience getting at least a few minutes of what they seemed to want.

Then there is an interview—Hendrix sits on the 21st floor of the Regency Hyatt House and does not want to be interviewed as he watches Joe Pyne[2] freak on the tube. We begin slowly, phones ring, doors knock, the rest of the band comes in, and they are good people in a better mood than Hendrix, we stone, we spray aerosol cans, wc indeed finish slowly with Hubert Humphrey's red and blue face on the color tube. We leave stepping over four or five afro kids sitting in the hall by the star's door—strange—the elevators are a gas, though. We stop at every floor and freak for Regency guests. What follows is in the past.

* * *

BIRD: Well, do you have to tour to keep things going?

HENDRIX: No man, that's just another hang up, another scene I have to think about. It's great playing but when you come to actual things like this, people coming up saying, "Well, you're supposed to be an entertainer, so you're supposed to be this to us and we're buying your records and we're making you this and we're making you that." They think they have us for the rest of our lives. Who wants to go through all that?

BIRD: How was the afternoon performance?

HENDRIX: I really didn't feel really up to it, you know, because we were pretty tired. Very, very tired as a matter of fact. We just got straight off the plane and came over here [and] had free time for about an hour and a half. It's just like having recess in school. The first show was a drag, it was a bore. The people were waiting for flames or something, and I was waiting to get through to those people by a music way.

[*The next comment follows immediately after the above; whatever question was asked—probably about how Hendrix felt when fans asked him to burn his guitar—was not printed in the article.*]

HENDRIX: Yeah, right, and that's what we're trying to avoid. That's what makes things uptight. I'd like to see anyone come to a show, but don't forget we're trying to get it across. Who wants to sit in a plane eight days-a-week and come down and see people's faces saying "Are you going to burn your guitar tonight?" What's that shit about? Just because we did it about three times in three hundred gigs.

BIRD: Who are the people you dig now?

HENDRIX: I just dig different things, you know. I was digging some of the things Cream was doing and I was digging some things by this cat E. Power Biggs[3] on the harpsichord and I was digging Muddy Waters. I dig anything that holds my interest, you know.

BIRD: Do you think all this constant travelling is hurting your music?

HENDRIX: Right. It sure is. It's hurting our new LP as a matter of fact. That's the reason it's not released yet. It was supposed to be put on July 21.

BIRD: How did you get started? Did you play with B. B. King?

HENDRIX: We did some jam sessions and I did some shows and tours with him. I'd like for you all to get into the other cats too. You're not going to be like the rest of them, are you? You ought to be down in Noel's room and Mitch's room. Spread out, like we try to do in our songs.

BIRD: How do you feel about having to go to England to get started?

HENDRIX: I didn't have to. That's just some other hogwash you hear. It's just something that happened. I just decided what in the hell was I doing playing behind other people, so I got my own group together in the Village, and almost immediately we got offers from Epic and CBS, and then I just happened to want to go to England. I never been there, and I'm glad I went because the group I had here wasn't half as good as the one we have now. So I went to England and we had a jam and Mitch came down. There were about 20 drummers there and like we just had a jam session at this club. Noel came down with a guitar to audition for the new Animals, and someone asked him to play bass and he's been playing bass ever since, and like we got our little group together.

BIRD: Do you get much into what's happening with black people?

HENDRIX: I don't get a chance, man. I'm not thinking about black people or white people. I'm thinking about the obsolete and the new. Some people weren't made to live together anyway. And that's more personal-type things that comes out in riots and frustrations and so forth. It's so screwed up. Everyone's like sheep now, almost, in America.

BIRD: What kind of things are going to be on your new record?

HENDRIX: Well, let's see. I don't know. It's what they call funk melodies. It's slightly electric funk every once in a while, and it goes into blues and it goes into hard rock and it goes into complete opposites on some songs, complete fantasy, you know, which is the easiest thing to write about. Tell it the way you would like to see something.

BIRD: Do you dig doing things like "Red House" more than like head things?

HENDRIX: It all depends, man. I like to listen to anything that holds my interest, so therefore we like to play things that hold our interest. Blues just doesn't make it all night long or rock doesn't make it all night long.

BIRD: Who did the writing on the new album?

HENDRIX: Noel's going to have a couple of songs on it, and we're going to do a song by Dylan, and the rest are like ones that I wrote.

BIRD: What's your Dylan one?

HENDRIX: It's "All Along the Watchtower." I think it's going to be a single. It'll be released as soon as possible.

BIRD: Do you ever talk with Dylan much or see him?

HENDRIX: I only saw him once and we were both stoned out of our minds, so, you know.

BIRD: Have you ever jammed with [Al] Kooper?

HENDRIX: Yeah. He's going to be on one of our songs too. He's going to be on one but his piano is almost drowned out. It just happened that way so the piano is there to be felt and not to be heard.

BIRD: Do you dig the covers you've had for your albums?

HENDRIX: All that's in the past, completely in the past.

BIRD: What are you going to do for the new one?

HENDRIX: Well, we have this one photo of us sitting on Alice in Wonderland, a bronze statue of it in Central Park, and we got some kids and all. First I wanted to get that beautiful woman, about [six] foot [seven]—Veruschka—she's so sexy you just want to *hmmm*. Anyway, we wanted to get her and have her leading us across the desert, and we have like these chains on us but we couldn't find a desert 'cause we was working and we couldn't get hold of her cause she was in Rome.

BIRD: A lot of people aren't sure about that interview thing on the second album, that spacy interview.[4]

HENDRIX: We just felt like saying it. You're really going to be disappointed when you hear our first track on our new LP, because it's like "When the Gods Made Love,"[5] and it's, you know, maybe I should play it. Can I play it for you?

---

1. Eire Apparent.
2. Joe Pyne was a mostly conservative radio and TV talk-show host who supported the Vietnam War and ridiculed hippies, homosexuals, and feminists.
3. E. Power Biggs (Edward George Power Biggs) was a concert organist and recording artist from England.
4. The interviewer was referring to the first track on *Axis: Bold as Love*, called "EXP," where Hendrix plays an alien from another planet being interviewed on the radio.
5. Hendrix was referring to "And the Gods Made Love."

INTERVIEW WITH JIMI HENDRIX

GUS GOSSERT | From the original 1968 interview recording.

The JHE performed six concerts from October 10 to 12 at San Francisco's Winterland Auditorium. KMPX, the legendary local "underground" FM station, sent DJ Gus Gossert to interview Hendrix backstage during the six-show run.

Gus Gossert: This is Gus Gossert on KMPX, and we're talking with Jimi Hendrix. Let me get an ID from you. Say, "This is Jimi Hendrix on KMPX." We'll use it in a produced tape. [*Gossert hands Hendrix the microphone.*]

Jimi Hendrix: But you just said that though. You can get it together some kind of way, I know.

GG: I was rapping with Buddy [Miles] on the air the other night about where he thought music was going. . . . What do you think?

JH: It's a birth of what's going to happen later on, maybe. When this generation grows up hearing this kind of music on the radio . . . it's like a backbone, what you can call the early blues. This is probably the same scene . . . it's taking millions of directions. A lot of people wonder what happened to modern-day poetry. Most of it's on records today anyway. Some people have the open-mindedness to combine both the sound and words together . . . I'm playing a more mature type of thing right now. I write songs all the time, and I have words in my head for the songs. If I have personal faith in a song, I'll run it down to [the group] in the studio. But sometimes I won't. We'll just mess around and see what we come up with . . . I have a basic idea of how I want it to go . . . sometimes we'll jam it with our friends and hear different interpretations of it.

GG: When you first started to play, did you play blues guitar?

JH: I was diggin' everything like Billy Butler who used to play with Bill Doggett . . . all the way up to Muddy Waters and Eddie Cochran [*laughs*] . . . to bring every-body down on the cross . . .

GG: You had a run with Curtis Knight for a while.

JH: Yeah, that was just a scene . . . one of the cats I used to play with, but like there's millions of Curtis Knights around. . . . They try to capitalize off of our name, which is very embarrassing because we don't try to think about that. Otherwise you waste too much time, and you don't have time to get your music together . . . and then he comes around with this big scene . . . that's why it's all settled over here. Hardly any of those tapes I was playing on . . . there's one tape where I was playing about three seconds on, and they edited it . . . and threw in the words here and there . . . and threw in my name, which is so embarrassing.

GG: And the albums have you blasted all across the front.

JH: Yeah, that shows you what's happening right there. Even our LPs don't go through that scene.

GG: How long did it take you to do the *Electric Ladyland* album?

JH: We was working on it for about three months . . . off and on because we was like gigging and touring at the same time and it was really hard to get anything together like that. So that's why I said we might as well go ahead and make it funky or something—electric funk, electric church music.

GG: You first started in San Francisco, right?

JH: No, I started all over the place . . . I came out here before. Yeah. I played at the Fillmore with Ike and Tina and Little Richard about four or five years ago.[1]

GG: Where do you think people are going?

JH: I've given up on people en masse. It's really the people that have some feeling for themselves or belief in themselves that are the people we try to help along the best way we can. Sometimes I feel like a messenger. I can't necessarily get my own personal things together, but [I] try to give peace of mind to other people . . . I might be able to do that. Since we've been noticed as far as music goes . . . we can use that. Maybe you can come to the concert and wash your souls in electricity . . . and then dissect it later on after . . . you get home.

GG: Like the scene in San Francisco . . . like the scene down in the Haight now for example . . . do you think dope changed the heads, or do you think people's heads can be changed as much without dropping acid? It might take a longer time . . .

JH: Acid shouldn't even been in the question of people getting their own selves together . . . I use it as entertainment to me. I get bored sitting in a movie house so I go on and do that. That's my own personal thing, and other people should try to take care of their own thing regardless of what the masses might do. It's really bad to base your whole life on a drug that you might run across and really love. It's just like a girl.

GG: Do you think the image of a man is changing?

JH: I don't know. That's why we're making all these supernatural things to see exactly where men are. Do you remember how Muddy Waters used to get into "Hoochie Coochie Man"? Like what they called black blues then, it was bringing the black person up higher . . . encouragement . . . just like you have Ulysses, and all the mythological-type things. . . . Well, we like to make that up representing man as our friends . . . it's a certain one-out-of-five scene.

---

1. Hendrix performed with Little Richard's band called the Crown Jewels at the Fillmore Auditorium on February 21, 1965. Ike and Tina Turner were the opening act.

"A JIMI HENDRIX DOUBLEHEADER"

JACOBA ATLAS | From HULLABALOO, February 1969.

After the Winterland concerts in San Francisco, the JHE flew to Los Angeles and spent the next two weeks of October in the studio recording a follow-up to ELECTRIC LADYLAND.

Jacoba Atlas was a student at UCLA and worked as a journalist for a variety of music magazines when she interviewed Hendrix. Her lengthy interview was split up between HULLABALOO and TEENSET.

The Jimi Hendrix Experience just spent six weeks in Los Angeles, ensconced in a rambling home in Benedict Canyon that was once occupied by the Beatles. If any house can be a celebrity, then this one is. The Beatles lived in it for a portion of the madness now known as Beatlemania—the summer of 1966. It was this house that was guarded by electronic fences and electric cops, this house that found itself penetrated by air by a rented helicopter.

Today, things are different with the "Beatle house." The once tightly locked gate is now open; the police are far away, the atmosphere congenial. As I approach Hendrix's temporary haven, the Experience's road manager, Jerry[1] [sic] (I forget his last name), opens the door and ushers me into a spacious living room very comfortably furnished in *House Beautiful* style.

Noel Redding, Mitch Mitchell, and various other people are sitting around not really watching daytime television. They are eating home-delivery chicken and throwing the bones into a large fireplace which is—strangely—burning in the 80-degree October heat. A sign on the kitchen door orders guests to stay out.

Jimi himself is in the bedroom, mulling over some tapes of the group's "live" performance at Winterland in San Francisco. He finally comes out, dressed in green and turquoise, and we retreat into the dining room for the interview. He seems reticent at first—the answers are short, guarded—but the mood quickly changes as the questions begin to touch on today's controversies.

Q.: Why do you feel that you don't get airplay on the rhythm-and-blues stations?

Jimi: It just takes time. We haven't been exposed in this one area as much as we have in other areas. But we're as open to it as we are to anything else.

Q.: But why don't we see you on the R&B charts?

Jimi: Well, it's all right. Our music may not be R&B to them; it may not be what they think of as R&B. It doesn't bother me. Everyone gets his chance.

Q.: Do you feel that people are too hung up on musical categories and won't listen to your records because of labels?

Jimi: Yeah. But sometimes they don't listen to something because it sounds completely alien to them and to what they've been used to. It's like if a colored actress wants to make it in Hollywood, she has to be twice as good. It's like that with us: we have to be 10 times as good to get the soul people to listen to us.

Q.: Why did you decide to use additional musicians on *Electric Ladyland*?

Jimi: They were just on a couple of tracks.

Q.: Do you mean that they sort of wandered into the sessions and that you thought they'd be good on a particular track?

Jimi: Yeah, like that. Al Kooper is on one track. Steve Winwood is on another. They just happened. There were also some cats from Kansas[2] who hung around while we were recording, and I used them, too.

Q.: Do you feel any limitations with a three-man group?

Jimi: No, it's not like that. You *do* have to work much harder. I may want to add some people after a while, but not as a permanent thing. I'll just add things when I need them.

Q.: Are you planning to cut down on your touring?

Jimi: No—because, first of all, I love playing. As I said before, a lot of people don't have a full understanding of us yet, and if we stopped touring, they'd never understand. Nobody would hear us.

Q.: Do you find it difficult to produce your own records?

Jimi: No—in fact, it's quite the opposite. It's not difficult at all because I know exactly what I want to do. I know exactly what I want to hear. Before, sometimes I'd finish a thing, and somebody else would come along and goof it—in the cutting of the record or in the pressing—they'd screw it up. Right now, I want to release a special cut for the R&B stations. I want to release "House Burning Down."

Q.: You just cut a "live" album at Winterland. How did it go?

Jimi: It was great. But I was out of tune a few times. We'll use one or two of the things, maybe three of them.

Q.: What are some of the problems in cutting a live album?

Jimi: Well, we can play, but I'm out of tune most of the time. I mean, you might not even notice it. Like, we start playing, but with the way I play the guitar, it might jump out of tune, and so I have to take away 30 per cent [*sic*] of my play-ing for three or four seconds to get the guitar back in tune to keep playing right. But it's all natural, you know. It's so groovy like that because you can get to the people just a little bit more.

Q.: Does an audience's response have an effect on your playing?

Jimi: Well, sure. Naturally, you try to play a little better when you get good feelings from an audience. I have to hold myself back sometimes, because I get so excited—no, not excited: *involved*.

Q.: Is the recording scene very different in London?

Jimi: In London, they have less equipment and it's not as good as the equipment they have here. Therefore, they work twice as hard. Even the engineers are involved in getting the best for you. Which is good. They have more imagination over there. It's groovy. Even the limitations are beautiful because they make people *really* listen—and the people are very, very, very good. They're almost critics themselves. It's all very positive. Over here, all an engineer does is his thing. He's a complete machine, just like the tape recorder he's working. But that's only in some instances. We have a good cat. He's on the ball.

Q.: I understand that the atmosphere in London is generally more free.

Jimi: Yes, that's what it is—the atmosphere *and* the engineering, everything. When you're with an engineer over there, you're with a human being. You're with someone who is doing his job. Over here, you feel that the human being is missing, that the studio isn't interested in anything but the bill, the $123 an hour. There's no atmosphere, no anything. We've never recorded seriously here yet. We did cut "Burning of the Midnight Lamp" and *Electric Ladyland* in New York, though. And the engineer was really together.

Q.: Why did you record in New York?

Jimi: Well, because we were doing some gigs there. We were on tour and we happened to be in New York.

Q.: *Electric Ladyland* took quite a while to finish, didn't it? Six weeks ago, I remember asking you when it would be completed, and you said, "Constantly." What was the problem?

Jimi: It was because we were on tour, because we were working at the same time. It's hard—because you want to do your best on an LP, you want to play and sing to the best of your natural ability and your natural talents. You have to have time. You can't rush through things.

Q.: If you could work with additional musicians right now, who would they be?

Jimi: Roland Kirk. Lee Michaels. I'd just jam, though. I wouldn't want to play with anyone too long. We jam all over the place. It's not to show that we can play, but it's a communication between musicians. It's just groovy to play with other people. As I said before, we're not trying to go in any particular direction. We're not hung up on ourselves. That's why we play with other musicians, why we play other music. Because it's fun, you know.

Q.: How did you get into electronic music?

Jimi: I don't know. [*Laughing*] With the feedback amplifier and the wah-wah pedal.

Q.: Do you want to do more of that sort of thing?

Jimi: I don't know. I'll do whatever the song calls for.

Q.: Do you have any interest in computerized music?

Jimi: Not necessarily, no. I like instrument music.

---

1. The JHE's road manager was Gerry Stickells.

2. Hendrix was referring to organist Mike Finnegan who is featured on *Electric Ladyland*. Finnegan's band was called the Serfs; they were from Wichita, Kansas, and were recording at the Record Plant when Hendrix was there.

"JIMI HENDRIX, BLACK POWER, AND MONEY"

JACOBA ATLAS | From TEENSET, January 1969.

The second half of Jacoba Atlas's 1968 interview with Hendrix was featured in TEENSET magazine. The controversial cover featured Grace Slick of Jefferson Airplane in blackface giving a gloved Black Power salute, similar to the one given by African American athletes Tommie Smith and John Carlos at the 1968 summer Olympics.

Jimi Hendrix, like most black performers who have made it in the white world, has long been the target of accusations claiming race desertion. Mitch Mitchell and Noel Redding, the Experience's drummer and bass guitarist, respectively, are not only white, but English. Hendrix therefore twice deserted his race: first in choosing England and second in choosing his sidemen. Blacks in this country have reciprocated by ignoring Hendrix's work and ignoring his attempts to aid various poverty programs. Hendrix has no soul, they say. He just ain't no James Brown, baby.

But the problem of communication between the black community and Jimi Hendrix is not just one of color, but also of location. Concert promoters rightly see little profit in playing poorer black community theatres, and concentrate instead in the rich, white, middle-class neighborhoods . . . the kids who come to see a Hendrix concert are not the ones who support Sam and Dave, The Temptations, or Gladys Knight and the Pips. Does Hendrix care about this lack of black faces in his audiences?

The answer has got to be yes. At the SOUL TOGETHER opus in New York, Hendrix contributed $6,000[1] [sic] to a scholarship fund for poverty students. He plans a concert at Harlem's famed Apollo Theatre—a place few whites would attend. When told of the Watts Summer Festival (held every year since the '65 riots) Hendrix made an immediate commitment to perform next year.

When accused of deserting his race, Hendrix mixes humor with exasperation, explaining he himself is a mixture of most every race, and therefore could not desert anyone. But derisive blacks have made Hendrix uneasy and have prompted more direct action. When they joked in Harlem about Jimi's "playing the guitar with his teeth," Hendrix cut that bit of theatrics from his act. When militants insisted that whites couldn't play the blues, Jimi forced some "brothers" to sit down and listen to a Cream album—the reaction? The blacks simply couldn't believe three white boys could get all that down.

Hendrix was in Los Angeles to finish his last album, *Electric Ladyland*, when he sat down with me in his rented house in Benedict Canyon (once referred to as the Beatle house—vintage '65) and rapped about race, poverty and getting it together. He wanted people to know . . . to hear what was in his head. The pity is that the kids in Harlem and Watts won't be reading this, won't know how the man feels.

"We're not played on R&B stations because it takes time. We haven't been exposed in this one area as much as we have in other areas. We're as open about that as anything, but maybe the publicity hasn't been as together as it might have been. I dig playing at the Apollo Theatre . . . we want to do a free show there.

"People are too hung up on musical categories, they won't listen to something because it sounds completely alien to what they've been used to or something. So therefore it takes twice as long, three times as long. It's like if a colored actress wants to make it in Hollywood she has to be ten times as good, like us. We have to be ten times as good for the soul people to even notice us. Not fakey good, I mean actually, naturally good. But that comes in time and developing your own thing. Like our next step in music is gonna be today's problems—you know, whatever's happening today. It's going to be just basically the way I see what's happening today. Not exactly a protest.

"There's this song I'm writing now that's dedicated to the Black Panthers (a black militant paramilitary group) and that's the sort of thing we might go into, not pertaining to race but pertaining to . . . like symbolism and today's things and what's happening.[2] By the time we start to do the new album the President will be elected. We plan to make it a whole new thing regardless of who's elected.

"Like I was digging America so much until I went over there (England) and came back and then went over there again, and went all over Europe and came back here and saw why people [are down on America]. It (America) has so much good in it, but it has so much evilness, you know, and it's because it's based on money mostly. And that's really so sick. I still love it, quite naturally, but I see why people [are down on] it.

"Now, people are losing peace of mind, and they're getting so lost in all these rules and laws and uniforms. For instance, New York: I mean as a physical city it's doomed completely, demoralized, like Pompeii. It's nothing bad though. It's just what happens when people get lost . . . Change of time. That's what happens when human beings get lost when there's no more time for 'thank you' or 'yes please' and 'how ya do.'

"If people would just take three or five minutes a day completely by themselves for peace of mind, to find out what they want to do and why, and then, as I say, everyday . . . you'd get something together by the end of the week.

"If people would stop blaming—you can see how frustrating it is, you take the black person who argues with the white person that he's been treated badly for the last 200 years, but now's the time to work it out instead of talking about the past. We know the past is all screwed up, and so instead of talking about the past they should get it all together again. Then the white man will argue something else, but that's all little child games. Arguments . . . that's for kids, you know where the truth is. The truth is that it's the time to get together now! For instance they say well there's no jobs to pass on to everybody, the job is to clean up the slums. You get people out there to do their own thing. Not necessarily the same old things . . . you could get the government together to issue some tools; get some money together if they really wanted to help this problem . . . if they didn't want this problem anymore.

"You see, America's supposed to have this money thing and all this, which is one bald-faced lie when we don't give a damn about helping anybody. I think America has on its mind to let other groups really suffer badly and then put them away somewhere. It's very sick, but that's what I think is going on. Some people around here are naturally sick in the head anyway. And half of those people are running things. It's based on the laws, and you might say well, what can I do to get all this together, but you can even start with music, like having mixed bands.

"And they can have little neighborhood committees that sign petitions for problems and then send someone up to the government to try to get things done, and if it doesn't happen, try again; have patience. Do it about three or four times, and then if it doesn't happen then get your Black Panthers and your little army groups, not to kill anybody, but to scare them. It's hard to say . . . I know it sounds like war but that's what's gonna have to happen, it has to be a war if nobody is going to do it peacefully. Like quite naturally you say, make love not war and all these other things, but then you come back to reality and there are some evil folks around and they want you to be passive and weak and peaceful so that they can just overtake you like jelly on bread.

"It's good to be passive and all this, but there are these people on the other side, like I said before, who want you to do these things and you're gonna get screwed in the end, you and me, regardless. So you have to have something to back it up. Some people have to be scared into it. You have to fight fire with fire.

"You have to do something—not frustrated like throwing little cocktail bottles, you know, here and there, breaking up a store window. That's nothing, especially in your own neighborhood. You should have people like the Black Panthers who are trained, commanders, only together, like the National Guard—not to fight maybe, but to harass. I mean, like they have the Ku Klux Klan that's running all over. You have to take advantage of getting yourself mentally and physically together. Like there might be some white people who are on your side that you might kill off which is very hurting, especially when you're fighting for peace of mind.

"What I'm saying is if you just want to sit around and talk about this you can go forever . . . for the rest of your life. That's what I'm trying to say. Somebody has to make a move. The others are just waiting around until you turn to jelly and they are gonna tick you off, you know, wash you down the street like you would do jelly. Somebody has to make a move and we're the ones that are hurting most as far as peace of mind and living is concerned.

"Maybe if you scare half the people, just common sense. Not saying yes or no, just the truth. You sit glued to the TV and you're seeing the fantasy side of life, but the problems are still there. Out in the street, that's still there.

"I'm doing the best I can. Everybody's just gonna have to get off their ass. All I can say is common sense. We're gonna use our music as much as we can. We're gonna start if people will start listening."

---

1. The actual amount Hendrix donated was five thousand dollars.
2. Hendrix may have been referring to the song "Machine Gun," which was also inspired by the Vietnam War. On the CD *Live at the Fillmore East*, Hendrix introduces "Voodoo Child (Slight Return)" as the Black Panthers' national anthem.

"A JIMI HENDRIX DOUBLEHEADER"

TONY GLOVER | From HULLABALOO, February 1969.

On November 2, the JHE performed on a bill with Cat Mother & the All-Night Newsboys at the Minneapolis Auditorium. Journalist Tony Glover interviewed Hendrix before and after the concert. Part I was featured in HULLABALOO.

It wasn't much over two years ago when Jimi Hendrix was Jimmy James, playing at the Cafe Wha? in the Village. Chas Chandler, bass man for the Animals heard him and talked him into going to England. In January of 1967, "Hey Joe," his first single, was on the English charts, and by late spring, he was a full-fledged star. His first LP, *Are You Experienced*, was released in early summer, and the Jimi Hendrix Experience returned to America for the Monterey Pop Festival and a tour. Since then, of course, you all know what has happened (you can tell by the different shape your head's been in lately, if by nothing else).

This fall at the beginning of their fifth American tour, Jimi and the Experience played Minneapolis, and I made arrangements to meet him. We got to the hall in time to catch part of the opening act, Cat Mother & the All-Night Newsboys, a hard-rock group with folk tinges that Hendrix will be producing (they will probably have been recorded by the time you read this). Backstage in the auditorium were the usual crew of road managers, friends, and bored-looking stage hands—and Albert B. Grossman, super-manager, who had spent a few days traveling with the tour. Ten minutes before they were due on stage, the Experience arrived: Noel, cool and easy, walking close to his chick; Mitch, grinning at everybody; and Jimi, dressed in whiter shades of pink, super-cool.

From everything I'd heard and read, I was ready for the worst. I expected Hendrix to be an egomaniac and very hard to talk to, but when the introductions were made and after we rapped a while, I had to change my mind: in all of my years with and around musicians, he's one of the nicest most cooperative cats I've ever seen. (And the same goes for Noel and Mitch.) We headed for a curtained-off dressing room even further backstage, but it was pretty loud there, and Jimi, concerned that I'd get a good tape, suggested that we go upstairs (which we did) to the third floor. Hendrix flipped through some magazines, Glover turned on the tape machine, and it went like this.

TONY: How's the tour doing?

JIMI: Outasight—it's really good, you know. We're getting through to a lot of people we normally wouldn't have reached if we weren't on tour.

TONY: How do you dig the audiences here compared to those of England and Europe?

JIMI: They're the same, once you get into it. The first thing is a sound of surprise, but then we come through again later. And most people just hit it off with us right away because they've heard of us before. It's groovy to play to people who listen—the response comes *afterward*; they show their appreciation in groovy ways. You can feel it on stage, even though you can't see them.

TONY: You produced most of *Electric Ladyland* and did the mixing, right?

JIMI: Yeah, we did it all.

TONY: It's a very good mixing job.

JIMI: Thank you. As I said before, we had a tiny bit of trouble. We were recording while we were touring, and it's very hard to concentrate on both. So some of the mix came out muddy—not exactly muddy but with too much bass. We mixed it and produced it and all that mess, but when it came time for them to press it, quite naturally they screwed up, because they didn't know what we wanted.

Tony Glover interviews Hendrix backstage at the Minneapolis Auditorium in Minneapolis, Minnesota, on November 2, 1968. MIKE BARICH

There's 3-D sound being used on there that you can't even appreciate because they didn't know how to cut it properly. They thought it was out of phase.

TONY: Where was the track with Jack Casady and Steve Winwood cut? "Voodoo Child"?

JIMI: Except for "All Along the Watchtower" and "Burning of the Midnight Lamp," it was all recorded at Record Plant Studios in New York. What we did was, we just opened the studio up to our friends, who came down, like, after a jam session. We wanted to jam somewhere so we went to the studio—it's a good place. And we brought about 50 of our friends along.

TONY: How did you like Record Plant? It's 12-track, isn't it?

JIMI: It's great, yeah, I dug it. Everybody was telling me that it's supposed to be obsolete because it doesn't adapt to today's figures. I don't know, but for what we were trying to get across, it was perfect.

TONY: How do you fill up 12 tracks?

JIMI: You don't have to fill 'em all up. Like, for instance, on "Voodoo Child (Slight Return)," I was playing lead guitar, Mitch drums, and Noel bass, and then I added on maybe two more things. We put the drums on three separate tracks and sometimes the vocal on two to spread it out. How many tracks is that?

TONY: The stereo thing is really nice. I've got earphones and it just flows right through your head.

JIMI: Yeah, sometimes we'd, what you'd call, "pan the echo," and that's when you need 12-track. You can put the echo on a complete separate track of its own. You don't always use up all 12 tracks. Quite naturally, the sound is bigger if you don't.

TONY: Are you going to do any more Dylan material?

JIMI: Yeah, if I can feel it, yeah. There are two other songs of his I really want to do. I can really feel 'em, feel 'em like I wrote . . . them a long time ago or something.

TONY: Which ones?

JIMI: "Like a Rolling Stone" is one of 'em—that's the third one, actually. To tell you the honest-to-God truth, I can't remember the names of the other two. They're on this tape that hasn't been released yet.

TONY: The tape with "the band." *(This is a tape which Dylan recorded at Big Pink so that other artists could hear some of his new material and decide whether or not they wanted to record any of it. It was not made for commercial release.)* Yeah, it's really nice.

JIMI: There's this one song that's really outasight. I think we could put it across really well.

TONY: I dug the way you did "Watchtower." The rhythm guitar is laying down all the basic changes, and the other stuff is on top. You can see the structure.

JIMI: What we used on that was a solo guitar with about four different types of sounds—like, as a slide, then as a wah-wah, and then straight.

TONY: You were the first guitarist to use the wah-wah pedal, weren't you?

JIMI: I guess so, but I wouldn't really care. We used it on "I Don't Live Today" on *Are You Experienced*.

TONY: Are you going to be doing more blues material? Some of the tracks that I like the best are blues.

JIMI: Definitely. There are all different sides to it, millions of sides that we haven't even seen yet, and it would take, like, five more LPs before we really could do it. But what we're doing now is using the three-piece unit and exhausting it. We'll use it until we can't get what we want from it at a particular time.

TONY: Then, are you going to augment?

JIMI: Yeah—but whenever we feel it, though. But the blues, man, I've written millions of 'em. If we were going to use all of 'em, the whole last LP would have had to have been a blues LP. We're going to release another double album.

TONY: All blues?

JIMI: Not necessarily. There'll probably be seven tracks of blues on it. We're going to try to make it about 26 tracks.

TONY: How do you feel about having to go to England to get to be successful?

JIMI: No feelings about it at all. It's just that I had never been to England before, so I decided to go over there. Before that, I had a group in the Village with Randy California, the guitar player for the Spirit now, and we got offers from Columbia, Epic, you know, the whole record scene. But I didn't feel that we were completely ready as a group, so I just happened to go to England. These cats asked me to go over there.

TONY: What's Chandler doing these days?

JIMI: He wants to settle down. He's married, and that's his scene.

At this point, [Gerry Stickells], Hendrix's road manager, entered to say that it was performance time. The group went on stage to tune behind the curtains, and we headed out front, where the air was full of expectancy. Jimi came on like gang-busters (with a Confederate flag tied to his left arm), and he and the Experience did 10 numbers, mostly from *Are You Experienced* and *Axis: Bold as Love*. It was during "Are You Experienced?" (which Hendrix dedicated to "the narcotics and plainclothes cops and any other bastards who happen to be in the audience") that the audience, or at least a younger segment of them, rushed the stage in a frenzy. People were getting elbowed, stepped on and shoved. One girl fainted, and another was cut badly on a railing. The fire marshal threatened to stop the show, and the house lights were brought up. The emcee, a local "underground" DJ, pleaded with the kids to go back to their seats so that the show could go on. A few did, enough so that the concert was resumed. But as soon as Hendrix pointed at a chick and stuck out his tongue at her, the rush was on again.

Jimi then did "Red House," a blues number from the first English LP, in a 15-minute version, which had people applauding his solos. He really proved himself a master of the electric guitar and laid down some very heavy stuff. Later, the group did "Sunshine of Your Love" as an instrumental then closed with "a riff of the national anthem" (it sounded the way it should have been played in Chicago, and if Nixon's hip, he'll have Hendrix at the inaugural—but, of course, he's not), which later turned into "Purple Haze." It ended with a thick shower of feedback, and the curtain fell with the audience yelling for more. I cut back upstairs, and we continued the interview.

TONY: Does it bother you when an audience rushes the stage?

JIMI: No, man. I used to do it for Fats Domino. And I wasn't about to sit down just because somebody told me to!

TONY: Has it been like this much lately?

JIMI: Yeah, the last few days. Oh, you mean with the people. *(Jimi had had amp trouble all night and, at one point, walked off the stage in disgust while the equipment men made frantic adjustments. They never did get it fixed completely.)* Not necessarily. We don't judge by the people alone, we just judge by how well we get across music-wise, you know. If we're not laying down anything, and they're screaming and hollering and thinking we're good, that makes me feel bad. I didn't play so well tonight. *(Tony Glover begs to differ!)* Like I said, I was only playing out of about three speakers. Damn!

TONY: I heard that you were going to be producing Cat Mother.

JIMI: Yeah. Did you hear 'em tonight?

TONY: Only about a third of their set.

JIMI: They're really solid. I can hardly wait. I'll be proud to produce them. Right now, I'm producing the Eire Apparent, a hard-rock Irish group. There's a tinge of folk in it—Irish folk—but it's hard-rock.

TONY: Will you be doing more producing?

JIMI: Yeah, I'd love to.

TONY: More than playing music?

JIMI: No, not more than playing. I just like to do it when I can, when I get the chance.

The limousine was waiting, and it was time to go into the bowels of the building where a hidden garage (remember the Batcave?) was hidden. We made arrangements to meet Noel back at the hotel and later had a good, relaxed rap with him. (But that's another story. Maybe you'll read about it in HULLABALOO.)

Hendrix is a showman. He can probably play the guitar underwater—and if he wants to, I'm sure he will—but don't forget that in addition to being a freak-out artist and a master of spooky sounds, he's also a damn good musician. He can *play*, and so can Mitch and Noel.

One more thing, best said by a chick I know, after the concert. "Mick Jagger is a sexy little boy, but *Hendrix*, he's a *man!*"

"HENDRIX"

TONY GLOVER | From CIRCUS, March 1969.

When HULLABALOO folded and became CIRCUS in March 1969, the magazine ran the second part of Tony Glover's 1968 interview with Hendrix.

Part Two of my rap with Jimi Hendrix was concluded just before the elections in November. It is interesting to compare Hendrix's concepts of America with those of Noel Redding.

TONY: What are you working on right now?

JIMI: There's one song I'm writing that's dedicated to the Black Panthers, and that's the sort of thing we might go into. It doesn't just pertain to race but to symbolism and today's things and to what's happening today. By that time the president will be elected.

TONY: That will mean either a lot of change or absolutely no change at all.

JIMI: Well, we plan to make it a whole new thing, *regardless* of who is elected.

TONY: Living in London as you do, do you get a different perspective of America?

JIMI: I was digging America so much until I went over there (to England) and came back and then went over there again and went all over Europe and came back here and saw why people put this country down. I still love America—quite naturally—but I can see why people put it down. It has so much good in it, you know, but it has so much evil, too, and that's because so much of it is based on money. That's really so sick. People here are losing their peace of mind—they're getting so lost in all of these rules and regulations and uniforms that they're losing their peace of mind. If people would just take three to five minutes a day to be by themselves to find out what they wanted to do, by the end of the week, they'd have something. If people would only stop *blaming*. You can see how frustrating it is—the black person argues with the white person that he's been treated badly for the last two hundred years. Well, he has—but now's the time to work it out, instead of talking about the past. We *know* the past is all screwed up, so instead of talking about it, let's get things together now. But that's all child's games. You know where the truth is. Quite naturally, you say. "Make love, not war" and all of these other things, but then you come back to reality, there are some evil folks around, and they want you to be passive and weak and peaceful that they can just overtake your life like jelly on bread. You have to fight fire with fire. I mean, I'm getting myself personally together in the way of music—and what I'm going to do.

I'd like our next album to be a double set again and to have about twenty tracks on it. Some tracks are getting very long, that's why you can only get about twenty tracks—our type of tracks, anyway—onto two records. But, you see, our music doesn't pertain to one thing. It just happens that the white people can dig it all of a sudden because some of them are very freaky and have imagination as far as different sounds are concerned. I love different sounds as long as they're related to what we're trying to say—or if they touch me in any way I don't like them to be gimmicky or different just for the sake of being different.

It's all going to come about soon, but the way that America is going now, it's all getting kind of lost. Those three to five minutes of contemplation I was talking about, that's how you can get yourself together and be friends with your neighbors—maybe even say hello and see if you can knock down all of those complexes. You have to go down into a really bad scene before you can come up with light again. It's like death and rebirth. After you've gone through all of the hell of dying, you've got to find out—and face—the facts to start a nationwide rebirth. But I'm not a politician, you see. All I can say is what I've been seeing: common sense.

TONY: But the masses are saying just the opposite.

JIMI: You know who is *really* living in fantasy land? It's the damned masses. *The masses.* The point is, *who* is wrong and *who* is right. *That's* what the point is—not how many people.

TONY: But the amazing thing is, is that the masses feel that we are the ones who are living in fantasy land, that we are the sick ones . . .

JIMI: That's what I'm saying. If you want to sit around and talk about it, you can go on like this for the rest of your life. What I'm trying to say is that somebody has got to make a move. The others are just waiting around until you run to jelly. Then they tick you off.

TONY: How much contact have you had with the Black Panthers?

JIMI: Not much. They come to the concerts, and I sort of feel them there—it's not a physical thing but a mental ray, you know. It's a spiritual thing. But I don't care if people are white—let me tell you something, I don't care as long as people are doing their jobs, that's what it is. Our thing is completely wide open. I'm for the masses and the underdog, but not for just trying to get the underdog to do this or to do that—because I tried that before and I got screwed so bad millions of times. So now I'm for just anybody who can do the job.

TONY: Will things have to be destroyed before we can achieve a better world?

JIMI: Quite naturally, you have to destroy the ghettos. You have to destroy those. Physically.

TONY: What about the mental barriers?

JIMI: Maybe we can just scare half the people with common sense. Take cancer and cigarettes on TV—we don't say yes and we don't say no, we just tell the truth. You blind your head to the TV all of the time by watching some dreary program—*really* the fantasy side of life!—and then you say, "I'll just get a joint and do this." But the problem is still there. When you come back out, it's there, the street is there.

TONY: But who is going to do all of this?

JIMI: I don't know, man. I'm doing the best I can. Everybody's going to have to get off their ass. All that I can say is just common sense. We're going to use our music as much as we can. We're going to start, if people will start listening. Some things may not come yet—but they will.

TONY: Was it easier for you in Europe?

JIMI: Well, everyone has problems. In Europe, people have a little more contact with one another. There's a little more communication, and everything's not all freaked out. In just saying hello and good-bye, there's more warmth. I live all over, though, so no place is really my home.

TONY: When you want to relax, what kind of music do you put on?

JIMI: I dig anything that holds my interest.

TONY: Thank you for a fascinating interview.

JIMI: My pleasure.

PART V

January 1969 to June 1969

AS THE NEW YEAR BEGAN, Hendrix's frustrations with JHE's limitations were clear. He desired to expand the trio, replace members, and perform material that didn't fall into the pop category.

On January 4, 1969, the JHE were scheduled to perform two songs on the BBC's live TV show *Happening for Lulu*. Hendrix was to perform a duet with host-singer Lulu. Unscripted, Hendrix cut short "Hey Joe" and declared to the viewers that he wanted to "stop playing this rubbish." Technicians, cameramen, and most of all Lulu were confused. As Hendrix then dedicated "Sunshine of Your Love" to the recently disbanded Cream, the show's floor manager waved his arms furiously and threatened to pull the plug. As a result of the incident, the BBC's five o'clock news was late for the first time, and the JHE were punished by receiving a lifetime ban from appearing on the BBC.

Hendrix continued to expand his musical collaborations by recording with Eire Apparent and Cat Mother & the All-Night Newsboys, but most notably by contacting Billy Cox, his old friend and a bass player, to discuss the formation of a new band.

All future plans screeched to a halt on May 3, when a Toronto customs officer found drugs in Hendrix's carry-on bag. Hendrix was later released on bail, and the concert tour resumed—but the world-famous guitarist would have to return to Toronto for court hearings and a trial.

On June 29, the JHE performed their final concert at the Denver Pop Festival. Crowd violence disrupted the show, and police used tear gas to quell the uproar. The original trio would never perform again. Redding and Mitchell returned to England while Hendrix pulled together a new group.

"HENDRIX: AS EXPERIENCED BY JANE DE MENDELSSOHN"

JANE DE MENDELSSOHN | From IT, March 28–April 10, 1969.

This interview was done for the famous UK underground newspaper INTERNATIONAL TIMES. It was conducted over a two-day period sometime between February 27 and March 12 at Hendrix's new Brook Street flat.

De Mendelssohn later noted that most of the interview was conducted with Hendrix in bed while she sat on the side. Hendrix offered her hash, grass, amyl nitrate, and pills as well as bourbon and whiskey. De Mendelssohn was invited back the following day when the level of coherent conversation broke down.

JANE: Tell me about your Indian [Native American] heritage.

JIMI: Well, my grandmother's a full-blooded Indian, that's all. She used to make clothes for me. And everybody used to laugh at me when I went to school, you know, the regular sob story. And then, er . . . yeah, she is, she's full-blooded Cherokee [*laughs*].

JANE: And is she still around?

JIMI: Yeah. Up in Seattle, Vancouver, British Columbia now.

JANE: And does she live on a reservation?

JIMI: No, she lives in a groovy apartment building. She has a television and a radio and stuff like that. She still has her long silver hair, though.

JANE: Can't you tell me something about the whole Indian heritage scene? I don't know much about it.

JIMI: It's just another part of our family, that's all. There's not too much to know. There's a lot of people in Seattle that have a lot of Indian mixed in them.

JANE: Do they still take peyote?

JIMI: Oh yes, it's all over the place. It's mostly around the Southwest and all that, around the desert areas, you know. But you know all Indians have different ways of stimulants, their own steps towards god, spiritual forms, or whatever . . . which it should be kept as, nothing but a step, mind you.

JANE: What I'd really like to ask is . . . well, you're very big these days, you've become a real pop giant . . .

JIMI: Oh, don't tell me those things [*laughs*].

JANE: Everybody's writing about you, talking about you, you won the *Rolling Stone* magazine Performer of the Year award. I want to know how it all affects you as a human being.

JIMI: Well, I'm trying not to let it affect me at all. It's nothing but a brand, it's the way the public identifies me probably with them, but I don't think that way and it's like anybody else, I just happen to have a chance to be heard.

JANE: Does it touch you?

JIMI: Yeah, it touches me and so forth.

JANE: Do you feel that it cuts you off at all?

JIMI: Yeah, a lotta times. I can't have fun like anybody else. I used to be able to go somewhere, down to the Wimpy or something like that, you know earlier on, but most of the time I go down there now there's always people asking for autographs, somebody looking at me really strange, you know, whispering and all that. So then, quite naturally you get complexes about that. . . . My head's in a position now where I have to take a rest or else I'll completely crack up pretty soon, in the next few hours or days . . . [*laughs*]

JANE: Do you think it's true that teenyboppers don't go for you so much as the sophisticated heads?

JIMI: I've found out that just by looking for myself you know, that you'll find almost anybody in our audience. You see a nine-year-old and you see a ninety-year-old—all ages. It used to be mostly the young people, young adults, you know, like around the Fillmore and the Forum and so, anywhere we play, but now it's anybody almost, you find all kinds of people there. You find a lot of straight people there, so therefore we play twice as loud just to see where they're really at, and they dig it, the louder the better, they're just not getting into the fact that it does make you drunk if you let it . . . just take you away, you know.

JANE: Do you get hustled a lot by people wanting bread and banging on your door?

JIMI: Oh constantly, yeah. I try to treat everybody fairly but if I did I wouldn't be able to buy another guitar. So therefore I just don't go around too much, except when I find a certain little scene going, and just go there if I want to go anywhere. But I stay in bed most of the time, or go to the park or somewhere. That's where I write some of my best songs—in bed, just laying there. I was laying there thinking of some when you came in. A really nice piece of music that I'm getting together for this late-summer LP that I'd like to do with this cat named Al Brown,[1] in America. It's called "The [*sic*] First Ray [*sic*] of the New Rising Sun," and it gives my own . . . you know, anybody can protest for instance, like in records or whatever you use music for, anybody can protest but hardly anybody tries to give a decent type of solution, at least a meantime solution, you know.

JANE: You've got the reputation for being moody. I was almost afraid to come.

JIMI: Moody? Oh, that's silly, you fall into the same . . . [*laughs*] I shouldn't say that. That's what you're supposed to think. . . . The establishment, they project a certain image and if it works, they have it made. They knock down somebody else for instance, you know, like saying I'm moody or so-and-so is evil or saying blah blah, woof woof is a maniac or something, so that everybody gets scared to actually know about me. So that's part of the establishment's games.

JANE: You were quoted in the Sunday *Mirror* as saying that it was time for a change from the pretty songs the Beatles made, time for something else.

JIMI: Aah. I don't know if I said that. Which paper is that in? Sunday *Mirror*. Well, most of those papers are all screwed up anyway, they come over here and they do their interviews, we turn the cats on, you know, give 'em wine and all that, and they go back and they're so stoned they don't know what they're writing about. No, I didn't say nothing like that. I wouldn't, there's no reason to.

JANE: What do you think about the Beatles?

JIMI: I think they're excellent and fantastic writers and musicians and so forth, you know.

JANE: Do you think their era of enormous influence has passed? Do you think another big influence is moving in?

JIMI: Well . . . yeah, people are starting to get a little more hep to music nowadays. It's not so easy to throw hogwash on anybody. The Beatles are doing their thing. I think they're going towards the past a little more. Like for instance their last LP was . . . I consider it to be like an inventory of the past ten years, rock music you know. There's a lot of people that's waiting for something else to happen now anyway.

JANE: Don't you think it's you? I've got this feeling.

JIMI: Me? [*Laughs.*]

JANE: Well, it seems to me to be moving down to the animal, and that's what you are. The Beatles aren't animal.

JIMI: The Beatles are part of the establishment. They're starting to melt that way too. We must watch out. It's just like a young cat protesting in school, for instance, saying, "That's not right, this is not right," so he goes out and says something about it and everybody says, "Yeah man, that's what it's about man, we're with you." Soon as he reaches about twenty-five years old and starts getting into the establishment scene, you know, he got his degree and all this, and now he's a lawyer or whatever he wants to be, and all this feeling for everybody else, well he forgets it himself because he's comfortable now, he's nice and fat and got his little gig together, so then he just forgets about the younger people, all his friends, what they used to say when they were in school, and he melts into part of the establishment. And that's not saying nothing bad about a person at all, it's just the scenes some people go through. Compare that with the Beatles' music, that's the way I look at it. It's like a person who starts out with something really on fire, you know . . . but now they're still good, as a matter of fact they're better than they used to be, you know, but they seemed a little . . . closer to the public beforehand. Now they're doing things, like for instance "Happiness Is a Warm Gun," bang bang shoot shoot, and all these little songs.

JANE: D'you dig that?

JIMI: Not necessarily, no.

JANE: What about violence?

JIMI: I don't dig it too much, no. It's best to have violence on stage and watch it through TV than do it yourself. So what we do, we get up there and like, I found that it worked both ways; we'd do our thing, you know, and so many people would dig it, would really be turned on by it, and they don't bother their old ladies as much when they get home. They don't beat their old ladies up as much [laughs] because there's hardly anything left in them. We try to drain all the violence and that out of their system. That's why you watch wrestling matches and football games, you get it all out of your system, unless you want to do it for real yourself, and then you'd be a violent person. Bad. Bad.

JANE: Well, what about violent trends in America today, the Black Power scene saying, we've tried everything else, now we're going to slam you, baby . . .

JIMI: Well, that's what the establishment's waiting for, for people to start fighting against their own selves like for instance black against white, yellow against pink and all that. But that's not the idea of the thing, the idea is against the new and the old, and the establishment causes this by playing games, by turning different colors against each other to make the younger generation weak. So what they do is they let you fight, they let you go out into the streets and riot and all that, but they'll put you in jail . . .

JANE: Well, in fact the establishment seems to get frightened by all this violence in the States because . . .

JIMI: Propaganda, propaganda, everyone has their own brand of propaganda . . .

JANE: It still seems that if you burn down a few warehouses in the States today . . .

JIMI: Oh they should burn down more, I think.

JANE: Well right! That's what I was asking you!

JIMI: They should burn down the whole area.

JANE: Would you do it if you were there?

JIMI: Well if I wasn't a guitar player I probably would, yeah. I'd probably be in jail, 'cos . . . I get very stubborn, like with the police. I used to get into arguments with them millions of times, they used to tell me to be quiet and I just can't be quiet, there's no reason to be, especially if I have something to say. So I'd probably wind up getting killed. But I have to feel those things. I hear about violence and all that, but really for me to say anything about that . . . I just can't jump on the bandwagon just because it might be happening today. 'Cos like for instance how they exploit and prostitute the groupie scene, you know, that's a violent scene, it's the same thing.

JANE: But you must have an enormous amount of energy and if it weren't coming out through your music, maybe you'd be very violent.

JIMI: Well, I am very violent anyway, in defense, you know.

JANE: How liberated do you think you are?

JIMI: You mean free? I don't know. That's pretty hard to say. In music we get to do anything we want to do. But I get restricted when I get around a lot of people sometimes, or even with one person too long.

JANE: What, on a head scene?

JIMI: Yeah, like for instance on a love scene. If I stay with one person too long, if I feel more obligated than I do pleased, that makes me, as it were, have to get away. So I don't know how free feeling like that is if every time you turn around you might be with somebody. Like if you're writing a song or something like that, and you want to get the words down or you're thinking about something, and all of a sudden these people pop up . . . not saying you, because I'm digging this interview. And at least it's a different face. [*Laughs*.]

JANE: It was surprisingly easy to get an interview with you. I mean if you want one with Paul McCartney it can take weeks to set it up.

JIMI: Well, maybe 'cos I'm not Paul McCartney. You get a lot of . . . oh no, I shouldn't say that.

JANE: Why not?

JIMI: There's a lot of things I shouldn't say. But you have time, don't you? Great, we can get into a whole lot of things. There's this thing I was writing, LP sleeve notes for one of our LPs. We've got about three lined up now. Now we're trying to get them released but everybody else wants us to be released stars and so forth, so now we have to do this film, like 'round in August or something like that, and then before that we have to do an American tour—April and May—and we'll only have just a few weeks to edit these recordings that we did. Can I play some of those from the Albert Hall to you? Yeah? Can I? Is that all right? What was the question? I forgot. What was we talking about? Oh yeah, about being hard to see folks and all that. That's silly, that's the stupidest game you could ever play. It's not like, "Oh, can't see you today, far too much on, tomorrow baby . . ."

JANE: All your songs seem to be directed at chicks. Is that from personal experience? For instance, there's one phrase, "I wanna make you mine." What d'you mean?

JIMI: Oh, just the cat would like to make love to you, that's all, whoever's singing the song, you know.

JANE: D'you see him as somebody else, outside of yourself?

JIMI: Well, sometimes. I don't look at it as me singing the song, I look at it as anybody singing the song. It's hard to say. I just don't put myself in all those positions 'cos I've already been through them already, all the things I like to get into myself personally, but in the meantime I can write down some other experiences, yeah, you're right, like you say. But I don't necessarily use those direct words when I'm talking to somebody [*laughs*]. I don't say, "I wanna make you mine . . ."

JANE: When you write songs, is it the music you hear before the words?

JIMI: Sometimes, it all depends. A lot of times I write a lot of words all over the place, anywhere, on matchboxes, or on napkins, and then sometimes music comes across to me just when I'm sitting around doing nothing, and then the music makes me think of a few words I might have written, you know, so I go back to those few words if I can find them and you know, just get it together. Sometimes it all happens at the same time. All depends on what you might want to say. Different moods you might be in . . .

JANE: But do you sit down and think "I want to say this to them" and then compose the song around what you want to say?

JIMI: Yeah, definitely. Sometimes, there's things I'd like to say. A lot of songs are fantasy-type songs so that people think you don't know what you're talking about at all but it all depends on what the track before and after might have been. Like you might tell them something kinda hard but you don't want to be a completely hard character in their minds and be known for all that 'cos there's other sides of you and sometimes they leak onto the record too, you know, that's when the fantasy songs come in. Like for instance "1983"—that's something to keep your mind off what's happening today but not necessarily completely hiding away from it like some people might do, with certain drugs and so forth.

JANE: But is this awareness actually conscious when you write the song, or do you write it, listen to it, and then realize what motivates you afterward?

JIMI: Well, honest-to-God truth, on the first LP I didn't know what I was writing about then. Most of the songs, like "Purple Haze" and "[The] Wind Cries Mary," were about ten pages long, but then we're restricted to a certain time limit so I had to break them all down, so once I'd broken the songs down I didn't know whether they were going to be understood or not. Maybe some of the meanings got lost by breaking them down, which I never do anymore. It's such a drag.

JANE: Your songs don't tend to be analyzed and intellectualized by reviewers like for instance the Beatles' songs.

JIMI: Mmm, which is kinda good, because our songs are like a personal diary.

JANE: Well, it's just this basicness [sic] in your music that makes me see you as the innovator of a new era.

JIMI: Yeah, but that's how it should be in any scene, though. Like I said about the carpenter, if he really digs that he should put all his heart into really getting that together, if it means going to school or whatever it means. And in music, you gotta say something real just as quick as you can. I just say what I feel, you know, what I feel, and let them fight over it, if it's interesting enough. But that's the idea of it: make it very basic. During a certain age which was past [sic] not so long ago they started getting really superficial, and the music started getting too complicated, and in order to get into that you have to really be true to yourself, and none of those cats were doing that, they just put sounds here or sounds there.

It doesn't seem like I'm busy 'cos I'm just sitting here, but after all, being busy can be just sitting here in this kind of scene, you know. I haven't had no time off to myself since I've been in this scene . . . and anything that doesn't have to do with music, I don't think about it too much, like shirts and stuff. People just make me so uptight sometimes, but I can't really let it show all the time because it's not really a good influence on anybody else. Oh no, don't take any pictures now 'cos my hair's all messed up. I just hate pictures. It always comes back on me later on. People are always saying, "D'you remember that picture that was in the so-and-so?" and I say, "No I don't fucking remember it." . . . Some music is such bullshit nowadays, and that's why there's so many good groups going towards establishment because it's comfortable there, it's not so hard, you don't have to keep scuffling for the rest of your life. I couldn't even save up some money and go to the hills, because there's always problems, you know, always hang-ups. Most people would like to retire and just disappear from the scene which I'd love to do, but then there's still things I'd like to say. I wish it wasn't so important to me, I wish I could just turn my mind off, you know, forget about the scene. But there's so much rubbish going by and for us trying to do our thing, there's so much rubbish said about us. I'd like to get things straight in this interview. I spend most of my time just writing songs and so forth, and not making too much contact with people 'cos they don't know how to act. They act just like the . . . the pigs that run these places, you know . . . countries. They base everything on the status thing, that's why there's people starving, because humans haven't got their priorities right. I don't feel like talking to most people because they're just bullshitting, they don't even know the difference between us and the Cream, for instance, or Blue Cheer.

JANE: Do you still take acid?

JIMI: Not necessarily, no. I don't get a chance to get into all that because I'm writing songs and so forth. Anyway I just used it for certain things, as a step towards seeing it both ways, if you like.

JANE: Do you feel good onstage?

JIMI: Oh yeah, I love to be onstage—not necessarily onstage but I love to play, that's why we play so loud 'cos it makes us feel good anyway.

JANE: Does the atmosphere in the audience affect you to the extent of changes the way you play?

JIMI: It never changes me to a negative feeling. I just ignore the negative feeling 'cos I know exactly what I'm doing when we're onstage, you know. And if the audience doesn't dig it, well, I don't know, there's nothing else we can do. Like you say, music is what it's all about, it's not us three up there facing about fifteen thousand people, it's the sounds we make that are important. Oh, I can't explain, you know what it is, you're not daft.

JANE: Well, I know what it is to me, your music is something in the middle between us, a medium between human beings, and the groovier the music the faster the communication.

JIMI: It's all spiritual. Except when the eardrums come in [*laughs*].

JANE: Can you get outside of yourself enough to see the picture other people must see?

JIMI: Yeah, I can do that a lotta times. That's what makes me stay away from them, 'cos most of them have dirty minds anyway. What I see them seeing is really useless. I talked to a lot of old ladies one time, seeing exactly how they think, and wow, their impressions must really be weird.

JANE: Do you like kids?

JIMI: Yeah, I like kids. I guess I like them any age. It's a drag to grow up because you're not really growing up, you're just losing. You're only as old as you think you are, as long as your mind can still function openly you're still young.

JANE: D'you mind getting older?

JIMI: Not at all, no.

JANE: Can you think of yourself as being eighty?

JIMI: Not too much, no. I don't think I'll be around when I'm eighty. There's other things to do besides sitting around waiting for eighty to come along, so I don't think about that too much.

JANE: And death. Does it bother you?

JIMI: No, not at all. This is only here we're going through, you're not even classi-fied as a man yet. Your body's only a physical vehicle to carry you from one place to another without getting into a lot of trouble. So you have this body tossed upon you that you have to carry around and cherish and protect and so forth, but even that body exhausts itself, so you get into a whole lotta other scenes, which are bigger. This is nothing but child's play—so-called grownups. Children don't play games. Well they do, but adults play the more serious games that can get people killed for no reason at all. People who fear death—it's a complete case of inse-curity. That's why the world's screwed up today, because people base things too much on what they see and not on what they feel.

JANE: They don't even know what they feel.

JIMI: Right. Well, it's time for a direction.

JANE: And did you have this awareness before you made it or has money made a difference?

JIMI: Well, listen, I could have stayed at home. I could have stayed in L.A., but I just couldn't stay in one place too long because I wanted to see other things. That's why I went in the army beforehand when I was sixteen [*sic*], so I could really get all that mess over with and concentrate on the music I play, which calls for traveling all over the place in my own way. I travel most places without any money actually. And so when the money comes along, well, it's just another part of living really. I don't dig the way the world's going these days, but it's nice to get experience out of it, that's the money, that's what I consider riches.

JANE: And do you believe that you can change anything, anybody?

JIMI: Well, the idea is trying. But I'm just gonna do it, and if it works, great!

JANE: It's really down to your music, isn't it?

JIMI: Yeah, that's it, that's what we're talking about. Music. Talking isn't really my scene. Playing is. There's certain people on this Earth that have the power to do different things, for instance in the Black Power movement they're using it wrongly. But in the musical movement you can't call that using it wrongly 'cos that's a natural talent. Protest is all over with. It's the solution everybody wants now, not just protest. The Beatles could do it, they could turn the world around, or at least attempt to. But you see it might make them a little more uncomfortable in their position. But me, I don't care about my position. What I have to say I'd be glad to say it. You see, it comes out in my music, and then you have to go through scenes like the releasing of an LP and you can't release one every month, and you can't do this and you can't do that. And all the public-image bit . . . in my book it doesn't have to move along. People should get out of images and all that, and start getting into their own gigs, and give forth whatever they can, in their own bags, you know. Instead of laying back and digging someone else and saying "Oh Wow! Oh wow! Look at that! Such imagery!" and all that shit. That's what made me cut my hair off, because of this being a slave to the public and all that, you know . . . I used to dig all those scenes with the clothes and the hair and all that but then people start misusing those scenes as our image and all that— which it is, but it's nothing to talk about, it's just the way I felt like going through according to my own taste. But then people start trying to prostitute that idea, and it gets to be a hang-up. You find yourself almost running away. You have to grab hold of yourself. People, they don't give me inspiration except bad inspiration, to write songs like "Crosstown Traffic" and all that, 'cos that's the way they put themselves in front of me, the way they present themselves . . .

---

1. Al Brown was a close musician friend of Hendrix's; he offered Hendrix his Fifty-Seventh Street apartment as a retreat when he was in New York.

"THE JIMI HENDRIX EXPERIENCE: SLOWING DOWN AND GROWING UP"

JOHN LOMBARDI | From DISTANT DRUMMER, April 17–23, 1969.

The JHE returned to America in mid-March. After a series of recording sessions and jams, their US tour began on April 11, 1969. The following day, Philadelphia's underground paper sent its assistant editor to interview Hendrix.

Kneeling down like that, close to the crackery colors of the Holiday Inn's impersonally designed walls and rugs, Jimi Hendrix didn't look at all like Superspade. His voice, soft, but running its syllables and ends of sentences together like clusters of notes at the climax of a guitar riff, didn't sound much like the bull Negro who turned on masses of emerging young white chicks with the leotard-tickling totally free announcement:

"Move over Rover / and let Jimi take over."

Gone was the enormous corolla of hair that, along with his similarly coifed sidemen Noel Redding and Mitch Mitchell, had changed hip hairstyles across the country from Beatle-straight and Dylan-curly to Post-Frankenstein electric, transcending the historical gap of 19th century Edwardian and Bret Harte wild western; bringing the 'lectric guitar home, baby. Jimi's "roots" go no deeper than Joe Turner's sax man's breaks and that is, you know, okay. But the hair was gone now, and the soft voice, down on its knees, close to the floor, was asking the Holiday Inn room service boy to please come up and take away the dirty dishes. Mitch Mitchell, with his blond hair no longer electrically amplified, was arriving from a Chestnut Street shopping spree, carrying a slim volume of Hieronymus Bosch, and even Noel Redding, smiling his usual wicked smile behind his little red glasses, was slightly subdued. Redding had on his suede bells, but his Plaster Caster tee shirt was nowhere to be found.

"Hiya," Hendrix said. "I'm kinda tired."

The Experience was on its fifth [sic] stop in a 19-city tour, and the boys had just done a one-nighter in Raleigh, North Carolina. ("We really turned the crackers on," Redding joked later.) They had been on tour, more or less, for two years. The day's concert was scheduled for the Spectrum in South Philadelphia, a huge sports arena with lousy acoustics, but great seating capacity, and was scheduled to begin in just four hours, at 8 PM. The band arrived only 15 minutes before the first reporters.

"Do you mind a few photographs?" Hendrix was asked.

"No, the same shit happens every day, so fuck it," he said listlessly.

He was wearing an all-black outfit with Indian belts and bracelets and big rings. Standing, he looked about six feet tall and was thin—thin and very tired.

"My hair? I cut it short in protest. There are too many long-haired people running around whose heads aren't anywhere." (He looked at me a trifle too long, I thought.) Then, fingering his dry looking mop, he added: "But I think I'm gonna grow it again."

The standard questions to ask when interviewing rock superstars have to do with the evolution of rock, the lifestyle it represents, and where the particular person you are talking to thinks he fits in. Hendrix's reputation as the biggest cockman in the pop music business is legend, reinforced of in-group tales, nude posters and other photos, and most recently by articles in *Rolling Stone* and the *Realist* showing his member as the biggest in a row of five, "casted" (blown and then molded in plaster) by the famous Plaster Casters of Chicago. The cover of his latest LP, *Electric Ladyland*, released in England but banned in the States, has a group of about 20 totally nude young ladies lolling about on it. Hendrix's famed feather boa and Mitch Mitchell's frequently unisexual postures contribute to the image. Imagery then seemed a likely place to begin.

"Many rock musicians have been influenced by your style, but would you agree your huge success (Hendrix albums always sell 300,000 to 400,00 copies) is perhaps not really based on your music, but rather what you represent?"

He sat down on the bed, and then got up and moved to a sofa, looking pained:

"I don't consider myself a success. I haven't even started yet. The scene puts you through a lot of changes . . . you get involved in images. I didn't have nothing to do with that stupid LP cover they released, and I don't even want to talk about it . . . it's mostly all bullshit."

"Well what about your act on stage? Setting the guitar on fire, going through the motions of intercourse?"

"We did those things mostly because they used to be fun . . . they just came out of us. But the music was still the main thing. Then what happened, the crowd started to want those things more than the music. Those little things that were just added on, like frosting, you know, became the most important. Things got changed around. We don't do that stuff as much anymore."

I asked about the recent Jim Morrison incident in Miami Beach,[1] if Hendrix thought the Doors had perhaps gotten carried away.

"Well, if it happened, it is flipped out, but I've only heard reports. I guess you'd have to ask Morrison about that. I don't want to talk about it. You know, we used to try to defend against some of the publicity, but we don't anymore. They just ignore what you say anyway, and the people who know where you're at know without asking questions. They know from the music . . . I dig music.

"Listen," he said, "you want to talk about music? That's what I really know about. I don't want to say nothing about comparisons with other groups because if you do that puts you higher or lower than them, and that's just the same old cycle. Our music is in a very solid state now. Not technically, just in the sense that we can feel around the music and get into things better. We don't have any answers this time, but we'd love to turn everyone on to all we know . . . we know for instance that Jesus was starting to get it together quite nicely, but that 10 commandments thing was a drag. The bogey man isn't going to come get you if you don't tie your shoe. You don't have to be afraid to make love to one of your boyfriend's wives. Brand-name religions like Buddhism and Zen are just clashes. The Catholic Church is spreading and vomiting over the earth. The Church of England is the biggest landowner in England. Your home isn't America, it's the earth, but things are precarious, man. America could start getting together and China or Russia could go and we'd all be even heavier slaves. You know my song, 'I don't live today, maybe tomorrow?' That's where it's at.

"But I want to talk about music. Things were getting too pretentious, too complicated. 'Stone Free,' you know that? That's much simpler. That's blues and rock and whatever happens happens. People were singing about acid itself, man. Things start to rule you. Images. Drugs. Everybody forgets what happened to God.

"You know when you're young, most people have a little burning thing, but then you get your law degree and go into your little cellophane cage. You don't have to be an entertainer or anything to get it together. You can do the family thing. I've wanted to do that at times . . . I've wanted to go away to the hills sometimes, but I stayed. Some people are meant to stay and carry messages . . ."

"You think of yourself as a messenger?"

The question offended Hendrix.

"No, man, nothing like that." He paused, scratching his long nails on the acetate of his black shirt. "I didn't want to do this interview because I was tired and I never get any time to myself. I wanted to relax, write a song. But how can you say that to someone?"

Gerry Stickells, the Experience road manager, came into the room. "You've got to get ready soon." Jimi nodded.

"Listen, I'm tired but this is what I'm trying to say. If you prostitute your own thing . . . you can't do that. We was having a lot of fun with that stuff we used to do, but the more the press would play it up and the more the audience would want it, the more we'd shy away from it. Do you see where that all fits?

"When I'm on stage, playing the guitar, I don't think about sex. I can't make love when a beautiful record comes on. When I was in Hawaii, I seen a beautiful thing . . . a miracle. There were a lot of rings around the moon, and the rings were all women's faces."

Hendrix had been staring toward the window, over the heads of the people in the room. His glance came back reluctantly.

"I wish I could tell somebody about it."

Nearby, Neil Landon, Jimmy Leverton and Eric Dillon, members of the Fat Mattress, Noel Redding's own group, were beginning to get ready for the evening's performance. The Mattress would precede the Jimi Hendrix Experience at the Spectrum. The three boys, a little younger than Mitchell, Redding and Hendrix, looked healthy—joking a lot. They hadn't been on the road as long as the Experience. Redding, pencil-thin with a Kentish accent and a James Dean squint, squatted on a bed, going over some of the ground Jimi had declined to touch on:

"We got together a couple of years ago when Chas [Chandler] brought Jimi over from America. I was auditioning for the Animals and we got to talking and then jamming. He asked me if I could play bass, I told him no. He showed me a few things, and the next day we were playing. I pick up things quick.

"It was a great deal of fun at first. We used to do a lot of raving and rolling on the floor, sure. But it gets to be a drag when you got to a city and people start expecting things from you, doesn't it? When they stop listening to the music?

"My new group is more commercial than the Experience. What? Sure, it's a bitch working two sets on the same tour, but we'll be touring when the Experience finishes this current trip, and the Experience hasn't been working that much anyway. Taxes and all. Besides I don't like to sit around, and I'll do anything if I'm drunk enough." A flash of the old Experience lit up in Redding's eyes, behind his red glasses.

In the other room, Hendrix's mood had changed. He was talking to an attractive black girl, and she was persuading him to call one of her friends. The friend, a girl named "Beefy," was in the hospital, she said, and was just crazy about Jimi Hendrix. He picked up the phone and spoke smoothly and quietly for 20 minutes.

The floor of the Spectrum was swarming by 8 PM, the little girls from the northeast and the deep South sides of the city all giggling in their French undershirts from Ward's Folly. The giggles changed to screams at 8:15 when Mr. Noel Redding's leather bells slithered out of the basketball exit up the steps to the revolving stage. They kept on screaming, right through the entire Fat Mattress act and on into Hendrix, who arrived wearing a velvet sash around his head, de-emphasizing the short hair.

He did "Let Me Stand Inside [sic] Your Fire" and "Red House," then drove everybody totally mad with "Foxey Lady" and "I Don't Live Today."

But then, with all the little girls panting and waiting, he announces a song for "Beefy, in the hospital," and it was a slow blues—"Hear My Train a Comin'"—and was completely out of context. It broke the sexy undercurrents, and although Jimi played with his teeth and got down on his knees in subsequent numbers, he failed to "do" his guitar or any of the other things the kids had turned out for.

When it was over, they tried to tear at his sash anyway, but the cops had a relatively easy time getting him out.

"It wasn't like that last year," one little cherub was telling another as they adjusted their eye shadow in the mirror next to the big Schlitz beer sign near the press box. "I wish the Doors would come in."

Both kids had obviously been experienced, and were, like everyone else in the world, growing up.

---

1. After a Doors concert on March 1, 1969, the City of Miami issued six warrants for the arrest of Jim Morrison: a felony charge of lewd and lascivious behavior and five misdemeanors, which included two counts of indecent exposure, two of public profanity, and one of public drunkenness.

"THE EGO OF JIMI HENDRIX"

JIM BRODEY | From SAN DIEGO FREE PRESS, June 13–27, 1969.

The JHE performed at the International Sports Arena in San Diego, California, on May 24 to a very rowdy crowd. After two hundred fans smashed the Sports Arena's glass doors and entered without paying, police arrested eighteen adults and twelve juveniles and attended to security guards who were trampled in the rush. In the middle of the confusion, Hendrix gave a pre-concert interview to the local underground paper.

James Marshall Hendrix, completing a two-month concert tour of the U.S., gave the *Free Press* an exclusive interview last week. Jimi, who was recently busted in Toronto for "illegally possessing narcotics," goes to trial in a couple of weeks. The Canadian bust was made at the airport by the Royal Canadian Mounted Police (the Mounties always get their man) who searched his luggage and discovered several small packages in a small bottle. Circumstances leading to the arrest could indicate a frame. The New Musical Express had reported that Jimi was going into retirement for a year. This and the bust were among some of the topics discussed in a small dressing room at the rear of the Sports Arena prior to his performance.

FP: Tell me about your bust in Toronto.

JIMI: I can't tell you too much about that because my lawyer told me not to. Anyway, I'm innocent, completely innocent.

FP: Do you think it was a frame?

JIMI: It must have been or either it was just a very bad scene, because it ain't anything it was. But, anyway, I can't talk too much about it now.

FP: How about your retirement? I understand you're going to . . .

JIMI: Oh well, see this is what the negative folks are trying to tell you. That's what the establishment is telling you. They're trying to blow us all up and give us awards and all that so that they can just dust us away, but we're not here to collect awards, you know, we're here to turn people on to the right way because there is some really strange scenes coming up though. . . . Hey I can't do this with other people in the room.

FP: You mean the rumor then about your going into a year's retirement . . .

JIMI: No, I don't think it'll take that long actually because now is the time when a year's retirement would be just completely wasted, you know, at the rate our pace is going now.

FP: What objective do you have? Just sort of to get back together again?

JIMI: No, no, not again. There's other moves I have to make now, you know. A little more towards a spiritual level through music. It's not that the idea of basing yourself on different religions and so forth. There's no such thing really. All those are nothing but games they play upon themselves, but you know the drag of it is there are a lot of good people that are aware of the games being played. They play just as many but are not doing anything about it, you know, for their own selves. Not necessarily taking violent means; that's just another game. That's what they want you to do. They want you to be extra weak; fight amongst yourselves—so they can have complete control, you know . . .

Some of the vibrations people claim they are getting now, it is true considering the fact that the earth is going through a very, what do you call it, physical change soon. A physical change basically. I mean like since the people are part of [the] earth, they are going to feel it too. In many ways they are a lot of the reason for causing it.

There really are other people in the solar system, you know, and they have the same feelings too, not necessarily bad feelings, but see, it upsets their way of living for instance, and they are a whole lot heavier than we are. And it's no war game because they all keep the same place. But like the solar system is going through a change soon and it's going to effect [*sic*] the earth in about 30 years, you know. And I'm not talking about just this room; I'm talking about the earth itself. This room is just a crumb from the crust of the pie. And like there's no moving from any one land to another to save yourself in that respect.

So I think a person should try to get his own thing because he should get a certain faith with one link. There's a whole lot of religions. Just one link because there's only a few chosen people that supposedly are to get this across; these chosen people, in the process, are now being distracted and they are drowning themselves. So, therefore, they've got to take a rest. Not a rest, but a break from people. In order to properly save them, they've got to take a break from people. There's no good people or bad people, it's actually all lost and found. That's what it all boils down to. There's a lot of lost people around and like there are only leaders in times of crises, but that's what's happening now. It's not just a fad that's going on; it's very serious.

If you revert back in time, there's Egypt. It's very dusty now, but it used to be green. It's that they had a great flood and the world used to be flat, so they say, I mean, you know. And like they found memorandums on the moon, but no telling when they are going to get there, but when they do, they are going to find memorandums from other civilizations that have been there before and think nothing of it because the moon is there in the first place.

I mean, it's hard to say really quickly, but all they can do . . . the only answer they can find is through music now. That's not a good scene or a bad scene, this is the truth. They have to face up to the complete, constant truth. Music is in a state now where it's getting rid of all the rubbish, and in order to do these things, mostly the musicians that are here for a purpose are not out to satisfy themselves because in that case, that is when they get distracted with the fame, imagery, and all that stuff. Actually this is when the kids get more distracted by trying to follow the changes that a musician might go through because they look like that person. Like when they come here to see us, which is wrong. That is what we are trying to get across. It's very easy right now because, like I say, I haven't had this time to get away yet.

FP: Will it actually be an absence from the rock scene then?

JIMI: I don't look at things like the rock scene and folk scene. I don't look at those terms at all. But, therefore, nothing can explain what I'm going to do later on. I will have to use some sort of brand name. So like, I guess I will call it the spiritual scene. But it's not a hazy thing out of frustration or bitterness that I'm trying to build up. It's out of what's directing me. What I was here in the first place to do. It does mean I am going to strip myself from my identity because this isn't my only identity. I was foolish to cut my hair, but that was part of the step of me learning what I was really here for. I see miracles every day now. I used to be aware of them maybe once or twice a week, but some are so drastic that I couldn't explain them to a person or I'd probably be locked up by this time.

FP: Through what means do you see these miracles?

JIMI: From all different types because you may not necessarily be one of the chosen few ones to help. Everybody can't or else there would be nothing but every single person having his own different religion, and pretty soon they would wind up fighting and we would go right back to the same thing again. I'm not better than you in this sense. It's just that maybe I'm not going to say it until a wider range of people see it. It's a universal thought; it's not a black or white thing, or a green and gold thing.

FP: It might be used as a vehicle . . .

JIMI: Yeah, I would like to say to close, there are a few chosen people that are here to help to get these people out of this certain sleepiness that they are in. There are some people running around with long hair preaching the word "love," and they don't know what the fuck they are talking about because there's no such thing as love until truth and understanding come about. All they're doing is making themselves weaker and weaker until their negatives come and just take them away. And that's what's gonna happen. Then you are going to have no world to live on. The establishment's going to crumble anyway. This only happens when a person has his own thing. If he is a carpenter, for instance, or whatever, he has to work towards what he really digs. Like someone is going to have to go back to his childhood and think about what they really felt, really wanted before the fingerprints of their fathers and mothers got a hold of them or before the smudges of school or progress . . . Most of them are sheep. Which isn't a bad idea. This is the truth, isn't it? That's why we have some sheep fighting under the form of Black Panthers and some sheep under the Ku Klux Klan. They are all sheep and in the beginning they were all following a certain path.

FP: But you feel the Black Panthers are necessary, though?

JIMI: Yeah, only to the word "necessary." You know, in the back of their minds they should be working towards their own thing. They should be a symbol only to the establishment's eyes. It should only be a legendary thing.

FP: Is it necessary as a step on the road to liberation and freedom?

JIMI: It all depends on what freedom means. Some people don't even know the meaning.

FP: How about for each individual that's involved in the Black Panthers?

JIMI: No, see, most of that comes from any kind of aggressive group like that. It's good when you start adding up universal thoughts, and it's good for that second. The rest of it should probably be in a legendary figure. In a, what do you call it, a symbol, or whatever. So what they are doing now is fighting amongst their individual selves. There's nothing we can explain to them. Most of it is from bitterness. There's no color part now. There's no black and white. It's very small. It's just like animals fighting amongst each other—then the big animals will come and take it all away.

FP: But someone who has been crippled for years?

JIMI: Other people have no legs, have fought in wars and have no eyesight.

FP: Psychologically crippled.

JIMI: Right, that's what it's all about. They have to relax and wait to go by feeling. If you are going to be psychological, you have to go by the psychological feeling. If you start thinking negative, it switches to bitterness, aggression, hatred, whatever.

At this point the interview was interrupted by promoters and someone with a "love" medallion. Top forty radio station KCBQ had sponsored a contest in which entrants who had made the "grooviest love" medallion would win a free ticket to the concert and present their love beads to Hendrix in person. Jimi, who knew nothing of the contest, refused to save face for the bumbling KCBQ and wouldn't see the winners.

Later that evening at the cocktail lounge at the Hilton Inn, Hendrix further discussed his philosophies of life. The lounge seemed symbolic of everything within the establishment, which Hendrix was so against. Perhaps Jimi's view of life may be different from ours; certainly in his position he sees a different view. Fame, money and success can put strange emotions into one's head and Hendrix does fall into this category. He is part of the game, surely. But I doubt he is the leader he thinks he is; I doubt that music is as powerful a force as he would have us believe.

What happens to the Experience now doesn't look certain. The possibility of personnel changes isn't unlikely. A new album will be released before the end of summer and before the "retirement" happens. Live material will be used on the album. (Saturday's concert was recorded, but most likely won't be used.)[1]

---

1. The 1969 San Diego concert was eventually released as part of a box set called *Stages* in 1991.

INTERVIEW WITH JIMI HENDRIX

NANCY CARTER | Excerpts from the original 1969 interview recording.

Nancy Carter was not a reporter—rather, she was a student doing her masters thesis at the University of Southern California and wanted to incorporate Hendrix and the Los Angeles counterculture scene into it. The interview took place on June 15 at the Beverly Rodeo Hotel. The JHE had only two gigs left to play before they split up on June 29. The following is an excerpt from Carter's interview.

Nancy Carter: If you had the chance to communicate one general idea to the American public, what would it be?

Jimi Hendrix: I guess it would be understanding and communication between the different age brackets. There's no such things as age brackets; not in my mind, 'cause a person's not actually old in numbers of years, but how many miles he's traveled, you know? How he keeps his mind active and creative. And I guess that'll be one general idea, there's millions of them though . . .

NC: What social implications do you feel rock music has brought to your generation?

JH: . . . Younger people . . . their minds are a little keener and they can figure this out. Since they can't get a release and respect from the older people they go into these other things, and music gets louder, and it gets rebellious because it's starting to form a religion. You're not going to find it in church. A lot of kids don't find nothing in church. I remember when I got thrown out of church because I had the improper clothes on. I had tennis shoes and a suit, and they said, "Well, that's not proper." I said, "We don't have no money to get anything else." So I got thrown out of church anyway. It's nothing but an institution. They're not going to find nothing there . . .

NC: In your opinion, what is the future of pop music?

JH: I don't like the word "pop" in the first place. All it means to me is pilgrimage of peace.

NC: Well, what do you think the sound of the future will be then?

JH: I don't know . . . I'd like to get more into symphonic things, so that kids can respect . . . traditional [music], like classics. I'd like to mix that in with the so-called rock today. But it's always changing according to the attitude of the people . . .

"THE GYPSY SUN JIMI HENDRIX"

RITCHIE YORKE | From HIT PARADER, January 1969.

On June 19, Hendrix appeared at the Toronto Court House for a preliminary hearing regarding his recent drug bust. A trial date was set for December 8. Before returning to Los Angeles, Hendrix gave an upbeat interview and expressed his outlook on his career's future.

Jimi Hendrix is about to shed some of his Experience. His next three albums will not feature either bass guitarist Noel Redding or drummer Mitch Mitchell. He will, however, continue to appear with the Experience on all live concert gigs.

In a recent interview—the first which Hendrix had agreed to in 1969 [*sic*]— the 26-year-old Seattle-born guitar master said: "The group isn't breaking up because we'll continue together on gigs."

Hendrix was in good humor and seemed pleased to talk about anything we cared to mention during the interview. He said that he'd been spending his time thinking, day dreaming, making love, being loved, making music and digging every single sunset.

"I plan to use different people at my sessions from now on; their names aren't important. You wouldn't know them anyway. It really bugs me, man, that there are so many people starving, musicians who are twice as good as the big names. I want to try and do something about that.

"I feel guilty when people say I'm the greatest guitarist on the scene. What's good or bad doesn't matter to me; what does matter is feeling and not feeling. If only people would take more of a true view and think in terms of feeling. Your name doesn't mean a damn, it's your talent and feeling that matters. You've got to know much more than just the technicalities of notes, you've got to know sounds and what goes between the notes."

Hendrix made it abundantly clear that he is fed up with people constantly expecting things of him. "I don't try to live up to anything anymore," he said, laughing at his new-found freedom. "I was always trying to run away from it. When you first make it, the demands on you are very great. For some people, they are just too heavy. You can just sit back, fat and satisfied.

"Everyone has that tendency and you've got to go through a lot of changes to come out of it.

"Really I'm just an actor—the only difference between me and those cats in Hollywood is that I write my own script. I consider myself first and foremost a musician. My initial success was a step in the right direction, but it was only a step, just a change. It was only a part of the whole thing. I plan to get into many other things."

The current clash between body and beat was bound to come in Hendrix's colorful and erotic career. The Hendrix we all first saw—all dashing and devastating and sizzlingly defiant—was an image maker's dream. The way he performed it looked as though every twitch of the busy eyebrows, every thrust of the velvet-panted knee, every shake of the tousled hair, had been meticulously formulated by a bunch of assorted PR and promotion types. His act, with the biting of the guitar strings and the complete overshadowing of all that had gone down before in rock, was as precise as a missile countdown. It whipped the audience into a frenzy and left them as limp as a rose on a boiling summer's day.

Initially it wasn't so much that he was a skilled guitarist. No one really seemed to notice, they were too busy digging his freaky almost unlawful aura and his wild uninhibited stage act.

On his most recent North American tour, Hendrix tried vainly to take his audiences through the same sort of changes that he'd been through. He did some of the anthems—the Hey Joe's, the Purple Haze's, the Foxey Lady's—but he also tried to work in a lot of the more complex and intricate things from *Electric Ladyland*. But in many cases the audiences were apathetic towards the guitar gymnastics.

"Yeah," said Hendrix, when I mentioned the matter. "But instead of getting mad, we have to talk a little more, sometimes a little more than we really want to.

"What it all comes down to is that albums are nothing but personal diaries. When you hear somebody making music, they are baring a naked part of their soul to you. *Are You Experienced* was one of the most direct albums we've done. What it was saying was, 'Let us through the wall, man, we want you to dig it.' But later, when we got into other things, people couldn't understand the changes. The trouble is, I'm a schizophrenic in at least twelve different ways, and people can't get [used] to it.

"Sure, albums come out different. You can't go on doing the same thing. Every day you find out this and that and it adds to the total you have. *Are You Experienced* was where my head was at a couple of years ago. Now I'm into different things."

One of the things which Jimi is into very deeply these days is the relationship between the earth and sun and people. "There's a great need for harmony between man and earth. I think we're really screwing up that harmony by dumping garbage in the sea, and air pollution and all that stuff.

"And the sun is very important; it's what keeps everything alive. My next album, coming out in late summer, will be called *Shine On Earth, Shine On*, or *Gypsy Sun*. The Christmas album will be called *First Rays of the New Rising Sun.*

"There might also be a couple of other albums in between. A live album which we cut at the Royal Albert Hall in London, and a Greatest Hits thing. But I have no control over that sort of thing. All I know is that I'm working on my next album for summer release.

"We have about 40 songs in the works, about half of them completed. A lot of it comprises jams—all spiritual stuff, all very earthy."

Not long ago, a report that Hendrix planned to quit pop for a year went the rounds. The report suggested that Hendrix was fed up with it all and wanted to get away for a rest and to get himself together.

"I couldn't possibly take a year off," he said. "Even though I am very tired. In reality, I might get a month off somewhere but there's no way for a year. I spend a lot of time trying to get away but I can't stop thinking about music. It's in my mind every second of the day. I can't fight it so I groove with it." Although he many not be taking a year off for any significant length of time, Hendrix does have one big trip in mind. "I'm gonna go to Memphis, Egypt," he said, in a curious tone. "I had a vision and it told me to go there. I'm always having visions of things and I know that it's building up to something really major."

"I think religion is just a bunch of 'crap.' It's only manmade stuff, man trying to be what he can't. And there's so many broken-down variations. All trying to say the same thing but they're so cheeky, all the time adding in their own bits and pieces. Right now, I'm working on my own religion, which is life.

"People say I'm this and I'm that, but I'm not. I'm just trying to push the natural arts—rhythm, dancing, music. Getting all together is my thing."

It was inevitable that we should get around to discussing other musicians and other groups, and Hendrix appeared more than ready to pass expert judgment.

Blood, Sweat & Tears—"I think it's a bit pretentious. But with hard work, they'll get out of that. Right now, it's very plastic, a very shiny sound. All the music is written out, and you can see so much of the endless circle in it. They're trying to prove to themselves that they're very heavy. But I do think their intentions are good. One day they'll find themselves."

Crosby, Stills, and Nash—"I really dig them. They've gotten right into their own thing. They have a great awareness of themselves. I think they're really great."

Iron Butterfly—"They're really trying man. I like them for the fact that they are trying."

Stevie Winwood—"I think he's great."

Blind Faith—"Their name tells me what they're gonna do."

Creedence Clearwater Revival—"I think they're very good, and I hope [they] stick to what they're into. I can hear a spiritual aura in what they're doing. I hope they don't lose it.

"I like Dylan and all the other people, but you can't play them all the time. You have to learn to understand things like that. I like records of Bach and Handel and Sly and the Family Stone, they're really getting to be themselves."

On pop in general, Hendrix said he would like to see Dylan get back into it. "I think too many people are getting on bandwagons. Now is the time to do your own thing. You know, man, sometimes I can't stand to hear myself because it sounds like everyone else. I don't want to be in that rat race."

Hendrix is not really knocked out by the current moves to link up rock and classics.[1] "To each his own," he said. "In another life, the people who are trying to do it may have been Beethoven or one of those cats. But this is a rock 'n' roll era, so the people get into rock. Every era has its own music.

"What I don't like is this business of trying to classify people. Leave us alone. Critics really give me a pain in the neck. It's like shooting a flying saucer as it tries to land without giving the occupants a chance to identify themselves. You don't need labels man, just dig what's happening."

I suggested to Jimi that he seemed to be a lot happier than he used to be. "Yeah, man, and I'm getting more happy all the time. I see myself getting through all the drastic changes, getting into better things. I like to consider myself time-less. After all, it's not how long you've been around or how old you are that matters; it's how many miles you've travelled.

"A couple of years ago all I wanted was to be heard. 'Let me in' was the thing. Now, man, I'm trying to figure out the wisest way to be heard."

---

1. Released in March 1969, *Switched-On Bach* was a top-ten album by Walter Carlos. It consisted of pieces by Johann Sebastian Bach that were performed on a Moog synthesizer.

PART VI

July 1969 to December 1969

ON JULY 30, 1969, HENDRIX LEFT NEW YORK for a brief vacation in Morocco, where he stayed with friends, traveling to Marrakesh, Essaouira, and Casablanca. Hendrix went unrecognized, though a few locals mistook him for the French-Moroccan R&B singer Jean Claude Vigon.

After Morocco, Hendrix rented an estate in upstate New York where he could relax and regroup. Plans were already under way for a major music festival in the area, with Hendrix as headliner. A diverse group of musicians was invited to the house to jam and rehearse, and a multiracial group emerged that Hendrix called Gypsy Sun and Rainbows. Hendrix was the highest-paid performer on the Woodstock bill, and he was scheduled to close the show on Sunday, August 18. However torrential rainstorms caused delays, and the band didn't play until early Monday morning.

Gypsy Sun and Rainbows played the Greenwich Village club Salvation on September 10, in an event billed as "the Black Roman Orgy." The group broke up in October, and Hendrix began sessions and rehearsals with Buddy Milles and Billy Cox. The trio would become the Band of Gypsys.

Hendrix celebrated his twenty-seventh birthday by watching the Rolling Stones perform at Madison Square Garden. In early December, he flew to Toronto for his drug-possession trial. After receiving a not-guilty verdict three days later, Hendrix returned to New York to rehearse for the Band of Gypsys' upcoming New Year's Eve performances at the Fillmore East.

THE DICK CAVETT SHOW
INTERVIEW (JULY)

DICK CAVETT | From THE DICK CAVETT SHOW, July 7, 1969.

With a new band still in the works, Hendrix made a rare solo appearance on ABC-TV's THE DICK CAVETT SHOW. Prior to the televised interview, Hendrix wrote down eight topics he felt comfortable discussing with the host and gave them to a staff member. Most of the subject matter was covered, with the exception of the upcoming moon landing, air pollution, and justice.

Dick Cavett: My next guest is one of the superstars of the pop music world. His name is Jimi Hendrix, and he is not here with his group, but he's here himself, which is a thrill for us. Rather than try to describe the Jimi Hendrix experience, if you've never had it, here's a piece of film from D. A. Pennebaker's film, *Monterey Pop*, to do it for me . . .

[*The last few minutes of "Wild Thing" are played, showing Hendrix lighting his guitar on fire and then smashing it.*]

DC: That isn't all he does, but he is here tonight, as I say, without his Experience. So here is a naive and innocent Jimi Hendrix.

[*Hendrix enters as the Bob Rosengarden Orchestra plays "Foxey Lady."*]

DC: Nice to meet you. That's not the only thing you do on stage, for those who have never seen you before, if there are any, and of course there happen to be a few. What is the meaning of destruction on stage when you do it like that?

Jimi Hendrix: Hmm, let's see.

DC: You can reject this question.

JH: I was in such a trance then when I did it, but I can't remember, but let's see if I can remember. It's a thing like, when you bring your girlfriend there, and you watch us play and so forth, you can get it out of your system then by watching us do it, making it into a theatrics instead of putting it into the streets. So, when you get home with your family or your girlfriend you have all this tension out of the way. It's nothing but a release, I guess.

DC: Possibly a safety valve to some kinda violence?

JH: Yeah, you can call it that.

DC: Do you hate to be asked what things mean? I realize you almost have to apologize to ask someone who's considered an artist as you are what they mean by something because you're asking them to reinterpret something they've already done. Do you think music has a meaning?

JH: Oh, yeah, definitely, it's getting to be more spiritual than anything now. Pretty soon I believe that they're going to have to rely on music to get some kind of peace of mind, or satisfaction, direction, actually, more so than politics, because like politics is really an ego scene, you know, that's the way . . . I look at it anyway . . . It's on a big fat ego scene, for instance.

DC: Ego scene?

JH: Well, yeah, the . . . art of words, which means nothing, you know. So therefore you have to rely on a more of a earthier substance, like music or the arts, theatre, you know, acting, painting, whatever.

DC: I bet you didn't wear this in the paratroops.

JH: Not necessarily. [*Laughs.*]

DC: You were a para— What is it? A paratrooper or a parachutist? Or shoutist?

JH: It doesn't make a difference. One Hundred and First Airborne, Fort Campbell, Kentucky.

DC: We almost wore the same things tonight. It would've been embarrassing.

[*The audience laughs and applauds as Cavett points to Hendrix's turquoise kimono-like top.*]

DC: I turn him on. It's really amazing . . . I want to clear something with you. I heard you use the expression "an electric church" as an ambition you had. Was this speaking metaphorically or poetically, or do you really wanna . . .

JH: [*Sighs.*] Oh, let's see . . . It's just a belief that I have . . . we do use electric guitars. Everything is electrified nowadays. So, therefore the belief comes into . . . through electricity to the people, whatever. That's why we play so loud. Because it doesn't actually hit through the eardrums like most groups do nowadays. They say, "Well, we're gonna play loud too, 'cause they're playin' loud." And they got this real shrill sound, and it's really hard. We plan for our sound to go inside the soul of the person, actually, and see if they can awaken some kind of thing in their minds, 'cause there's so many sleeping people. You can call it that if you want to.

DC: What do you like to hear if somebody comes up after a concert, what kind of compliment do you like?

JH: I don't know. I don't really live on compliments, matter of fact it has a way of distracting me, and a whole lot of other musicians and artists that are out there today. They hear all these compliments; they say, "Wow, I must have been really great." So they get fat and satisfied, and they get lost, and they forget about the actual talent that they have, and they start livin' into another world, you know.

DC: That's an interesting problem isn't it? Someone said about Janis Joplin, who's a superstar now. You know Janis I expect . . .

JH: Superstar? Oh, yeah.

DC: Yes, she certainly is in my heart.

JH: I'm Super Chicken,¹ and don't you forget it. [*Laughter.*]

DC: And don't I forget it? Now I was going to say, the problem of succeeding is a hard one for you if your basis is, say, in the blues, or something like that, and you suddenly make hundreds of thousands of dollars a year. Someone said it's hard to sing the blues when you're making that kind of money. This assumes you can't be unhappy and have a lot of money.

JH: Well, sometimes it gets to be really easy to sing the blues, when you're sup-posed to be makin' all this much money, you know, 'cause, like, money is, it's gettin' to be out of hand now, you know, it's, you know, and, like, musicians, especially young cats, you know. They get a chance to make all this money, and they say "Wow, this is fantastic," and like I said before, they lose themselves, and they forget about the music itself, they forget about their talents, they forget about the other half of them. So, therefore you can sing a whole lot of blues. The more money you make, the more blues, sometimes, you can sing. But the idea is to use all of these hang-ups and different things as steps in life . . . it's just like drinking coffee; well, you don't drink it every day, or else you go into another scene with it, like escapes, and all this.

DC: I don't know, but it sounds good. Do you consider yourself a disciplined guy? Do you get up every day and work?

JH: Oh, I try to get up every day. [*Audience laughs and applauds.*]

DC: That in itself is a discipline.

JH: I'm still trying today too. [*Audience laughs.*]

DC: Do you write every day?

JH: Oh, yeah, yeah.

DC: Do you wanna leave a call?

JH: [*Uses silly voice*] What does that mean? What are you trying to say?

DC: That's hip talk. I wouldn't have time to explain it.

JH: [*Laughter as Hendrix pretends he's trying to look up the word "hip" in a book.*] Hmm. Hip? Oh, yeah, I see. Right.

DC: Listen, Hendrix. I'm told you're going to perform for us, which I still don't believe, because I don't know how this is possible. But if you would, there would be more than one grateful person on the premises. Oh, by the way, good night to my guests in case I forget later, in case you don't want to come to a stop.

JH: For him. [*Laughs and holds up three fingers, indicating that Cavett has made three jokes on his behalf.*]

DC: Have you understood *anything* I've said?

JH: I think so. I've been watching you. . . . I talk through music anyway. Maybe if I get my guitar together, I can get something together.

DC: Great. OK. Your stage is ours.

[*Hendrix plays "Hear My Train a Comin'" with the orchestra. After a commercial break, Hendrix returns to the guest chair alongside Cavett.*]

DC: Thank you, Robert Downey, Jimi Hendrix, Garson Kanin, and Gwen Verdon for being here tonight. Jimi, thank you for making your network debut here.

JH: Thank you very much.

DC: We have twenty seconds left to which you can tune up. We'll be back tomorrow. Good night. See you then.

---

1. Hendrix was a fan of Saturday-morning cartoons. The animated crime-fighter show *Super Chicken* ran on ABC-TV from 1967 to 1970.

THE TONIGHT SHOW INTERVIEW

FLIP WILSON | From an audio recording of THE TONIGHT SHOW, July 10, 1969.

Comedian Flip Wilson filled in for host Johnny Carson on this episode of THE TONIGHT SHOW. Wilson used the opportunity to promote his July 11 concert at Madison Square Garden, called SOUL '69, that featured Joe Tex and Wilson Pickett, who were also guests on the evening's show. Hendrix had met Wilson the year before at a private birthday party for Hendrix.

Hendrix now had bassist Billy Cox on the payroll but no new drummer, so he requested Ed Shaughnessy for the job. Shaughnessy was Carson's house-band drummer, whom Hendrix had recently seen perform with jazz legend Charles Mingus.

Flip Wilson: Glad you could make it, man. Glad you could make it.

Jimi Hendrix: I am too.

FW: Fine. So many people have been asking, because they've heard that you regard your performance as a spiritual experience. So, if there are any comments you'd like to make about that, we'd all be very interested.

JH: Let's see now, spiritual . . .

FW: I can dig it. I can *dig* it. [*Laughter.*]

JH: Well, somebody's going to have to.

FW: I'll dig it.

JW: It's a thing that I don't know, after . . . goin' to church for a few times an' gettin' thrown out of there because you've got tennis shoes on with a blue-and-black suit . . . brown shirt, the works . . .

FW: Yes.

JH: And then after politics tell you this hogwash about this and that, you know, you decide and say, "Well let me get my own thing together," you know, and so music is my scene. My whole life is based around it. So quite naturally it comes to be even more than a religion. And so what I learn, through the experience of it, I try to pass on to other people, you know, through our music, so it won't be so hard for them to go around. Like for instance all this violence, people runnin' 'round through the streets, you know. I can understand their point but, like, uh, if they dig the sounds and let the spiritual . . . look, it's like church actually, you know.

FW: Yes.

JH: It's like church, how you go to a gospel church and we're tryin' to get the same thing through, modern-day music, you know . . .

FW: I can dig it, very easily. There's no problem, not at all. I was checking, doing a little research on you. You're Sagittarian also . . .

JH: Constantly. [*Laughter.*]

FW: When I'm very interested in people I try to check them out, and find out as much as I can.

JH: What date are you?

FW: December eighth.

JH: The twenty-seventh is mine.

FW: The twenty-seventh of . . . November. Sammy Davis, myself . . . let's see. On December eighth is Sammy Davis, Winston Churchill, Kirk Douglas, myself. Sinatra's on the seventh . . . and who else? Maurice Chevalier . . .

JH: I know quite a few of 'em. [*Laughter.*]

FW: That's the sign of great entertainers—Sagittarius. That's why I checked you out.

JH: Yeah . . .

FW: I can dig it. I feel we all have something to offer, and we each have to find our thing. And *we* represent, in my opinion, God, and what we give to each other . . . and we're all supposed to come here and put something in the pot, and go.

Unidentifiable guest: Yes! Amen!

FW: Don't just come here and suck up all the air.

JH: We're all a temple of God anyway, you know . . . that's why you have to have some kind eye dreams on yourself, regardless of what you're like outwards, you know?

FW: Yes.

JH: And, like, once you carry God inside yourself, well then you're part of him, he's part of you, you know?

FW: Well, Jim, it's my pleasure to extend an invitation to you to whip a light sermon on us. [*Laughter.*] Great. Yes. Jimi Hendrix! Ladies and gentlemen.

JH: I'd like to say first of all this is Billy Cox, our new bass player. We'll do a thing called "Here Comes Your Lover Man." Out the window, I can see him . . .

[*Just as Hendrix's solo begins, his amp blows. Cox and Shaughnessy continue to play in hopes the sound would be quickly restored.*]

FW: We're going to switch amps, and get it together. Jimi will be back with us in a minute. . . . The amplifier went out . . . while he was cooking so hard. . . . That's right, he burned it up, and we're switching amplifiers. Are we just about ready? The main thing to do in a situation like this is to keep talking. I'm gonna run my mouth till the amplifier starts. After all, people don't want to waste their time lookin' in and nothin's goin' on. How's the amplifier comin' along? . . . OK, ladies and gentlemen . . . What?

[*The amplifier and guitar make feedback sounds.*]

FW: *You* ask Jimi, I got to keep talkin' to the people. Don't forget, *The Joey Bishop Show* is just a notch away. We don't want to lose anybody. Maybe I'll cut this watermelon up and pass it out. We'll have a commercial and get things squared away . . .

[*Commercial break*]

FW: This is what makes shows like this exciting, because it's *real*. And people want the truth . . . and the truth will now be given to you by way of the Jimi Hendrix Experience. Jimi Hendrix!

[*The trio plays "Lover Man," which is followed by applause. Hendrix then returns to be seated with Flip Wilson and the other guests.*]

JOE TEX: Damn, Jimi. Wow! Sock it to 'em.

FW: Sorry about that little difficulty.

JH: Don't worry about it. It's all right.

JT: It's all the experience. That was too much, Jimi.

JH: It better be too much, or my snake pants will jump up and bite you.

FW: Because you're an explosion of love, so I have nothing to fear from your snake pants.

JH: I was scared every day for five years. I was scared to death of them. . . . every day for five years I used to fall on them, almost, in my dreams. What is that from anyway?

FW: I don't know. Sagittarians? Snakes? Well, possibly. Horses are our thing. We're very closely related to the horse, and the horse is very much afraid of the snake.

JH: Some horses are some of my best friends.

FW: I love horses because they're big and they're gentle and they have all their strength and they're so cool. . . . I like cows too.

JH: Cows can't fly.

FW: Cows can't fly?

JH: I'm glad they can't.

FW: A cow can fly if you put some LSD in their grass.

[*Wilson invites Hendrix to stay and have some lemonade as he introduces Wilson Pickett, the next act.*]

JIMI HENDRIX'S POST-WOODSTOCK COMMENTS

From a Canadian radio broadcast, August 18, 1969.

Gypsy Sun and Rainbows, Hendrix's new six-piece band, was scheduled to close the three-day Woodstock festival on Sunday, August 17, but due to numerous complications they didn't perform until the early hours of the following day. Hendrix was sick, tired, and insecure that the band didn't know the songs well enough. After the concert, a reporter asked Hendrix about his thoughts on the event.

HENDRIX: The nonviolence . . . the very, very good brand of music . . . the very true brand of music . . . the acceptance by the long-awaited crowd. They had to sleep in mud and rain, and get hassled by this and hassled by that, and still come through saying it was a successful festival. That's one of the good things. There's so many stories you can add up on this thing . . . if you add them all up you'd feel like a king. They're tired of joining the street gangs. They're tired of joining the militant groups. They're tired of hearing the president gab his gums away. They're tired of this and tired of that, they want to find a different direction. They know they're on the right track, but where the hell is it coming from?

UNITED BLOCK ASSOCIATION PRESS CONFERENCE

From an audio recording of the August 1969 press conference.

To promote Hendrix's upcoming benefit concert for Harlem's United Block Association (UBA) on September 5, 1969, a press conference was scheduled in late August at Frank's Restaurant on 125th Street in New York. Hendrix sat with several UBA representatives and had six microphones placed in front of him.

[*A voice in the room announces that the cameras are rolling.*]

Question: Is there anything you want to say?

Jimi Hendrix: Pardon? I can hardly wait till the gig comes because I'm more comfortable with a guitar in front of people. This whole thing is under the benefit of UBA, and we hope to do some more gigs, some more benefits for it. What we're trying to stress also is that music should be done outside in a festival type of way. Just like they do it anywhere else. And like, if they can have more gigs like this in Harlem, where you play outside, say for instance, three days, and the fourth day you play half the day outside, for instance, and maybe the other time in the Apollo, four shows or whatever, you know. 'Cause a lot of kids from the ghetto, or whatever you want to call it, don't have enough money to travel across country to see these different festivals, what they call festivals. I mean, seven dollars is a lot of money. So, I think, more groups that are supposed to be considered heavy groups should contribute more to this cause.

Q: Can we ask you what your thoughts may be after White Lake [*site of the Woodstock festival*]?

JH: Well, I was pretty tired . . . very tired . . .

Q: Do you think this is going to have an influence on future festivals?

JH: Well, the idea of nonviolence, and the idea of when your attendance is over the thing [the record], you should let everybody else in free. Yeah, that idea, yeah, and the idea of people really listening to music over the sky, you know, in such a large body. Everybody thinks that something is gonna go haywire or somethin', but that's always brought on by the police. Always.

Q: You say that this is a success, but there [were] 300,000 people. Isn't that pretty large to really be a success?

JH: It sure is, and I'm glad it is a success. . . . It was a success for the simple fact it was one of the largest gatherings of people in the musical sense of it. It could've been arranged a little . . . tighter, but it was a complete success compared to all the other festivals that everybody tries to knock here and there. I'd like to see the same thing happen, and see some sort of chartered bus thing come from different areas of town, because I'd like everybody to see these types of festivals and have everybody mix together. You wouldn't believe it. You really wouldn't.

Q: Do you think that anything significant was stated by this gathering?

JH: It just seems to me that . . . [*he pauses to listen to someone whispering in his ear.*] Oh yeah, that's true. Music has a lot of influence on a lot of young people today. Politics are getting . . . well, I don't know; you know how they're getting . . . a cat—they talk on TV, and a cat from Mississippi, a farmer in Mississippi, you can't barely understand him, except when he says, "America," you know. So then he's gonna vote for him. But through music it's all true . . . either true or false, such a large gathering of music must show that music means *something*, and then it breaks down to the arts of earth; the earth arts.

Q: Why did you play "The Star-Spangled Banner" in your set?

JH: Oh, because we're all Americans. We're all Americans, aren't we? It was written and played in a very beautiful, what they call a beautiful state. Nice, inspiring, your heart throbs, and you say, "Great. I'm American." But nowadays when we play it, we don't play it to take away all this greatness that America is supposed to have. We play it the way the air is in America today. The air is slightly static, isn't it?

Q: With all the bad reports about drugs, if it was held in the same place next year, would you appear again?

JH: What? Do you mean the festival? Held in the same place? Yeah, I'd love to appear, but the drug scene is going to be a little different by that time anyway. Everybody's gonna know the *truth* about that. By that time. *By that time.* Harlem's going to have beautiful round buildings . . . in comparison . . .

Q: What is your comment on drug use at the Wallkill[1] festival?

JH: I don't know. Well, some people believe that they have to, you know, do this or do that to get into the music. I have no opinions at all. Different strokes for different folks. . . . Sly and the Family Stone, I think, said that. [*Laughter.*]

Q: How do you think the benefit that you're gonna do in Harlem will be compared to the Woodstock festival?

JH: I don't know. I might be living in the wrong time, but I don't go by comparison, I just go by the truthness or the falseness of the whole thing. The intentions of, whatever it might be. Forget about comparing, that's where we make our biggest mistake, is trying to put our ego against another person's. That's why I can't find out who's better, B. B. King or Segovia. They're both masters. They're both kings.

Q: Mr. Hendrix, why the United Block Association? Why did you pick the United Block Association?

JH: It's a start, man. What's wrong with it?

Q: Do you think that this kind of assembly marks a change in American culture?

JH: There's been some changes marked, even before the times of King, Dr. [Martin] Luther King, you know, it's been a whole lot of changes. But some people after the excitement, or the backwash of the change slows down, they say, "Yeah, that was groovy. Let's see what else can we feast upon now?" One of them things. It's a whole lotta changes happening, but now it's time for all these changes to connect, to show them that it's leading up to love, peace, and harmony for anybody, and a *chance* for anybody.

Q: Mr. Hendrix, a lot of people found the Wallkill assembly startling, even surprising. What would you say to them?

JH: Well, from now on a whole lot of people are going to find things ten times more startling, and ten times more surprising. It depends on where their head's at. Just pretend a flying saucer is coming down. Instead of checking it out, or really seeing what it's about, they gonna try to shoot it down first of all. In other words, not knowing a thing. So *this* is unknown, a surprise, isn't it? They should get into it and see what it's really about. Just like smoking and cancer. It got so bad they had to put it on TV. Didn't they? Find out the yeses and nos, what's the actual link up. Well, it's the same thing with these festivals and gatherings. I hope it happens in art, hope it happens in community sports, and whatever.

Q: You taught yourself to play.

JH: People taught me to play, man. The movement of people and the way they carry on from this or that. . . . Anyone can do anything; it's up to themselves . . . with the right intentions.

---

1. The three-day festival was originally scheduled to be held in Wallkill, New York, but was banned by the town's zoning board because the portable toilets did not meet code.

THE DICK CAVETT SHOW
INTERVIEW (SEPTEMBER)

DICK CAVETT | From THE DICK CAVETT SHOW, September 9, 1969.

Hendrix was originally scheduled to appear on Cavett's Woodstock special on August 18, along with several other groups that played the festival, but he was too exhausted after performing that morning. Instead, he made his second appearance on the program in early September.

Hendrix debuted a portion of his new band, Gypsy Sun and Rainbows, featuring Billy Cox, Juma Sultan, and Mitch Mitchell.

Dick Cavett: There seems to be something making noise back there. I hope it's all right. Some of you might remember that some weeks back we did our rock show, and James Hendrix was not on that program. After playing a terrifically long set that night and all into the morning[1] at Woodstock, he collapsed in his room and was not able to be there. He's had odd things happen to him. Once fifty girls jumped into the pool between the stage and the audience when he was appearing, and we assume that will not happen here tonight. Anyway, he's recovered enough to join us tonight, and will you welcome the inimitable Jimi Hendrix Experience, Jimi Hendrix!

[*Hendrix, Cox, Mitchell, and Sultan perform a medley of "Izabella"/"Machine Gun." After the song concludes, the Bob Rosengarden Orchestra plays "Foxey Lady" while Hendrix walks over to sit with Cavett.*]

DC: So it's really you at last. How are you?

JH: I'm pretty tired, I've been recording so much.

DC: You're tired now?

JH: Yeah! I haven't had any sleep for all night. We've been working on our last LP.

DC: How much sleep do you need to be alert?

JH: Alert? I guess about . . . eight. [*Laughs.*]

DC: Eight hours?

JH: Yeah, I had about eight minutes. [*Makes clock-ticking noises with his tongue.*]

DC: Eight minutes? I slept longer than that in my monologue.

[*The band's amps are humming audibly offstage.*]

DC: Want to cut the racket off on the sound here? Nice gentlemen. . . . What is that sound that we hear irritating us so dreadfully?

JH: Well, it sounds something like the New York street. It's like today the air is all static, so the amplifiers are static. Music is loud, the air is loud. . . . We trying to settle things down a little bit, but it's going to take like a rest.

DC: I asked a practical question and got a philosophical answer. [*Laughter.*]

JH: Is that philosophical?

DC: I thought it was . . . with the static in the air today and all . . .

JH: Well, I was just trying to get a point across before we take our rest. [*Makes a snoring sound.*] Oh, I'm sorry. We're still on.

DC: We're both gonna sack out. Mr. Young, will you . . .

Robert Young: Carry on?

DC: What really happened to you that night at Woodstock? Did you stay on so long you were just . . .

JH: No, we were playing in the morning, and it was announced that it was canceled, that *The Dick Cavett Show* was canceled, and later on it was announced that it was on. I was so exhausted. It was like—what do you call those things? A nervous breakdown?

DC: A physical breakdown. Have you ever had a nervous breakdown?

JH: Yeah, about three of them since I've been in this group . . . since I've been in this business.

DC: Really? Gee. I didn't mean to pry, but since you brought it up. [*Laughter.*]

JH: It's all right.

DC: Everyone said they were amazed at the absence of violence. It's become a cliché now about that big festival and about the others. . . . Were you surprised at it?

JH: I was glad. That's what it's all about, you know. Try to keep violence down, keep 'em off the streets. Like a festival of five hundred thousand people was a really beautiful turnout. I hope we have more of them. It'd be nice.

DC: What was the controversy about the national anthem and the way you played it?

JH: I don't know. All I did was play it. I'm American so I played it. I used to have to sing it in school. . . . They made me sing it in school. . . . It was a flashback.

DC: This man was in the One Hundred and First Airborne, so when you write your nasty letters in . . .

JH: Nasty letters?

DC: When you mention the national anthem and talk about playing it in any unorthodox way, you immediately get a guaranteed percentage of hate mail from people who say, "How dare—"

JH: [*Interrupting*] Unorthodox? It isn't unorthodox!

DC: It isn't unorthodox?

JH: No, no. I thought it was beautiful, but there you go. [*Applause.*]

DC: Don't you find there's a certain mad beauty in unorthodoxy . . . [*Hendrix raises his hands and growls like a monster.*]

DC: Agh. I knew you'd do that some day. I knew you'd wig out on me. [*Laughter.*] Do they ever send that shirt back with too much starch in the collar? [*Laughter.*]

JH: I don't know nothing about it . . .

DC: That's the best shirt I've seen in a long time. Why do the super groups keep breaking up? There are always rumors that your group is breaking up, and Big Brother broke up . . .

JH: Probably because they want to get into individual things on their own, or they want to get into other things besides music.

DC: Do you mean guys in your group would want out of the music business?

JH: Not necessarily. Maybe they might want to get into their own music, 'cause what I was trying to do was like a today's type of blues, like "Manic Depression," and so forth. Noel Redding, he's into a more harmonic thing, like when you sing and so forth. He went to England to get his own group together.

Hendrix on **THE DICK CAVETT SHOW, September 9, 1969.** ABC PHOTO ARCHIVES

DC: Who's this?

JH: Noel Redding, the bass . . .

DC: Oh, Noel Redding.

JH: We have Billy Cox playing bass this time. I think this is the last job we'll do until we take a rest. We've been working very hard for three years.

DC: Can you tell some nights that you're just not making it at all? Do you have the urge to just walk off?

JH: That's why I hate compliments. Compliments are so embarrassing some-times, because you really know the truth. Sometimes people don't really try to understand. It's like a circus that might come into town . . . so wow, watch that!

And as soon as they fade away, they go and feed upon the next thing. But it's all right. It's part of life. I'm diggin' it myself. [*Laughter.*]

DC: You're considered one of the best guitar players in the world. [*The audience applauds as Hendrix hangs his head in embarrassment.*]

JH: Oh, no.

DC: Well, one of the best in this studio anyway.

JH: How about one of the best sitting in this chair?

DC: Do you have to practice every day the way a violinist does? I mean, if you're not working, say you're off in England, taking off a couple of months. . . . Do you have to keep in shape every day?

JH: I like to play to myself in a room, or before we go on stage, or when I ever feel down or depressed . . . I can't practice. . . . It's always constantly, what do you call it? Like a jam. It's hard for me to remember any notes because I'm always trying to create other things. That's why I make a lot of mistakes.

DC: Do you read music?

JH: No, not at all.

DC: Do you ever run into any of the guys from the old One Hundred and First?

JH: Yeah.

DC: Do they think your life is strange compared to what they're into?

JH: Yeah. It wouldn't matter really because there's so many different things going on now. I can't take time out and say, "I wonder what they're thinking about me there," and all this kind of stuff. I can't go through all that. . . . I've been going through it for three years. I think they're pretty well off if they ever get out of that stuff . . . to see me again in order for me to see them. I feel pretty lucky about that.

DC: You're still looking for that certain girl?

JH: Certain girl? What girl?

DC: The certain one! You're not married? Do you see yourself married ever?

JH: No, I hope not. [*Laughter and applause.*]

DC: But you'll never get a situation comedy on television.[2]

JH: By that time I think it'll be obsolete.

DC: We have to pause. We'll be back. Stay there, and Ralph Nader will be here.

[*Commercial break*]

DC: Jimi Hendrix left. He really felt lousy. He told me during the commercial, and I really want to thank him for coming here tonight. He felt somewhat obligated because he missed the other show, and I think he's a wonderful performer, and I'm really glad he came here tonight, and I hope he feels better . . .

---

1. Hendrix only played a morning set.

2. Cavett looked toward Robert Young as he said this to Hendrix, because Young was well-known for the sitcom *Father Knows Best*. With his back toward Young, Hendrix responded while slightly covering his mouth.

"JIMI HENDRIX: I DON'T WANT TO BE A CLOWN ANY MORE . . ."

SHEILA WELLER | From ROLLING STONE, November 15, 1969.

ROLLING STONE reporter Sheila Weller spent September 14 and 15 with Hendrix and friends at a rented house near Shokan and Boiceville, New York.

LIBERTY, New York—Records, film, press and gossip are collectively ambitious in creating the image of a rock superstar. With Jimi Hendrix—as with Janis Joplin, Mick Jagger and Jim Morrison—mythology is particularly lavish.

Unfortunately, it is also often irreversible—even when it's ill-founded or after the performer himself has gone through changes.

Several weeks ago, *Life* magazine described Jimi as "a rock demigod" and devoted several color pages to [a] kaleidoscopic projection of his face. Well, why not? The fisheye lens shot on his first album cover shows him in arrogant distortion: on the second album, he becomes Buddha. Lest anyone forget, Leacock-Pennebaker's *Monterey Pop* has immortalized his pyromaniacal affair with the guitar. Rock-media bedroom talk makes him King Stud of the groupies. Stories circulate that he is rude to audiences, stands up writers, hangs up photographers, that he doesn't talk.

What Jimi's really all about—and where his music is going—is an altogether different thing.

For most of the summer and early fall, Jimi rented a big Georgian-style home in Liberty, New York—one of Woodstock's verdant "suburbs"—for the purpose of housing an eclectic family of musicians: Black Memphis blues guitarists; "new music" and jazz avantgardists; "Experience" member Mitch Mitchell; and—closest to Jimi and most influential—Juma Lewis, a multi-talented ex-progressive jazzman who is now the leader of Woodstock's Aboriginal Music Society.

The hilltop compound—replete with wooded acreage and two horses—was intended for a peaceful, productive musical growth period. But hassles did come, sometimes sending Jimi off on sanity-preserving vacations in Algeria and Morocco: local police were anxious to nab "big-time hippies" on anything from dope to speeding; the house was often hectic with hangers-on; pressure mounted from Jimi's commercial reps to stay within the well-hyped image and not go too far afield experimentally.

But with it all, growth, exchange and—finally—unity was achieved among Jimi and the musicians, whose work-in-progress was evidenced in occasional public appearances in the New York area (at the Woodstock/Bethel Festival, Harlem's Apollo Theater, Greenwich Village's Salvation discotheque, and ABC's Dick Cavett show) and has been recorded for Reprise on an LP which will be released in January.[1] The name of the album, *Gypsies, Suns and Rainbows,* epitomizes the new Hendrix feeling.

With close friends of Jimi, I drove up to Liberty on a quiet September weekend. The mélange of musicians and girls had departed. In a few weeks, Jimi himself was to give up the house, woods and horses for less idyllic prospects: a Manhattan loft and a November hearing on the narcotics possession charge he was slapped with in Toronto, May 3rd.

Photographs have a funny way of betraying his essentially fragile face and body. He is lean. Almost slight. Eating chocolate chip cookies on the living room couch in this big house—"furnished straight and comfortable"—he seems boyish and vulnerable.

He offers questions with an unjustified fear of his own articulateness that is charming—but occasionally painful. "Do you, uh—where do you live in the city?" "What kind of music do you like—would you care to listen to?" He is self-effacing almost to a fault: "Do you ever go to the Fillmore? No?—that was a silly question, sorry." "I'm sorry, am I mumbling? Tell me when I'm mumbling. Damn . . . I always mumble."

It becomes uncomfortable, so one says: "Jimi, don't keep putting yourself down. There's everybody else to do that for you." He attaches to that statement, repeats it slowly, whips out the embossed Moroccan notebook in which he jots lyrics at all hours of day and night, and scribbles something down.

Fingering through his record collection (extensive and catholic: e.g., Marlene Dietrich, David Peel and the Lower East Side, Schoenberg, Wes Montgomery), he pulls out *Blind Faith*; *Crosby, Stills and Nash*; and *John Wesley Harding*. The Dylan plays first. Jimi's face lights: "I love Dylan. I only met him once, about three years ago, back at the Kettle of Fish [a folk-rock era hangout] on MacDougal Street. That was before I went to England. I think both of us were pretty drunk at the time, so he probably doesn't remember it."

In the middle of a track, Jimi gets up, plugs in his guitar, and—with eyes closed and his supple body curved gently over the instrument—picks up on "Frankie Lee and Judas Priest," riding the rest of the song home with a near-religious intensity.

He talks intently to Juma and his girl. He cherishes real friends and will do anything for them. They, in turn, feel protective toward him. "Poor Jimi," one says. "Everyone's trying to hold him up for something. Those busts . . . Even the highway patrol exploits him. They know his car: they stop him on the road between New York and Woodstock and harass him. Then they have something to gloat about for the rest of the day. Once a cop stopped *me* on the highway and started bragging: 'Hey, I just stopped Jimi Hendrix for the second time today.'"

On the bookcase is a photograph of a Fifties Coasters–type R&B group: processed hair, metallic-threaded silk-lapel suits, shiny shoes. The thin kid on the far left in a high-conked pompadour, grinning over an electric guitar: is it? "That's okay," Jimi smiles at the impending laughter. "I don't try to cover up the past; I'm not ashamed of it." But he is genuinely humble about the present. For example, he'd been wanting for some time to jam with jazz and "new music" avantgardists, but worried that such musicians didn't take him seriously enough to ever consider playing with him. "Tell me, honestly," he asked a friend, "what do those guys think of me? Do they think I'm jiving?"

We are listening now to the tape of such a session, the previous night's jam: Jimi on electric guitar, avantgarde pianist Michael Ephron on clavichord, Juma on congas and flute. A beautiful fusion of disparate elements, disjunct and unified at alternating seconds. Now chaotic, now coming together. "Cosmic music," they call it. Ego-free music. Not the sort of stuff the waxlords make many bucks off. Not the kind of sound guaranteed to extend the popularity of a rock superstar.

"I don't want to be a clown anymore." "I don't want to be a 'rock and roll star,'" Jimi says, emphatically. The forces of contention are never addressed but their pervasiveness has taken its toll on Jimi's stamina and peace of mind. Trying to remain a growing artist when a business empire has nuzzled you to its bosom takes a toughness, a shrewdness. For those who have a hardness of conviction but not of temperament it isn't a question of selling out but of dying, artistically and spiritually. Refusing to die yet ill-equipped to fight dirty, many sensitive but commercially-lionized artists withdrew. I watch Jimi quietly digging the pictures of faraway people and places in a book, *The Epic of Man* ("South America wow, that's a whole different world. Have you ever been there?") and I wonder just where he will be and what he will be doing five years from now.

We crowd into Jimi's metal-fleck silver Stingray ("I want to paint it over, maybe black") for a sunrise drive to the waterfalls. ("I wish I could bring my guitar and plug it in down there.") The talk is of puppies, daybreak, other innocentia. We climb down the rocks to the icy brook, then suddenly discover the car keys are missing. Everyone shuffles through shoulder pouches and wallets. "Hey, don't worry," Jimi says. "They'll turn up. No use being hassled about it now." Jimi's taking pictures and writing poetry. "I want to write songs about tranquility, about beautiful things," he says.

Back at the house, he pads around, emptying ashtrays, putting things in order. "I'm like a clucking old grandmother," he smiles. "I've just gotta straighten things out a little." It's 7 AM and he has to be at the recording studio in Manhattan at 4 in the afternoon. Everyone's exhausted.

After a few hours of sleep, Jimi floats into the kitchen looking like a fuzzy lamb unmercifully awakened and underfed. He passes up the spread of eggs, pork chops, crescent rolls and tea: breakfast, instead, is a Theragran[2] and a swig of tequila in milk. "Jimi, you never eat . . ." Juma's girl worries aloud.

We pile into the car for the two-hour drive into Manhattan. Passing two Afro-haired guys in an Aston-Martin, Jimi turns and flashes a broad grin, extending his fingers in a peace salute. We turn up the radio on Stevie Wonder's "My Cherie Amour"; groove on Neil Diamond, Jackie DeShannon, the Turtles. Everything is everything: We're playing with a puppy, grateful for clear skies, clear road, clear AM station. What more could a carload of travelers in an inconspicuous blue Avis ask?

We pull into a roadside stop. No giggly bell-bottomed young girls in sight, Jimi gets out and brings back chocolate milk and ice cream for everyone. Truckers pay no attention. Middle-aged couples glare disdainfully.

The talk is of the session. They'll record at a studio on West 44th Street, then go somewhere else to mix it—maybe Bell Sound or A&R—because Jimi says the recording studio they're going to "has bad equipment . . . likes to take advantage of so-called longhair musicians."

Downtown traffic on the West Side highway is light at rush hour. The fortresses of upper Riverside Drive are handsome in the sun, but the air has lost its freshness. Getting off the highway at 45th Street, it's 4:45. The session, costing $200 an hour, was booked to begin at 4:00. But delay couldn't be helped; no hassle. A carful of teenagers alongside us has the radio turned up loud on "If 6 Was 9"—the cut being used as part of advertisement for *Easy Rider*. I ask Jimi if he's seen the film; he doesn't answer.

Turning around, I find him stretched out on the backseat, legs curled up embryonically, hands clasped under his cheek. Sleeping soundly.

---

1. Due to legal issues, Capitol Records released an album titled *Band of Gypsys* in March 1970.
2. A multivitamin supplement.

THE QUEEN VS. JAMES MARSHALL HENDRIX

Hendrix returned to Toronto on December 6, 1969, in preparation for his trial on December 8. Toronto lawyer John O'Driscoll represented him, and John Malone represented the Crown. The court would determine if Hendrix was guilty of two charges of possession of heroin and hashish. If found guilty, he would receive a sentence of up to seven years in prison on each count.

The following testimony excerpts are from the original 1969 court transcripts, which surfaced on the TORONTO STAR's website in 2001.

THE QUEEN VS. JAMES MARSHALL HENDRIX

Before: His Honour JUDGE KELLY

APPEARANCES:

Mr. J. Malone for the Crown

Mr. J. O' Driscoll QC for the Accused

Court Room No. 15, Court House, University Avenue, Toronto

JAMES MARSHALL HENDRIX, Sworn.

December 8, 1969

DIRECT EXAMINATION BY MR. O'DRISCOLL:

Q. Can you tell us, Mr. Hendrix, on one of these tours, when you check into a hotel, what happens; is it all peace and tranquillity, or what happens?

A. No, it is not peace. There are always a lot of people around, sometimes—a lot of fans, outside and in the lobby and even through the halls.

Q. Without any insults to anyone, can you perhaps guess as to what age bracket you are talking about when you talk about fans?

A. Well, I could say from about 13 to 35, not counting mothers and fathers that bring their kids for autographs and pictures.

Q. And I think you have already told us that these gifts that are handed to you—however they are put to you, either dropped or handed or thrown, you keep them?

A. Yes. Most of them we keep, yes.

Q. Is there any reason you do that?

A. Well, it is just being gracious, you know. If a fan gives you something it's a very good feeling. They are the ones that support us; they are the ones that buy our records, so there's no harm done to receive a gift from a fan or a friend.

December 9, 1969

CONTINUED DIRECT EXAMINATION BY MR. O'DRISCOLL:

Q. Now, Mr. Hendrix, this room in the Beverly Rodeo Hotel in Beverly Hills, California. Can you describe this room to us?

A. It was a small room. As you walk in, to your right there is a closet and about two feet of wall, and then there is a bed and straight ahead is a couch. To your left there is a TV and bathroom and straight ahead, behind the couch, is windows. There is a very small hallway—a small little hall passage.

Q. Now, looking at Exhibit 1 [Bromo-Seltzer bottle] and the contents of it, Exhibit 2 [heroin], do you know where they came from?

A. As far as I can remember it came from a girl that handed it to me.

Q. Let's go back. Where were you at this time?

A. I was in my hotel room.

Q. Where?

A. In Beverly Hills. It was crowded with a lot of people there . . .

Q. Were you alone?

A. No, I was not. There were a lot of people there.

Q. Do you recall any person in that room by name?

A. Yes. There was one person there—she was doing an interview with me, her name is Sharon Lawrence.

Q. Now, can you tell us what your physical situation was at the time; how were you feeling?

A. I didn't feel very good at all. There were so many people there and I had an upset stomach, plus I was trying to be nice to everybody, you know, and I just didn't feel very good at all. I wanted to see if I could get rid of everybody in the most polite way possible, so I could be to myself, and Sharon and I was doing an interview together and I made it known that I didn't feel so good. I asked everybody politely to leave—the door was open and everybody was coming in and out, the usual scene in hotels.

Q. The door was open?

A. The door was open, yes.

Q. And did anything happen?

A. Like I said before, I was trying to get rid of everybody and I think I told Sharon, and somebody said, "Maybe you might need a Bromo-Seltzer," and at the same time there was a girl at the door, she stepped in and handed me this bottle and said, "Maybe this might make you feel better," and I said, "Thank you very much." I didn't study the bottle, I didn't look at it too much. I threw it in my bag.

Q. Just a moment. You say what you received from this girl—can you tell us what you received from her?

A. Yes. The bottle in your hand . . .

Q. All right. Now, after this happened, did everyone stay or did everyone leave, or what happened?

A. No. Eventually everyone left, because I guess they finally picked up on how I was feeling. I didn't mean to be rude, but I was a bit rude when I threw the bottle in the bag. So . . . like, everybody was gradually leaving then. After they left I laid down and took a nap . . .

Q. Mr. Hendrix, you have told us you receive gifts. Do you get anything that might be called extraordinary types of gifts?

A. Yes. We get all kinds of gifts.

Q. Such as what?

A. I received a few paintings that was very big—about like this [*indicating*], and we have received teddy bears and even pieces of string, yarn . . .

Q. Yarn?

A. Yes. We get everything; fountain pens, scarves . . .

Q. Now, have you ever received—prior to what you have told us about—presents which were drugs?

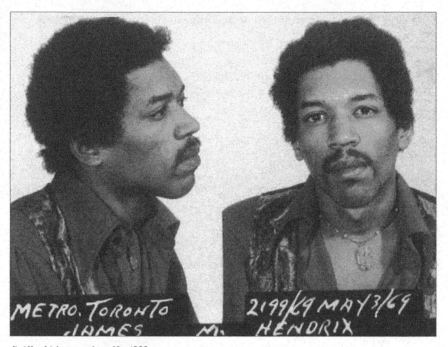

Jimi Hendrix's arrest photo, May 1969. STEVEN ROBY/STRAIGHT AHEAD ARCHIVES COLLECTION

A. Yes.

Q. Can you tell His Honour and the Gentlemen of the Jury in what form they came to you?

A. Well, sometimes we would get packages of marijuana, which would be either in cellophane or tinfoil, or maybe in little cookie packs or a cigarette box or something, and they might be rolled up in cigarette paper and we receive hashish sometimes in blocks or hash cookies or cakes . . .

Q. Hash cookies?

A. Yes.

Q. What do you mean by that?

A. Hashish that has been crumbled up and mixed in with a batter to make some cookies.

Q. And it comes to you in the form of cookies?

A. That's right. Sometimes cakes.

Q. Cakes as well?

A. Yes. I had a hash cake for my birthday one time in Ireland. I was celebrating my birthday and three or four cakes came in and there was one lump like that in the middle of a cake as we were cutting it.

Q. Now, what about the mails. Did you ever receive anything that way?

A. Yes. Well, I have received LSD through the mail.

THE COURT: What?

THE WITNESS: LSD, Your Honour, on blotting paper wrapped in tinfoil, through the mail, from France . . .

CROSS-EXAMINATION BY MR. MALONE:

Q. Mr. Hendrix, you told us this morning, earlier, that you have used marijuana?

A. Yes.

Q. And you have used hashish?

A. Yes.

Q. And you have used LSD?

A. Yes.

Q. And on occasion you have tried cocaine?

A. Right.

Q. What about amphetamines—speed?

A. No.

Q. Pardon?

A. No, no.

Q. And you denied using heroin?

A. Yes.

Q. When did you first begin using drugs, Mr. Hendrix?

A. Which ones do you mean?

Q. Well, any soft drugs, say marijuana, which I think was probably available first.

A. I guess I tried it once about four years ago. I really don't know—I guess about four years ago.

Q. I see. That would be about 1965—some four years after you started your band?

A. Four years ago—before, I guess.

Q. When was it that you got out of the service?

A. I can't remember the exact date.

Q. Can you remember the year?

A. It might have been in '63.

Q. Not until '63?

A. Or '62.

Q. Between say 1962 or 1963 and today, you have earned your livelihood as an entertainer. Is that correct?

A. Yes.

Q. And would you agree with me that, because of the nature of the work, traveling, and the audiences that you play before, and the places that you play, you would be exposed to what is known as "the drug scene"?

A. We would be exposed to it, yes.

Q. You would be exposed to it, even if you were not participating?

A. Yes.

Q. You would become quite knowledgeable as to say the language used and the source of supply and so on?

A. The language used, yes.

Q. It has kind of a language of its own, hasn't it?

A. Not really. It's the same English words.

Q. I suppose during your travels and your exposure to the drug elements, that you would know people who used heroin.

A. I have seen people that used heroin.

Q. And have you seen them use it?

A. To tell the truth, yes, I have. I have seen a person use it.

Q. On how many occasions.

A. About two occasions.

Q. I see. Now, I show you Exhibit 2 [heroin] and the contents of Exhibit 2. These are what are commonly known as "decks," aren't they?

A. That is what the Police Officer said to me. That's the first time I heard it. That's the term he used.

Q. When you were exposed to people using heroin, what did their material come in?

A. All I see was the person put the needle into his hand.

Q. You didn't see him prepare it?

A. No.

Q. And could you tell me—you saw him put the needle in and inject, but you wouldn't see him prepare?

A. No, I wouldn't.

Q. But they all happen at the same time, don't they?

A. I really don't know . . .

Q. This girl that you say handed you the bottle that you say was later found to contain heroin, did you know her?

A. No.

Q. Did you make any attempt to find her after you were charged?

A. No, I didn't.

Q. Now, relating to Exhibit 3, the pipe, was it the same girl that gave you this pipe with hashish on the end?

A. Not that I know of. No, it is not the same person.

Q. So you are suggesting two different people gave you narcotics on or about the same time?

A. As I said before, when I received the tube, I didn't know there was anything in it—you know. Somebody gave me the tube approximately about the same time or within a week of one another.

Q. Well, we are speaking of the tube; you say you got it and you put it in your bag. Is that right?

A. Yes.

Q. Well, can you suggest to me any possible use for that—ordinary use?

A. A pea-shooter. Maybe?

Q. A pea-shooter?

A. Yes.

Q. Yes, I suppose it could be used for that, but would you normally put pea-shooters in your bag?

A. I normally put gifts in my bag.

Q. What would you use that for; why carry it around?

A. I don't know. It was a gift; we accept gifts . . .

Q. And this person, whose name we don't know, did she say what it was when she gave it to you?

A. No. All she said was, "Maybe this will make you feel better."

Q. That's all?

A. Yes.

Q. And presumably she was a fan of yours. Is that right?

A. Yes.

Q. You are suggesting that fans of yours give you hard narcotics without telling you what it is?

A. I really don't know. You know—we had a lot of gifts and they didn't tell us what it is. They say different things here and there when they give it to us.[1]

---

1. The trial lasted three days, and on Wednesday the eleventh, a jury deliberated for eight and a half hours before coming to a verdict of not guilty on both counts of possession. Hendrix's first words out of the courtroom were: "I feel good, happy as hell" (from the *Telegram*, December 11, 1969).

"HENDRIX AND HIS BAND OF GIPSIES"

BOB DAWBARN | From MELODY MAKER, December 20, 1969.

Ecstatic with the positive verdict, Hendrix gave a telephone interview to UK reporter Bob Dawbarn on December 11, 1969, from his room at the Four Seasons Hotel in Toronto.

"No, you didn't get me out of bed, man. I'm in bed," said Jimi Hendrix, relaxing in his Toronto hotel after being acquitted of the drugs charges that had been hanging over his head for months.

Even over 3,000 miles of transatlantic telephone cable it was obvious he wasn't too keen to talk about the case. When I said how delighted we were at the MM [*Melody Maker*] that things have worked out OK for him, he contented himself with: "I've been having kind of a hard time over it all."

I let the matter drop and told him the MM had reported that he was trying to get Noel Redding and Mitch Mitchell—the other two-thirds of the Experience—back with him for a major tour.

"I've been thinking about that for a long time," he agreed. "All I'm waiting for is for Noel and Mitch to make up their minds and we can get everything fixed.

"I saw Noel at the Fillmore and I think everything is working out fine with him. Now I am looking forward to seeing Mitch. He has been over there in England getting himself together."

Will the tour include England if Noel and Mitch agree to return for the six weeks necessary—at a reported figure of half a million pounds?

"It would certainly include Britain and I'd hope to be there around February, or maybe March, at the latest. The way I see it is, we would start in England then do the rest of Europe, America, Hawaii, Canada and maybe end up back in England.

The conversation halted while Jimi went into paroxysms of sneezing that must have had the cable writhing on the ocean bed.

"'scuse me," he snorted when silence finally reigned. "Seems like I've got a chill."

I asked what he'd been doing recently, apart from worrying about the court case. "We've been recording with my new group, the Band of Gipsies [sic]," he said. "It's a three-piece and we have Buddy Miles on drums and Billy Cox on bass. How to describe the group? Very funky! Sort of a blues and rock type of thing.

"Hey, what's happening, over there in England? Who's making it happen? Somebody sent me a record by that Blue Mink. Nice. I need to get back there. I need to hear some of those new groups. And I need some new vibrations."

I wondered if Jimi had found any time to write new material recently.

"I've been writing a whole lot of things," he told me, after another, but lesser, bout of sneezing. "In fact, we've got enough material now for another two LPs. We are trying to decide what to release and at what time.

"We've started recording and you should be receiving a single around the end of January. The title? It should be either 'Trying to Be a Man' or 'Room Full of Mirrors.'"

Jimi repeated that he was looking forward to playing with Noel and Mitch again. I said Buddy Miles wasn't exactly a bad dep.

"Buddy is more of a rock drummer," he replied. "Mitch is more of a classic drummer—more of a funky R&B-type drummer."

Jimi has always been a man for catching up on what other groups and musicians are doing. I asked him if he had heard anyone new in the States that we ought to know about.

"I don't know about anybody new, I'm still digging Jethro Tull," he told me. "I heard them here and I was impressed.

"Have you heard of the Blues Image?"

I admitted that I hadn't.

"Or Eric Mercury?"

This time I was able to say that Peter Frampton had mentioned in last week's MM that Humble Pie have been working with him in the States.

"He's like all the R&B figures you ever heard all wrapped up together," said Jimi.

"To be honest, I'm not too up to date on what's been happening here. I've been working too hard rehearsing and recording with the Band of Gipsies [*sic*]. We are really getting it together now."

I thanked him and said good-bye.

"Hey," came Jimi's voice. "Just tell everybody over there a happy new year and a merry Christmas from me and I'm really looking forward to coming back home."

INTERVIEW WITH JIMI HENDRIX

SUE CASSIDY CLARK | From THE SUPERSTARS: IN THEIR OWN WORDS, 1970.

Upon returning to New York City on December 12, Hendrix gave an interview to Sue Cassidy Clark, a contributor to ROLLING STONE. The interview took place at publicist Pat Costello's apartment; Buddy Miles, Mike Jeffery, and photographer Douglas Kent Hall were also present.

Quotes from Clark's interview were published in the 1970 book, THE SUPERSTARS: IN THEIR OWN WORDS. The following is a selection of Hendrix's responses.

Three or four different worlds went by within the wink of an eye. Things were happening. There was this cat came around called Black Gold. And there was this other cat came around called Captain Coconut. Other people came around. I was all these people. And finally when I went back home, all of a sudden I found myself bein' a little West Coast Seattle boy—for a second. Then all of a sudden when you're back on the road again, there he goes, he starts goin' back. That's my life until somethin' else comes about.

There are a lot of things you have to sacrifice. It all depends on how deep you want to get into whatever your gig is. Whatever you're there for. So like the deeper you get into it the more sacrifices you have to do, maybe even on your personality or your outward this and that. I just dedicate my whole life to this whole art. You have to forget about what other people say. If it's art or anything else, whatever you really, really dig doing, you have to forget about what people say about you sometimes. Forget about this or forget about that. When you're supposed to die or when you're supposed to be living. You have to forget about all these things. You have to go on and be crazy. That's what they call craziness. Craziness is like heaven. Once you reach that point of where you don't give a damn about what everybody else is sayin', you're goin' toward heaven. The more you get into it, they're goin' to say, "Damn, that cat's really flipped out. Oh, he's gone now." But if you're producin' and creatin' you know, you're gettin' closer to your own heaven. That's what man's trying to get to, anyway.

What's happening is, you, we, we have all these different senses. We've got eyes, nose, you know, hearing, taste and feeling and so forth. Well, there's a sixth sense that's comin' in. Everybody has their own name for it, but I call it Free Soul. And that's more into that mental kind of thing. That's why everything is beyond the eyes now. The eyes only carry you so far out. You have to know how to develop other things that will carry you further and more clear. That's why the fastest speed . . . what's the fastest speed you can think of? They say the speed of light is the fastest thing—that's the eyes—but then there's the speed of thought, which is beyond that. You can get on the other side of this theme in a matter of thinkin' about it, for instance.

Sometimes you might be by yourself writing something. And you come across some words and you just lay back and dig the words and see how that makes you feel. And you might take it at practice or rehearsal or something like that, and get together with it there, in music—see how the music feels. Or either sometimes you might be jammin'—when I mean you, I mean the group—the group is jammin' or something, and then you might run across somethin' really nice. And then you keep runnin' across that, then you start shoutin' out anything that comes to your mind, you know, whatever the music turns you on to. If it's heavy music, you start singin' things.

Once you have the bottom there you can go anywhere. That's the way I believe. Once you have some type of rhythm, like it can get hypnotic if you keep repeating it over and over again. Most of the people will fall off by about a minute of repeating. You do that say for three or four or even five minutes if you can stand it, and then it releases a certain thing inside of a person's head. It releases a certain thing in there so you can put anything you want right inside that, you know. So you do that for a minute and all of a sudden you can bring the rhythm down a little bit and then you say what you want to say right into that little gap. It's somethin' to ride with, you know. You have to ride with somethin'. I always like to take people on trips.

That's why music is magic. Already this idea of living today is magic. There's a lot of sacrifices to make. I'm workin' on music to be completely, utterly a magic science, where it's all pure positive. It can't work if it's not positive. The more doubts and negatives you knock out of anything, the heavier it gets and the clearer it gets. And the deeper it gets into whoever's round it. It gets contagious.

Bach and all those cats, they went back in there, and they had caught a whole lot of hell. All they could do was get twenty-seven kids and then dust away. Because the way the society was they didn't respect this. They didn't know how to say, "Well, yeah, he's heavy. We'll go to his concerts. We'll dig him on the personal thing." But like, see, you're not supposed to judge a musician or composer or singer on his personal life. Forget about that. I like Handel and Bach. Handel and Bach is like a homework type of thing. You can't hear it with friends all the time. You have to hear some things by yourself. You can listen to anything that turns you on, that takes you for a ride. People want to be taken somewhere.

I wish they'd had electric guitars in cotton fields back in the good old days. A whole lot of things would have been straightened out. Not just only for the black and white, but I mean for the cause!

They keep sayin' things are changin'. Ain't nothin' changed. Things are going through changes, that's what it is. It's not changes, it's going through changes.

That's the way evolution happens. You have little bumps here. That's why you have the number seven after six. You have six smooth and all of a sudden a little bump. There's gonna be sacrifices. You get a lot of Black Panthers in jail, a lot of—what do you call that war thing?—the moratorium. A lot of those people who are goin' to get screwed up, for instance, here and there. But the whole idea, the whole movement is for everybody to appreciate. It's not only for young people to get it together by the time they're thirty. It's for anybody who's livin' to really appreciate.

It's just like a spaceship. If a spaceship came down if you know nothin' about it, the first thing you're goin' to think about is shootin' it. In other words, you get negative in the first place already, which is not really the natural way of thinking. But there's so many tight-lipped ideas and laws around, and people put themselves in uniform so tightly, that it's almost impossible to break out of that.

Subconsciously what all these people are doin', they're killin' off all these little flashes they have, like if I told you about a certain dream that was all freaked out, and you'll say, "Oh wow, you know, where is this at?" That's because you're cuttin' off the idea of wantin' to understand what's in there. You don't have the patience to do this. They don't have the patience to really check out what's happenin' through music and what's happenin' through the theater and science.

It's time for a new national anthem. America is divided into two definite divisions. And this is good for one reason because like somethin' has to happen or else you can just keep on bein' dragged along with the program, which is based upon the past and is always dusty. And the grooviest part about it is not all this old-time thing that you can cop out with. The easy thing to cop out with is sayin' black and white. That's the easiest thing. You can see a black person. But now to get down to the nitty-gritty, it's gettin' to be old and young—not the age, but the way of thinkin'. Old and new, actually. Not old and young. Old and new because there's so many even older people that took half their lives to reach a certain point that little kids understand now. They don't really get a chance to express themselves. So therefore they grab on to what is happening. That's why you had a lot of people at Woodstock. You can say all the bad things, but why keep elaboratin'? You have to go to the whole balls of it. That's all you can hold on to, in the arts, which is the actual earth, the actual soul of earth, like writin' and sayin' what you think. Getting' into your own little thing. Doin' this and doin' that. As long as you're off your ass and on your feet some kind of way. Out of the bed and into the street, you know, blah-blah, woof-woof-crackle-crackle—we can tap dance to that, can't we? That's old hat.

We was in America. We was in America. The stuff was over and startin' again. You know, like after death is the end and the beginnin'. And it's time for another anthem and that's what I'm writin' on now.

PART VII

January 1970 to June 1970

NOT LONG AFTER THE BAND OF GYPSYS' Fillmore East concerts, the group recorded at New York's Record Plant and continued to experiment with the new material.

On January 26, Noel Redding and Mitch Mitchell flew to New York City to discuss an Experience reunion tour organized by Michael Jeffery. Two days later, the Band of Gypsys performed at Madison Square Garden in a benefit concert for the Vietnam Moratorium Committee. In the middle of their second song, Hendrix stopped playing and announced, "That's what happens when Earth fucks with space." Then he walked off the stage and retired to his dressing room. This was the final public performance of the short-lived group.

Michael Jeffery continued to push for the Experience to reunite and staged an interview with a *Rolling Stone* reporter in early February. Later in the month, Jeffery turned over a completed master to Capitol Records for the *Band of Gypsys'* live album.

Hendrix left New York for London in early March and recorded several songs for Stephen Stills and Arthur Lee of Love. On March 19, he returned to New York, as did Noel Redding, who hoped to attend Experience reunion rehearsals. Instead Redding learned that Billy Cox had replaced him.

The stereo single "Stepping Stone," backed with "Izabella," was released in America on April 8. It was oddly billed as "Hendrix Band of Gypsys" but was quickly withdrawn for its poor-quality mix. The *Band of Gypsys* LP, however, did well on the *Billboard* charts.

The Jimi Hendrix Experience—with Cox on bass—began a spring tour of the States on April 25 in Los Angeles. An agreement was reached to limit the tour to three-day weekends throughout the summer.

Hendrix's New York recording studio, Electric Lady, neared completion in late May, around the same time the movie *Woodstock* was released in theaters. A three-album set featuring live recordings from the concert also appeared in record stores and featured Hendrix's rendition of "The Star-Spangled Banner."

"SPACEMAN JIMI IS LANDING"

ALFRED G. ARONOWITZ | From the NEW YORK POST, January 2, 1970.

The Band of Gypsys made their debut at New York's Fillmore East, playing two shows per night on December 31, 1969, and January 1, 1970. In this interview, Hendrix seemed apprehensive about the group's acceptance by fans and critics.

Jimi Hendrix wants to come back down to earth, but will his audience let him? There were people who walked out on his first set last night, refugees from the noise, but there's music in Jimi's guitar as well as sensationalism. By the time the second set ended, at 3 this morning, the audience was on its feet, clapping to the music and singing along, "We got to live together . . . We got to live together . . ." After it was all over Bill Graham had to come up to the dressing room and tell him that it was probably the best set ever played on the stage of the Fillmore East.

Jimi had chosen the new year and, as he put it, the new decade to unveil his new trio, with Buddy Miles on drums and Billy Cox on bass. Jimi had met Buddy at the Monterey Pop Festival, and they had been wanting to play together ever since. As for Billy, he and Jimi used to be in the same group five years ago, when Jimi was a paratrooper stationed down in Clarksville [Tennessee]. What's the reason for this change?

"Earth man, earth," Jimi said. With his old group, the Jimi Hendrix Experience, the music had been too far out in space. "Now I want to bring it down to earth," Jimi said. "I want to get back to the blues, because that's what I am."

The new group has a new repertoire, but during his first set last night, Jimi was still waving his freak flag. Here is probably the greatest master ever to make an electric guitar stand up and do tricks for the people. He can play it with his teeth. He can play it behind his back. He can make it talk. Last night, he even had it doing sound effects. But Jimi knows there's a change happening in music. With the trend back to the acoustical guitar, what will he do with his three ampli-fiers?

During his first set, you could sense his struggle, trying to get back to simplic-ity but afraid it would not be accepted by an audience that had come to hear the same old Jimi. "That first set was really tight," Jimi admitted afterwards. He was sitting in his dressing room while the clock pushed four and he was still jiggling and humming to himself, even after nine encores, or was it ten?[1]

"It was scary," he said. "We spent 12 to 18 hours a day practicing this whole last week, straight ahead, and then we went to a little funky club and jammed down there to test it out and see how the air was. Buddy's going to do most of the singing from now on. I'd rather just play. I never sang before. In England they made me sing, but Buddy has the right voice, he's going to do the singing from now on."

At the volume Jimi plays, Buddy's voice cut through the sound much more easily than Jimi's. When Jimi sang you couldn't hear him. There were two shows on New Year's Eve and two shows last night, and Jimi had them videotaped and recorded. By the eighth [sic] encore this morning, Fillmore owner Graham was dancing in the wings ordering the house lights on, telling the footlights to play on the crowd, commanding that the white light show screen be lit and finally running out of ideas to let everybody present know that this was for the Fillmore East a very special event.

There had been plans for Jimi to go back on tour with the Experience, accom-panied once again by Mitch Mitchell on drums and Noel Redding on bass, but after the show, Jimi had changed his mind.

"With Mitch maybe, but not with Noel, for sure," he said. "That's another thing. This is more of a real thing. We are trying to get it on its feet. We're wait-ing for Stevie Winwood. If I can get ahold of him and he agrees to it, that'll be another voice. We'll have harmony for days."

The name of Jimi's new group, incidentally, is A Band of Gypsies [sic]. "That's what we are," said Buddy. "That's what all musicians are. Gypsies."

---

1. There weren't any encores after the first set.

"THE END OF A BIG LONG FAIRY TALE"

JOHN BURKS | From GUITAR PLAYER, September 1975.

Michael Jeffery invited ROLLING STONE reporter John Burks to interview the reunited Experience and discuss their new musical direction. Burks subsequently discovered that his tape recorder didn't consistently capture Hendrix's voice, so he consulted with photographer Baron Wolman about what he thought the correct responses were. Burks' ROLLING STONE article made the deadline, but it wasn't until 1975 that the recording was enhanced in a studio for a more accurate transcription, which appeared in GUITAR PLAYER magazine.

February 4, 1970, interview. Left to right: Noel Redding, John Burks, Mitch Mitchell, Jimi Hendrix, and Michael Jeffery.
BARON WOLMAN

On February 4, 1970, a day so cold and snowy that all the cabs in New York were occupied, John Burks (then managing editor of *Rolling Stone*, more recently with *Focus*, *City*, *Newsweek*, and the *San Francisco Examiner*), shivering in his California clothes trudged and skidded through frozen slush to a chic midtown apartment to conduct what proved to be one of Jimi Hendrix's last major interviews. In attendance were Jimi, Noel Redding, Mitch Mitchell, various management personnel, and Baron Wolman, the well-known photographer-journalist for *Rolling Stone*, *Rags*, etc. The meeting had been initiated by Hendrix's management primarily to trumpet the reunification of the original Jimi Hendrix Experience, which turned out to be a short-lived regrouping that ran concurrently with the Band of Gypsys.

Burks and Wolman remember sensing an anxiety on the part of the interviewees. "Though the setup was like you do for a fan magazine writer," John recalls, "they knew they could not manipulate the interview for their own publicity purposes because they were dealing with *Rolling Stone*. Moreover, that particular time jag contained memories of a disturbingly dull concert in January at a peace rally at Madison Square Garden, at which an uninspired Jimi had simply stopped playing.[1] Nevertheless, it is difficult to make a case for a depressed Hendrix, for if Madison Square had been a bummer, he also had the memory of a concert with the Band of Gypsys that Bill Graham described as the finest he'd ever heard at Fillmore East. Whatever the initial mood, cognac, a warm fire in the fireplace, and a relaxed pace of questioning loosened things up."

Obviously, it did not occur to John that the Hendrix portions of this interview with the Experience would be used five years later in a memorial edition of *Guitar Player Magazine*. In fact, the tape itself—a hissy jumble of voices interrupting voices, captured by a wobbly recorder—was so discouraging in quality that Burks snatched from it what phrases he could for a quick article and stashed it away in a box where it rested untranscribed, unpublished, but fortunately not erased for the last half-decade. When he learned of this special issue, John dug the cassette out, and we present here the discernible portions. Whenever possible, topical events, recordings, and individuals have been identified in brackets. Some elude clarification. Though it does not always dwell on areas normally covered by *GP*, this interview nevertheless provides a last intriguing glimpse of a guitar genius.

—DM [Don Menn]

Are you still living with a lot of musicians at your house?

No, I just try to have some time by myself so I can really write some things. I want to do more writing.

What kind of writing?

I don't know. Mostly just cartoon material. Make up this one cat who's funny, who goes through all these strange scenes. I can't talk about it now. You could put it to music, I guess. Just like you can put blues into music.

Are you talking about long extended pieces or just songs?

Well, I want to get into what you'd probably call "pieces," yeah—pieces, behind each other to make movements, or whatever you call it. I've been writing some of those. But like I was into writing cartoons mostly.

If the cartoon is in your head, do you have the music too?

Yeah, in the head, right. You listen to it, and you get such funny flashbacks. The music will be going along with the story, just like "Foxey Lady." Something like that. The music and the words go together.

When you put together a song, does it just come to you, or is it a process where you sit down with your guitar or at a piano, starting from ten in the morning?

The music I might hear I can't get on the guitar. It's a thing of just laying around daydreaming or something. You're hearing all this music, and you just can't get it on the guitar. As a matter of fact, if you pick up your guitar and just try to play, it spoils the whole thing. I can't play the guitar that well to get all this music together, so I just lay around. I wish I could have learned how to write for instruments. I'm going to get into that next, I guess.

So for something like "Foxey Lady," you first hear the music and then arrive at the words for the song?

It all depends. On "Foxey Lady," we just started playing actually, and set up a microphone, and I had these words [laughs]. With "Voodoo Child (Slight Return)" somebody was filming when we started doing that. We did that about three times because they wanted to film us in the studio, to make us [imitates a pompous voice] "Make it look like you're recording boys"—one of them scenes, you know, so "Okay, let's play this in E; now a-one and-a-two and-a-three," and then we went into "Voodoo Child."

When I hear Mitch churning away and you really blowing on top and the bass gets really free, the whole approach almost sounds like avant-garde jazz.

Well, that's because that's where it's coming from—the drumming.

Do you dig any avant-garde jazz players?

Yeah, when we went to Sweden and heard some of those cats we'd never heard before. These cats were actually in little country clubs and little caves blowing some sounds that, you know, you barely imagine. Guys from Sweden, Copenhagen, Amsterdam, or Stockholm. Every once in a while they start going like a wave. They get into each other every once in a while within their personalities, and the party last night, or the hangover [laughs], and the evil starts pulling them away again. You can hear it start to go away. Then it starts getting together again. It's like a wave, I guess, coming in and out.

For your own musical kicks, where's the best place to play?

I like after-hour jams at a small place like a club. Then you get another feeling. You get off in another way with all those people there. You get another feeling, and you mix it in with something else that you get. It's not the spotlights, just the people.

How are those two experiences different, this thing you get from the audiences?

I get more of a dreamy thing from the audience—it's more of a thing that you go up into. You get into such a pitch sometimes that you go up into another thing. You don't forget about the audience, but you forget about all the paranoia, that thing where you're saying, "Oh gosh, I'm on stage—what am I going to do now?" Then you go into this other thing, and it turns out to be like almost like a play in certain ways.

You don't kick in many amps any more or light guitars on fire.

Maybe I was just noticing the guitar for a change. Maybe.

Was that a conscious decision?

Oh, I don't know. It's like it's the end of a beginning. I figure that Madison Square Garden was like the end of a big long fairy tale, which is great. It's the best thing I could possibly have come up with. The band was out of sight as far as I'm concerned.

But what happened to you?

It was just something where the head changes, just going through changes. I really couldn't tell, to tell the truth. I was very tired. You know, sometimes there's a lot of things that add up in your head about this and that. And they hit you at a very peculiar time, which happened to be at that peace rally, and here I am fighting the biggest war I've ever fought in my life—inside, you know? And like that wasn't the place to do it, so I just unmasked appearances.

How much part do you play in the production of your albums? For example, did you produce your first [Are You Experienced]?

No, it was Chas Chandler and Eddie Kramer who mostly worked on that stuff. Eddie was the engineer, and Chas as producer mainly kept things together.

The last record [Electric Ladyland] listed you as producer. Did you do the whole thing?

No, well, like Eddie Kramer and myself. All I did was just be there and make sure the right songs were there, and the sound was there. We wanted a particular sound. It got lost in the cutting room, because we went on tour right before we finished. I heard it, and I think the sound of it is very cloudy.

You did "All Along the Watchtower" on the last one. Is there anything else that you'd like to record by Bob Dylan?

Oh yeah. I like that one that goes, "Please help me in my weakness" ["Drifter's Escape"]. That was groovy. I'd like to do that. I like his *Blonde on Blonde* and *Highway 61 Revisited*. His country stuff is nice too, at certain times. It's quieter, you know.

Your recording of "Watchtower" really turned me on to that song when Dylan didn't.

Well, that's reflections like the mirror. [Laughs] Remember that "roomful of mirrors"? That's a song, a recording that we're trying to do, but I don't think we'll ever finish that. I hope not. It's about trying to get out of this roomful of mirrors.

Why can't you finish it?

[Imitates prissy voice] Well, you see, I'm going through this health kick, you see. I'm heavy on wheat germ, but, you know what I mean [laughs]—I don't know why [takes a pencil and writes something].

You're not what I'd call a country guitar player.

Thank you.

You consider that a compliment?

It would be if I was a country guitar player. That would be another step.

Are you listening to bands like that doing country, like the Flying Burrito Brothers?

Who's the guitar player for the Burrito Brothers? That guy plays. I dig him. He's really marvelous with a guitar. That's what makes me listen to that, is the music.

It's sweet. It's got that thing to it.

[In a deep drawl] "Hello walls." [Laughs] You hear that one, "Hello Walls"? "Hillbilly Heaven."

Remember Bob Wills and the Texas Playboys?

[Laughs] I dig them. The Grand Ole Opry used to come on, and I used to watch that. They used to have some pretty heavy cats, heavy guitar players.

Which musicians do you go out of your way to hear?

Nina Simone and Mountain. I dig them.

What about a group like the McCoys?

[Sings intro to "Hang On Sloopy," which featured Rick Derringer on guitar.] Yeah, that guitar player's great.

Do you dig parodies like the Masked Marauders or the English radio program The Goon Show?

I never heard it [Masked Marauders]. I heard about it. The Fugs, they're good. I've heard they don't have it [*The Goon Show*] over here. They're masterpieces. Those are classics. They're the funniest things I've ever heard, besides Pinkie Lee. Remember Pinkie Lee? They were like a classic of a whole lot of Pinkie Lees together, and just flip them out together.

You a Pinkie Lee fan?

Used to be. I used to wear white socks.

Were you really rehearsing with Band of Gypsys twelve to eighteen hours a day?

Yeah, we used to go and jam actually. We'd say "rehearsing" just to make it sound, you know, official. We were just getting off; that's all. Not really eighteen hours—say about twelve or fourteen maybe [laughs]. The longest we [the

Experience] ever played together is going on stage. We played about two and a half hours, almost three hours one time. We made sounds. People make sounds when they clap. So we make sounds back. I like electric sounds, feedback and so forth, static.

Are you going to do a single as well as an LP?

We might have one from the other thing coming out soon. I don't know about the Experience though. All these record companies, they want singles. But you don't just sit there and say, "Let's make a track, let's make a single or something." We're not going to do that. We don't do that.

Creedence Clearwater Revival does that until they have enough for a record, like in the old days.

Well, that's the old days. I consider us more musicians. More in the minds of musicians, you know?

But singles can make some bread, can't they?

Well, that's why they do them. But they take it after. You'll have a whole planned-out LP, and all of a sudden, they'll make, for instance, "Crosstown Traffic" a single, and that's coming out of nowhere, out of a whole other set. See, that LP was in certain ways of thinking; the sides we played on in order for certain reasons. And then it's almost like a sin for them to take out something in the middle of all that and make that a single, and represent us at that particular time because they think they can make more money. They always take out the wrong ones.

How often will you space these concerts with the Experience so that you won't feel hemmed in?

As often as we three agree to it. I'd like for it to be permanent.

Have you given any thought to touring with the Experience as the basic unit, but bringing along other people? Or would that be too confusing?

No, it shouldn't be. Maybe I'm the evil one, right [laughs]. But there isn't any reason for it to be like that. I even want the name to be Experience anyway, and still be this mish-mash moosh-mash between Madame Flipflop and Her Harmonite[2] [*sic*] Social Workers.

It's a nice name.

It's a nice game. No, like about putting other groups on the tour, like our friends—I don't know about that right now; not at a stage like this, because we're in the process of getting our own thing together as far as a three piece group. But eventually, we have time on the side to play with friends. That's why I'll probably be jamming with Buddy [Miles] and Billy [Cox]; probably be recording, too, on the side, and they'll be doing the same.

Do you ever think in terms of going out with a dozen people?

I like Stevie Winwood; he's one of those dozen people. But things don't have to be official all the time. Things don't have to be formal for jams and stuff. But I haven't had a chance to get in contact with him.

Ever think about getting other guitar players into your trip?

Oh yeah. Well, I heard Duane Eddy came into town this morning [laughs]. He was groovy.

Have you jammed with Larry Coryell and Sonny Sharrock and people like that?

Larry and I had like swift jams down at The Scene. Every once in a while we would finally get a chance to get together. But I haven't had a chance to really play with him, not lately anyway. I sort of miss that.

Do you listen to them?

I like Larry Coryell, yeah.

Better than others?

Oh, not better. Who's this other guy? I think I've heard some of his things.

He's all over the guitar. Sometimes it sounds like it's not too orderly.

Sounds like someone we know, huh [laughs]?

Have you played with people like [tenor saxman] Roland Kirk?

Oh yeah. I had a jam with him at Ronnie Scott's in London,[3] and I really got off. It was great. It was really great. I was so scared! It's really funny. I mean *Roland* [laughs]. That cat gets all those sounds. I might just hit one note, and it might be interfering, but like we got along great I thought. He told me I should have turned it up or something.

He seems like a cat you might record particularly well with. I hear these bands like Blood, Sweat, and Tears and their horns, and CTA [Chicago Transit Authority], though I haven't heard them in person.

Oh yeah, CTA. In person, listen, that's when you should hear them. That's the only time. They just started recording, but in person. The next chance you get, you should check them out.

Do you listen to the Band?

It's there. They got their own thing together that takes you a certain place. Takes you where they want to go [laughs], you know. Where they want to. They play their things on stage exactly how they play it on record.

Have movie people tried to lure you into films by saying you'd be a hell of a gun-slinger or an astronaut?

Astronaut! [laughs] Fly in space! We have one called "Captain Coconut." No, well, you know. I'm trying to get the guitar together really.

Do you find American audiences more violent than those of other countries?

In New York, it's more of a violent climate. It's very violent, actually. They don't know it really. But Texas is really fine. I don't know why. Maybe it's the weather, and the feeling of it. I dig the South a little more than playing in the North. It's more of a pressure playing in the Midwest, like Cleveland or Chicago. It's like being in a pressure cooker waiting for the top to blow off. The people there are groovy, but it's just the atmosphere or something, you know? But the south is great. New Orleans is great. Arizona is great. Arizona's fantastic. Utah.

How did they treat you in Utah?

[Laughs] Well, once we're offstage, it's another world, but like the people are great. But when we play at the gigs they were really listening; they were really tuned in some kind of way or another. I think it was the air.

Your tastes seem broader than the typical rock and roll fan or listener.

This is all I can play when I'm playing. I'd like to get something together, like with Handel, and Bach, and Muddy Waters, flamenco type of thing [laughs]. If I can get that *sound*. If I could get *that* sound, I'd be happy.

---

1. Menn was referring to the January 28, 1970, Madison Square Garden concert called Winter Festival for Peace. After only a few songs, Hendrix told the audience, "That's what happens when Earth fucks with space," and sat down in front of his amplifiers. The rest of the performance was canceled, and this marked the final show for the Band of Gypsys.
2. Hendrix actually said, "Madam Flip-Flop and Her All-Night Social Workers."
3. March 8, 1969. Also at the jam with Kirk were Vernon Martin (bass), Jimmy Hopps (drums), and Ron Burton (piano).

"HENDRIX: 'I'D LIKE A HIT SINGLE . . .'"

KEITH ALTHAM | From MELODY MAKER, May 9, 1970.

Journalist Keith Altham interviewed Hendrix on April 15, 1970, while he was in New York. A new Band of Gypsys single had just been released in America, and selections from their Fillmore East concerts were featured on an LP that followed about a week after this interview.

Just over a year ago I talked with Jimi Hendrix in his London apartment and he told me that the Experience were in a musical cul-de-sac and seemed unlikely to play again.

Noel went into Fat Mattress although he now apparently feels they were strange bed-fellows. Mitch darted in and out of London clubs like a lemming in search of the sea.

Hendrix went into a brief period of hibernation both musically and physically in his New York apartment from which he seldom ventured out unless in the early hours of the morning. Following his acquittal over a drug charge in America,[1] he finally put in an appearance last New Year's Day with drummer Buddy Miles and bass player Billy Cox at the Fillmore East as "The Band of [Gypsys]."

The [Gypsys] were apparently destined to be an ephemeral group, which may be no bad thing, if I am any judge from the Capitol album I heard taken from that concert and shortly to be issued here. Miles is the kind of drummer who competes rather than complements, and despite Jimi's preference for Billy Cox I find his "solid style" seems to drag some tracks back by the tail.

269

Contribution

Side II and tracks like "Message of Love" and "Power of Soul" are a brilliant illustration of Hendrix walking on electric splinters but despite his attempts to twist the musical guts out of his guitar-child, they never really lift off.

What there is on the album to distinguish the brilliant from the best comes from Hendrix but it is not enough to make a whole or eclipse the memory of the Experience who, when they were together, were more together than anyone but the Cream. Their new single, "Stepping Stone" is better but the outstanding contribution is Hendrix's solo work towards the end of the disc.

All of which poses the question "What Now?" During a recent sojourn in New York I was able to dig Hendrix from his apartment block, where the residents are currently organizing a vigilante committee to have him extradited and I was able to find out.

He has not changed too much. The face is greyer from his recluse-like existence and a bout of swollen glands—he explained it, "My gland is broke"—but the hands still flutter to the mouth in mock alarm and the smile is full-teethed and whole-hearted. Neither had he lost his sense of humor.

He was about to go live again with a new band operating under the title, "The Cry of Love" on a tour of America and featuring Mitch Mitchell back on drums but replacing Noel Redding by Billy Cox.

"It was always my plan to change the bass player even back in the days after the Experience when there was no band," said Jimi abstrusely. "Noel is definitely and confidently out—Billy has a more solid style which suits me. I'm not saying that anyone is better than the other—just that today I want a more solid style. There's no telling how I feel tomorrow.

"I'm not sure how I feel about the Experience now. Maybe we could have gone on but what would have been the point of that—what would it have been good for? It's a ghost now—it's dead—like back pages in a diary. I'm into new things and I want to think about tomorrow, not yesterday.

"I wasn't too satisfied with the 'Band of [Gypsys]' album. If it had been up to me I would have never put it out. From a musician's point of view it was not a good recording and I was out of tune on a few things. Not enough preparation went into it and it came out a bit 'grizzly'—we all felt shaky. The thing was we owed the record company an album and they were pushing us—so here it is.

"There were some nice songs on the album—some nice ideas—particularly on side two, and we will be doing some of those on the tour. I'm not sure what Buddy is doing. I think he is getting together a new group—the Bouncing Thimbles! No—it's a joke. He has a band called 'Freedom Express' featuring TA TA TA TEE DUM—Buddy Miles!

"Is this a joke?" asked Jimi looking at [the] microphone. "Am I really live on TV—can I wave to the people?"

The new single "Stepping Stone!"

"I don't know how good it is—I can't tell any more. Some of the copies out here have no bass on them. I had to go out somewhere and told the guy to remix it but he didn't. Sure it matters—I'd like a hit single. It's nice to have people hearing your songs all over the world on the radio—nice to know. I wanted this out before people forgot about me.

"We're going to record the first few dates on the tour—get things like 'Rolling Stone' live on an album. I called the tour 'The Cry of Love' because that's what it is all about. The recording is really up to Mitch but I'd like to do it.

"I'd like to play some festivals but I wish they would break up the events a bit more for the audience. There's no reason why these huge crowds should not be entertained by side attractions as well. They should make them like three-ring circuses, booths, movies—even some knights jostling."

"You mean jousting?"

"Right—and Freak Shows!" he added, as an afterthought.

"Would you consider 'Hells Angels' as a security guard for any of your concerts?"

"PERLEASE!" said Jimi. "I don't even want to talk about Altamount [sic], it was so dreadful—the whole of America is going to pot whichever way you look at it!"

There are quite a few tapes in the can which Jimi has cut with Mitch Mitchell, Billy Cox and Buddy Miles including one monumental freak out which features one of the Irish porters of the Penn Garden Hotel (frequented by Jimi's tour manager Gerry [Stickells]) on bagpipes.

"This guy insisted on dressing up in his full regimental kit for the session," recalled Jimi. "He spent a few hilarious minutes trying to keep his cap on over the headphones but the track came out very well."

One less successful attempt was apparently after Jimi had been dropped at the studios by a taxi driver who recognized him and remarked that he played bongos. Jimi nonchalantly invited him down one evening to jam—the cab driver turned up half an hour later and completed a six hour session which had to be scrapped. Jimi apparently did not have the heart to ask him to leave.

Whatever happened to Jimi's plans for a huge orchestral album—"The Last [sic] Rays of the New Rising Sun"?

Reaction

"Whatever happened to your small-pox jab?" countered Jimi referring to a trip some years ago when we attended the Monterey Festival and I sustained a painful reaction to my innoculation. "It went away," continued Jimi answering his own question. "The pain went away—say how is this interview going. You should have got me when I was asleep!"

We talked briefly about some of the contemporary pop guitarists on the scene whom Jimi had heard—he was in no mood to be charitable.

"Alvin Lee—he should be in movies," said Jimi. "He's the Gene Vincent of the '70s, I hear. I don't think much of Led Zeppelin—I mean I don't think much about them. Jimmy Page is a good guitar player. I didn't like what Clapton was doing with Bonnie and Delaney—he should be getting his own thing together, not trying to carry other people. I did some work with Steve Stills while I was in London a few weeks back—just a few solo passages on some of his things—he has a very fine solo album coming out."

Finally Jimi excused himself on the grounds that he had to go out and buy a cushion to rest his gland upon, and he only had 11 days to rehearse his new act. We can expect him here to play around August and he may do the Isle of Wight Festival if it does not conflict with dates already booked in Japan.

It was almost four years previously that I first flew to New York with Jimi for his first American tour with the Experience. Passing through New York I found my own definition for the word "Impossible" while trying to get him a cab. One: they would not stop if you had long hair. Two: they would not stop if you were a hippy. Three: they were not keen if you were colored.

Hendrix now gets cabs a little easier, being famous. But he still has a long way to go.

-----

1. The trial was held in Canada, not the United States.

PART VIII

July 1970 to September 1970

ELECTRIC LADY STUDIOS WAS UP AND RUNNING by mid-June, and Hendrix recorded there in between July concert dates. He was so excited that he told the *Village Voice* he was writing a song called "Electric Lady" in honor of the new facility. An official opening party took place on August 26, 1970, only a day before Hendrix left for the Isle of Wight Festival in England.

The band's 1970 European concert tour got off to a rough start. Hendrix was fighting a cold, which worsened in the changing climate zones. At several concerts, amps picked up radio broadcasts and walkie-talkie conversations. And two former girlfriends announced he was the father of their children.

Like he did at the incomplete concert by the Band of Gypsys at Madison Square Garden in January, Hendrix walked off the stage again in Denmark on September 2 after only a few songs. Following concerts improved slightly, but insecurity, depression, and paranoia continued to plague both Hendrix and Cox. After Cox decided to quit the tour and return home, Hendrix and Mitchell discussed finding a replacement. Both Noel Redding and Rick Grech were considered.

During this downtime, Hendrix shared his management frustrations with Alan Douglas, a producer. Douglas agreed that he shouldn't renew his contract with Michael Jeffery, which was set to expire on December 1, 1970. Chas Chandler was also contacted about returning as his producer and finishing the next album.

Hendrix spent September 14 to 17 with Monika Dannemann, a woman he met while on tour in 1969. She'd rented a garden flat in the Samarkand Hotel in South Kensington, London, for the two of them.

On the morning of September 18, 1970, an ambulance was called, and Hendrix was taken from the hotel to St. Mary Abbot's Hospital. There, he was pronounced dead.

PART VII

June 1970 to September 1970

"ONE-NIGHTER GRIND IS OVER; ALL JIMI WANTS NOW IS A REST"

PAUL OMUNDSON | From the MIAMI HERALD, August 8, 1970.

The JHE's North American tour was winding down toward a much-needed break in Hawaii. Hendrix summed up his feelings about his touring and recording schedule during this interview, which was done at the San Diego Sports Arena on July 25, 1970.

HOLLYWOOD, Calif.—A very tired-looking Jimi Hendrix sat slump-shouldered in his dressing room and talked about New York, where he spent the previous week recording in 12- to 14-hour shifts.

"Man, what I need now is a good rest. It's going to be Hawaii this time. We'll be there a week, two weeks. Who knows?"

This is the Jimi Hendrix who has spent three years in almost constant travel. All the one-night stands, the endless recording sessions, are all there in the back of Jimi's mind as a bad nightmare that is finally over with.

"I was like a slave, man. It was all work. In the beginning it was fun and now it's time to get back to having it fun again."

With a smile, he says, "I'm retiring now, it's going to be pleasure first. No more work." He explained that this meant a lot more time jamming with his friends and just getting away from everything to a relaxed atmosphere.

When asked where he'd like to go, he replied: "Anywhere but the city."

The strains of being a rock star have indeed marked the man deeply. He started out as a guitarist for Little Richard [sic]. Then he left his native Seattle for England where he picked up bass player Noel Redding and drummer Mitch Mitchell.

His trio won attention mainly for Hendrix's bizarre way of playing guitar. Using up to eight amplifiers, and making use of feedback and distortion, he generated a sound, not unlike the high, shrieking sound of a landing jet.

Raw, lashing spirals of sound was the well-earned trademark of the Jimi Hendrix Experience.

It was the Monterey Pop Festival in 1967 that finally catapulted him into the limelight in this country. And ever since, he has been subjected to a god-like admiration from his numerous fans that has not yet subsided.

A more mature and mellowed Jimi Hendrix resents this idol image. He said, quite seriously, "As far as I'm concerned, I have no image."

His troubles came when he tried to live up to his tremendous reputation. As a result, The Experience broke up with Noel Redding forming his own band, Fat Mattress. Following this was a year of seeming inactivity. Yet Jimi himself was intensely occupied. He spent his time in Woodstock, jamming daily with various musicians who came and went. A result of this was the formation of a new group called Band of [Gypsys] featuring Billy Cox on bass and Buddy Miles as drummer. This union lasted for one album and then dissolved.

"The reason for the record," Jimi said, "was to fulfill an old record contract. We won't be back together again."

Two of the "one-nighter grind" concerts Hendrix performed on the 1970 tour. STEVEN ROBY/STRAIGHT AHEAD ARCHIVES COLLECTION

Now the Experience is back together with Billy Cox as the replacement for Noel Redding. And Hendrix seems satisfied with this arrangement and plans to keep it.

In the recording studio it is not unusual for the group to work a 14-hour day. In fact, some of their songs are played as many as 40 times before the final take. It's often a traumatic experience, as those who have worked with him will readily admit. Yet Hendrix is admired for his persistence in attaining exactly the sounds he wants.

One reason for the length of time in the studios is, as Hendrix said, "because we improvise almost all our songs. The final tape may be very different from what it started out to be."

He went on to explain the group's way of creating music.

"We start out with a basic foundation and we weave around it in various formulas. We go around and around it until a new song has branched off."

ENCOUNTER WITH JIMI HENDRIX

CHUCK WEIN AND PAT HARTLEY | From the film RAINBOW BRIDGE, late July 1970.

After a concert in Seattle on July 26, 1970, the JHE headed to the Hawaiian island of Maui for a free outdoor performance that would be part of a film titled *Rainbow Bridge*. Manger Michael Jeffery was given a $450,000 advance from Warner Bros., and he hired film director Chuck Wein. In the attic of Seabury Hall, a private school for girls, Wein had his film crew shoot an unscripted scene in which Hendrix was asked to talk about reincarnation. Hendrix, admittedly stoned, held a bottle of rosé in his hands as he rapped with Wein and New York model Pat Hartley. The following are excerpts from that scene.

Chuck Wein: Did you ever dream you were in a pyramid?

Jimi Hendrix: I got high one time over in Florida. I thought maybe it had something to do with a pyramid. I didn't know. Maybe in one of my past lives or something, whew. . . . Pardon? I'm stoned now, so I have a pillow.

Pat Hartley: Listen, if your past lives did you any good you wouldn't have to come back and do them again.

JH: Only *this* one? Is that all your livin' for? [. . .]

279

CW: You ever seen anybody from the third grade? Do you remember back that far? Who sat next to you in third grade?

JH: Yeah, my teacher sat next to me in third grade, because I was a dunce. She sat in the front office, like the front desk, and did a thing like talking about, [*in a silly voice*] "Now this is an example." At the same time she's saying, "This is an example," she's touching my kneecaps, *under* the table . . . I never could sit with everybody else. 'Cause she'd say, "How are you feeling?" and I'd say something kind of spacey like, "Well, that depends on what the people on Mars are doing." She'd say, "Well, you go to the front for that." So I'd go into a little cubbyhole just like the Gestapo motorcycles. You know, the little driver sits on the motorcycle and the commander sits in the cubbyhole, you know . . .

CW: You thought you were from Mars in the third grade?

JH: I didn't *think* it, actually, I just didn't know what else to say to her. I got tired of saying, "Fine, thank you."

Hendrix performing at an outdoor concert on the island of Maui, Hawaii, July 1970. BRIAN BYRNES

"HENDRIX—HE'S A BEAUTIFUL PERSON"

GILLIAN SAICH | From NEW MUSICAL EXPRESS, September 5, 1970.

On August 28, Hendrix met with various reporters in his suite at the Londonderry Hotel. All had high hopes for the Isle of Wight festival and how it might compare to last year's Woodstock.

The slogan "Black Is Beautiful" could have been made up specially for Jimi Hendrix. When I spoke to him at his luxury penthouse suite at the Londonderry Hotel last weekend my first impression, and the most lasting one, was of his quiet magnetism and extreme physical grace.

Gone is the wild, flashy Hendrix of a few years ago—his famous hair has been trimmed a great deal and he was sombrely dressed in tight-fitting black satin trousers and shirt which he had had specially made for him just before he left New York.

Back in Britain for the first time in over a year, the bewitching Mr. Hendrix wasn't particularly explicit about his past but very excited about the present and the future.

The most immediate prospect in his life at that time was his appearance at the Isle of Wight Festival. I was interested to know how he was feeling about it as he had already been quite ecstatic about open air pop after his memorable appearances at Monterey and Woodstock.

Oddly enough he admitted to being quite terrified at the prospect. "I think that the crowd will be much bigger than at any previous festival—even Woodstock. It's a fantastic place to have a show because it brings kids together from not only the British Isles but also the whole of the Continent."

Daylight

"Strangely, there were only 15,000 people left when we played at Woodstock as I insisted on playing in daylight which meant waiting until the 4th day and most of the kids had split by then."

Jimi was right—the crowds at the IOW exceeded expectations and the majority of them were still there to watch Jimi Hendrix play an electrifying set.

After a long absence from these shores this magical guitarist need not worry as to whether his fans have forgotten him—if they had, his reception at the festival well and truly replaced in the ranks he deserves.

We talked about America, which he expressed as "not my scene man! I don't want to go back until I really have to. I've been away from this country and Europe for such a long time, I want to show them all over again what it's all about."

The lineup has changed since the days of the Experience. Billy Cox now plays bass, and after a short experiment elsewhere Mitch Mitchell is back on drums and sounding better than ever.

"We have been committed to so many tours and college gigs in the States that it was utterly impossible for us to come over to England—believe me we wanted to!"

On Monday morning after his Isle of Wight performance Jimi and the boys flew off to Stockholm where they started a tour of Europe followed by Australia and New Zealand. "We really want to come back to England and do some main venues here, like, say, one big concert in each of the major cities."

With a beaming white smile he added, "Jim Hendrix at the Oval?"

A somewhat perplexed Jimi proceeded to enthuse about his new recording studio—called aptly—"Electric Lady Studios."

It is situated in Greenwich Village, New York where five years ago Jimi's talent first came to the notice of ex-Animal Chas Chandler.

"I have done great things with this place—it has the best equipment in the world, we can record anything we like there.

"It is capable of recording on 32 tracks which takes care of most things and I am working on a symphony production to be done there in the near future.

"There is one thing that I hate about studios usually and that is the impersonality of them; they are cold and blank and within a few minutes I lose all drive and inspiration.

"Electric Lady is different—it has been built with great atmosphere—lighting, seating and every comfort makes people feel they are recording at home. We have recorded a lot of material there from which we hope the next single will come in about six weeks."

The number that is most likely to be the A side is "Dolly Dagger" which is about a notorious lady . . . (so I didn't dare ask about the theme of the B side "Night Bird Flying"!).

Many Moons

It seems many moons ago since Jimi Hendrix played "Hey Joe" on "Top of the Pops," had a hit with it and caused a great uproar amongst viewers and parents who found his sexual, aggressive guitar playing a degrading attack on the pleasant harmonic sounds that they were used to.

Well, Jimi Hendrix is now an international star and many, many other musicians have taken a leaf out of his book to add to their own. He is very flattered that in some ways he started the whole flow of accepted progressive music in this country.

"I haven't changed very much in that time, my music is still as pulsating, perhaps a bit more varied. I either play very loud or very soft, there is no aural medium."

"HENDRIX TODAY"

ROY HOLLINGWORTH | From MELODY MAKER, September 5, 1970.

In a series of interviews given on August 28, 1970, Hendrix opened up with reporter Roy Hollingworth about his future plans for a larger band and improving his musical skills.

Jimi Hendrix, the man with the misleading reputation that had mothers locking away young daughters when he was in town, is talking again.

After six months of hiding in corners, crawling into cracks when people were around, and generally locking himself away from the world, our Jimi is back in business, and his mind is six months pregnant with ideas.

For Jimi the first long trip has come to an end. It's time to go back home, feed himself until he's fat again, and then set out on trip number two, which will be a longer trip, an intrepid exploration, and for Jimi a new experience.

"It's all turned full circle; I'm back right now to where I started. I've given this era of music everything. I still sound the same, my music's the same, and I can't think of anything new to add to it in its present state," Jimi told me as he sat tending an English cold in a lavish London Park Lane hotel.

"When the last American tour finished earlier this year, I just wanted to go away awhile, and forget everything. I wanted to just do recording, and see if I could write something.

"Then I started thinking. Thinking about the future. Thinking that this era of music—sparked off by the Beatles—has come to an end. Something new has got to come, and Jimi Hendrix will be there.

"I want a big band, I don't mean three harps and fourteen violins. I mean a big band full of competent musicians that I can conduct and write for. And with

285

the music we will paint pictures of earth and space, so that the listener can be taken somewhere.

"It's going to be something that will open up a new sense in people's minds. They are getting their minds ready now. Like me they are going back home, getting fat, and making themselves ready for the next trip.

"You see music is so important. I don't any longer dig the pop and politics crap. That's old fashioned. It was somebody's personal opinion. But politics is old hat. Anyone can go round shaking babies by the hand, and kissing the mothers, and saying that it was groovy. But you see, you can't do this in music. Music doesn't lie. I agree it can be misinterpreted, but it cannot lie.

"When there are vast changes in the way the world goes, it's usually something like art and music that changes it. Music is going to change the world next time."

Jimi couldn't fully explain what his new music would be like, but he put forth his visions of how the next music form would be born.

"We are going to stand still for a while, and gather everything we've learned musically in the last 30 years, and we are going to blend all the ideas that worked into a new form of classical music. It's going to take some doing to figure out all the things that worked, but it's going to be done.

"I dig Strauss and Wagner—those cats are good, and I think that they are going to form the background of my music. Floating in the sky above it will be the blues—I've still got plenty of blues—and then there will be Western sky music, and sweet opium music (you'll have to bring your own opium) and these will be mixed together to form one.

"You know the drug scene came to a big head. It was opening up things in people's minds, giving them things that they just couldn't handle. Well music can do that you know, and you don't need any drugs.

"The term 'blowing someone's mind' is valid. People like you to blow their minds, but then we are going to give them something that will blow their mind, and while it's blown there will be something there to fill the gap. It's going to be a complete form of music. It will be really druggy music. Yes, I agree it could be something on similar lines to what Pink Floyd are tackling. They don't know it you know, but people like Pink Floyd are the mad scientists of this day and age.

"While I was doing my vanishing act in the States I got this feeling that I was completely blown-out of England. I thought they had forgotten me over here. I'd given them everything I'd got, I thought maybe they didn't want me anymore, because they had a nice set of bands. Maybe they were saying, 'Oh we've had Hendrix, yeah he was okay.' I really thought I was completely through here."

About his future big band Jimi had talked a lot. But he was also eager to talk about thoughts on the three-piece outfit, which he believed could go on forever.

"It was fun, it was the greatest fun. It was good, exciting and I enjoyed it. But the main thing that used to bug me was that people wanted too many visual things from me.

"I never wanted it to be so much of a visual thing. When I didn't do it, people thought I was being moody, but I can only freak when I feel like doing so. I can't do it just for the sake of it. I wanted the music to get across, so that people could just sit back and close their eyes, and know exactly what was going on, without caring a damn what we were doing while we were on stage."

Could Jimi give any indication when he would start to form the big band?

"I don't know, but it won't be very long. Isle of Wight might be the last, or second to the last. But if the kids really enjoyed it, then it might carry on a little longer. But I will only carry on that way if I am useful, you know you have got to have a purpose in life."

His hair is a little tamer now. Did he feel he was a tamer person, a changing person?

"No I don't think so, although I feel as though I get little sparks of matureness every now and then.

"I think of tunes, I think of riffs. I can hum them. Then there's another melody that comes into my head, and then a bass melody, and then another one. On guitar I just can't get them out. I think I'm a better guitarist than I was. I've learned a lot. But I've got to learn more about music, because there's a lot in this hair of mine that's got to get out.

"With the bigger band I don't want to be playing as much guitar, I want other musicians to play my stuff. I want to be a good writer. I still can't figure out what direction my writing is going at the moment, but it'll find a way.

"I won't be doing many live gigs, because I'm going to develop the sound, and then put a film out with it. It's so exciting, it's going to be an audio/visual thing that you sit down and plug in to, and really take in through your ears and eyes.

"I'm happy. It's gonna be good."

"MAN, MYTH OR MAGIC? JIMI HENDRIX IS BACK, AND HAPPY, AND TALKING . . ."

NORMAN JOPLING | From MUSIC NOW, September 12, 1970.

In another Londonderry Hotel interview, Hendrix talked about his newly opened recording studio, a bootleg record of a 1969 jam with percussionist Juma Sultan and Mike Ephron, and high-priced concert tickets.

Jimi Hendrix was staying at a West End hotel prior to his appearance at the Isle of Wight Festival and his forthcoming European tour. Black clad, Jimi sprawled incongruously amidst the penthouse splendor . . . wild thing Hendrix and all that tasteless luxury (". . . not even kitsch," said Rob Partridge, doing the stint for *Record Mirror*). Jimi poured out chilled white wine to the string of reporters and photogs who kept trooping in, and occasionally used the hotel telephone to order various bits of food to munch while he answered questions, talked, laughed and gestured.

"I'm so very nervous about the Isle of Wight. You know, so nervous. I can't believe it. I really hate waiting around like this and that's what makes me so nervous. I think it would be better if I'd gone to the Isle of Wight and mingled . . . took a sleeping bag with me and mixed with the crowds, to identify with it all. It would be so much better than all this, but there are the usual problems. If

I do things like that the people keep coming up to me saying 'Look it's him' and 'C'mon, c'mon' and all that, prodding me.

"I dug the Woodstock Festival—especially Sly, and Richie Havens. And the guy from Ten Years After, yeah, I was just a little bit jealous when I saw him play. Have you heard the record? I don't know why they used those tracks of mine, I really don't."

Jimi was relaxed enough to treat the interviews as a floor show and he seemed particularly happy to be back in England.

"We'd been touring a lot in the States and we didn't think there would be the demand for us here after so long away. I wanted to come back, but the people said, well, you're playing in Boston on so and so day, and all that. So . . . there it was, but here we are now. I'd like to get an English tour going soon."

I told Jimi that I'd read in "Cashbox" about his own recording studio, "Electric Ladyland [*sic*]."

"Yeah, yeah, and this is a different kind of studio. Chuck Berry and Sly have been down there doing a few things. It's a very relaxing studio, and it doesn't have that typical studio atmosphere. There are lots of cushions and pillows, thick carpets, and soft lights. You can have any kind of light combination you like . . . just what you feel like. I think this is very important. There are many capable engineers around now, the problem is this atmosphere thing. And we have the best equipment too . . .

"I was saying earlier about the light and sound thing. I'm into this combination or music and color—it's an extra area of awareness. I'm thinking about a film using those techniques."

Jimi has some tentative recording plans, which include an album sometime in October, and a double album following that. The double album, he says, will be mainly instrumental.

The 'super-star' aura that has always surrounded Jimi isn't at all apparent in an interview, or a conversation. How much of it is hype? How much is it a part that Jimi plays?

"I wouldn't know how to play that part. But I get a lot of people trying to make me play it. I'm here to communicate, that's my reason for being around, it's what it's all about. I want to turn people on and let them know what's happening. Even if they have nine to five jobs and come back to the family and TV, that's what counts, to keep turned on."

Isn't it a responsibility to communicate—especially at such an open-minded level?

"Yeah, sure, but I keep doing fresh things. Kids listen with open minds but I don't want to give them the same things all the time. Different things visually, different songs."

Where do those songs come from?

"Oh, they come from anywhere. I spend a lot of time daydreaming, they come from there. And from the people, all around. From the traffic too. They all give me ideas for songs, everything out there.

"But I really want to play England again. Do about eight cities or so. I'd like to go to Stonehenge, for the vibes. They're cooler heads in England compared to America.

"Sometimes I feel we should do a free concert. I see the prices that the kids pay to see us, and it's just ridiculous . . . I have a bad habit of talking too much."

How does Jimi feel about the pirate tapes and records that are circulating?

"I haven't had many records out for a while. Those pirate tapes, you know, some cat went to a private practice session with a tiny tape recorder and made a pirate LP. The quality must be terrible. There are pirate tapes of the Woodstock thing around too. The only reason we put out 'Band of [Gypsys]' was that Capitol was pressing us for an LP—we didn't have anything ready at the time. So they got that."

Jimi will be backed by Billy Cox (an old friend of his from the USAF [sic]) and Mitch Mitchell on the European tour. And if he comes to doing an English tour, that's probably what we'll see.

How did he see himself with regard to working with a group in the future?

"Well, when it was the Experience there was more room for ego-tripping. You know? All I had to blast off stage were a drummer and the bass! But now I want to be able to step back and let other things come forward. This is the idea of my getting a band together . . . a big band to develop the new ideas. I don't know what my music will be like, I don't know if I'm playing differently now.

"No, I haven't been playing with the old Experience, certainly no official gigs or anything anyway. There might have been some jamming somewhere. Mitch will be playing with me—he's never been better than he is now. And Noel, when I first picked them for the Experience, I picked Noel because he could play *anything* on that bass."

Jimi's head is full of ideas, some half-baked and some matured. He may take some time getting them together, but it's likely that the outcome will be no less spectacular than the experience he's delivered to us over the past three years.

INTERVIEW WITH JIMI HENDRIX

KLAS BURLING | From a Swedish radio broadcast heard on September 4, 1970.

The next gig was on the tour at the Stora Scenen in Stockholm's Tivoli Gardens. On August 31, Hendrix and his entourage arrived in Stockholm. Still exhausted from the Isle of Wight, he often slurred his words during this interview. The following are excerpts from the Swedish radio broadcast.

Klas Burling: [What's] your point of view on the Isle Wight Festival where you played a few nights ago?

Jimi Hendrix: The people were really groovy, the people were very groovy. But I really hate to play at night. You know what I mean? You can't see them, especially outside . . .

KB: Tell us more Jimi, because we have not seen you for very long.

JH: Well, listen . . .

KB: What have you been doing really?

JH: I've been doing like Yogi Bear, I've been hi-ben-natin' . . . hibernating.

KB: Which means?

JH: They surprise me that they . . . you know, wanted us, they wanted us back here, you know?

KB: Why?

JH: 'Cause there's, 'cause we received a lot of static . . . in New York, a lot of aggravation in New York.

KB: Jimi, your music today, has it changed in Europe?

JH: Well most of like, most of the time we play like a . . . a whole vacuous, I mean a wall of sound, a wall of feeling, that's what we try to get across. You know what I mean? *Wh-sheoo!* We haven't been to sleep in two days, you know.

KB: But, Jimi, during all this time when you have not appeared in Europe, what have you been doing in the States?

JH: We've been working very hard on other projects too, you know.

KB: Tell us a bit about it please?

JH: Well . . . I've been doin' a lot of writing, and Billy Cox our bass player's been doin' a lot of songwriting.

KB: You've written songs along with him as well?

JH: Well, you know. We're startin' to do that now, we're startin' to really make good contact with each other, because we realize how important a friend is in this world . . .

"MR. HENDRIX IN A GOOD MOOD"

TOMMY RANDER | From GOTEBORGS-TIDNINGEN, September 2, 1970.

On September 1, Hendrix flew to Gothenburg, Sweden, for a show at Stora Scenen in Liseburg, with Cat Mother & the All-Night Newsboys as the supporting act. In addition to the interview, Rander commented on the concert.

"We present to you Jimi Hendrix, Billy Cox on drums and Motoh Miller on bass," the speaker at Liseberg said to the somewhat confused audience. He meant Cox on bass and Mitchell on drums. Thirty minutes later the new Experience started to play and it sounded a bit stiff in the beginning. The bass and drums wouldn't work together and Hendrix seemed to think it was cold, and it was. After a couple of opening songs, things began to work well, very well. Jimi Hendrix played in a way he hadn't done for years and he seemed to like it here. He got the audience on his side; of course "Hey Joe" and "Foxey Lady" made all 5,000 feel at ease . . .

Tommy Rander: Have you had any problems with hotels this time? (The last time he was in town he smashed up a hotel room at Opalen and wasn't allowed to leave the city for a couple of weeks until things were sorted out.)

Jimi Hendrix: No, everything is okay. But I must say that I haven't had such a nice time as when I walked around waiting for the trial in Goteborg [in 1968]. I met this girl and . . .

TR: Are you involved in politics? You donated fifty thousand [*sic*] dollars to the Martin Luther King foundation . . .

JH: No, but they needed the money. In the U.S. you have to decide which side you're on. You are either a rebel or like Frank Sinatra.

The reason Jimi stopped touring in 1968 was that he suffered from "psychic exhaustion," as he put it.

JH: I was tired and worn out, but now everything feels much better. The current band with Cox on bass and Mitchell on drums will probably stick together. If we don't have an airplane accident or something like that, we'll stick together for a while, but everyone is free to do whatever he wants, of course.

"I AM TIRED OF LYING DOWN"

JØRN ROSSING JENSEN | Originally titled "Jeg er træt af at ligge ned." From the AARHUUS STIFTS-TIDENDE, September 2, 1970.

On September 2, the tour continued to Århus, Denmark, for a show at the Vejlby-Risskov Hallen. In a preconcert interview, Hendrix talked about writing a book, his own brand of religion, and image.

Jimi Hendrix (in Århus this evening) feels mentally hollowed; he prefers reaction to revolution and is on his way towards a universal religion.

Maybe Vulgar—but Not Obscene

Wasn't it the Pentecostal movement, which stood there with its heavenly message in the little portico at the Big Stage at Liseberg? And while the light streamed from the angels' flame-thrower and the 32 salivated began singing, "Find your God," came Jimi Hendrix—the electric religion.

They sang for him. They wanted to greet him as a preacher, a prophet who will show us the right way to the gospel of beat music.

Jimi Hendrix, 25 [sic] years old. Half Negro, half Mexican [sic]—an outcast. But when he works himself into his sizzling elegies, he is called the best beat guitarist in the world.

What does he want?

—*I want to play my guitar, all the other things, I'll write in a book. When will it be published? Some time after my death.*

297

Feel for It

Last Sunday Jimi Hendrix and [*sic*] Experience (Mitch Mitchell and Billy Cox) played at the festival of Isle of Wight. Last Monday in Stockholm, Tuesday in Gothenburg. Tonight they will be on stage in Vejlby-Risskov Hallen. For the first time in a long time, Jimi Hendrix is on tour and it continues.

—I am tired of lying down and I feel mentally hollowed. Under all circumstances it can become different, even if the tour is lonely.

Did the Stockholm critics find the show boring?

—They must be the only ones. The audience was good, we noticed reactions. If something is going to work, you have to feel for it. And we did.

No Politics

Jimi Hendrix does not always show that he is politically involved—but still he sent a big check to the Martin Luther King Memorial Fund.

—They needed the money.

Maybe there were others who needed it too?

—Tell me, do you want me to give it to the Ku Klux Klan?

T-H-I-S

The Rolling Stones want revolution, they sing about uprising in the street, now it is time to change a sick society. But is Jimi Hendrix on the front line?

—No I am not. At one point you have to choose: Revolution or Frank Sinatra. For me it was Frank Sinatra—and the reaction. I want to urge people to a lot of things, t-h-i-s (and then Jimi Hendrix takes his guitar and plays back and forth for a couple of minutes). *I want to turn people on.*

—Yes, I have said that I am electric religion—because it is all about religion, not Christianity. It was the Christians who started most of the wars in this world. I see in front of me a universal religion, containing all beliefs, containing the essence of them all.

In that religion the children can grow up and feel free, they will not be programmed, like they are today. And they can go to college even as ten-year-olds.

The Place Found

I have been looking for a place, far away from this mechanical world, where cities and hotel rooms run into each other. I have found it, inside myself. Now I want to spread it.

My music needs love and understanding. Through music you get more religion than through anything else. Jimi Hendrix and [sic] Experience will play as long as they feel good—and when we do not feel that anymore, we will tell you three years ahead.

Not Obscene

—Is it true, that the Daughters of the American Revolution accused you of being obscene?

—*Me, obscene, I have forgotten. Should I be obscene?* (Looks at himself in a mirror.) *Maybe somewhat vulgar, but obscene* (again in the mirror). *You confuse me with Jim Morrison.*

—He is not a voodoo doctor, is he?

—*Bahhh, you can have an opinion about me, and I have heard many, but a witch doctor?—pushhh. There are no such things anymore.*

I do not feel like an outcast, as long as I am not treated as one. It has not happened today, but then I have been sleeping all the time.

They Stand There

Jimi Hendrix and [sic] Experience are due onstage. The entrance fee to Liseberg amusement park is raised from 1 Swedish crown to 19 Swedish crowns.

—*I hope you got what you wanted,* he says.

—Yes, I hope you will too.

—*I will—after the tour.*

—Groupies?

—*Hah. It is only people who are jealous who call them groupies. To me they are nice girls. And they will be there for sure.*

At the concert tonight, Cat Mother, an American rock group, which has not been to Europe before, will play first. Jimi and Cat Mother continue the tour to Berlin.

"JIMI HENDRIX: I AM NOT SURE I WILL LIVE TO BE 28 YEARS OLD"

ANNE BJØRNDAL | Originally titled, "Jimi Hendrix: Jeg er ikke sikker på, jeg bliver 28 år." From MOR-GENPOSTEN, September 6, 1970.

After performing only three songs at Vejlby-Risskov Hallen, Hendrix left the stage. The music was disjointed and lacked continuity. It was announced that Hendrix was exhausted, and the remainder of the show was canceled. The incident added further drama to the tour, as the night before Billy Cox had a bad reaction to LSD that lingered for days. After being interviewed by Anne Bjørndal for this article, Hendrix faked a marriage proposal to model Kirsten Nefer for a tabloid that ran with the headline WORLD STAR GETS ENGAGED TO DANISH MODEL.

Unfortunately the concert in Århus, with one of possibly the greatest rock guitarists, did not turn out as we had expected. Jimi Hendrix was exhausted physically and mentally due to a far too tight touring schedule. This caused him to give up, having struggled his way through two songs[1] [sic], and unable to complete the concert. It was a shame—for both him and us, because we know he can do it, but the day before yesterday it did not work out. Still it must be said that the two tunes, he did play, "Freedom" and "Message of Love" from the album *Band of Gypsys*, really made us appreciate the unique sound that characterized his music. The music was there, warm and vibrant and everything else ceased to exist.

"Welcome to the electric circus," Jimi Hendrix opened by saying, but it was to be short-lived. Still there was time to enjoy both Jimi's eminent guitar playing, Billy Cox's wonderful bass, as well as Mitch Mitchell's powerful percussion.

Since the concert ended so abruptly, Jimi Hendrix said he'd return soon for a free performance that everyone would enjoy.

Talkative

It was clear that Jimi Hendrix was tired. Before the concert he talked about canceling because it simply wasn't fair to the audience. Before the concert he even talked about how beautiful the Århus harbor was. He exclaimed: "Oh the harbor! This is the drag about being on tour constantly, we never get a chance to see the places we play, but it's all part of the machinery. I prefer to play in Europe, because here people listen and understand what it's all about, where as they freak out in the States. I don't like playing at night because I can't see the audience. This is the best part of big open-air festivals, it's daylight, and you can see the faces of the audience."

Religion Is the Thing

Jimi Hendrix talks a lot about supernatural phenomenona, and brings up Jesus and Genghis Khan: "In reality Jesus started off a lot of wars, not himself but the people who supported his cause. That is why Christianity's something of the past. Religion is the thing and it has to be found within yourself, you have to live with peace of mind. Most human beings are born for love and peace, but it's only their obligations in our society that make them dress gray and black."

"Why is it that I keep hearing Mick Jagger's name?" Jimi Hendrix asks. "We are into different things, but I suppose we have got certain things in common. I'd like to get involved in starting a record company with the Rolling Stones, which they've talked about. Music is my life. It's about life and feelings, and you must take time for it like in any other occupation. In my case, I sacrifice a part of my soul every time I play. There are also certain moments when I feel I've got to write, especially before I go off to sleep, when all the thoughts run through my brain. My guitar is my medium and I want everybody to get into it. I want to turn the world on. Music and sound waves are cosmic when they vibrate from one side to the other.

"I am not sure I will live to be 28 years old (he is 25 [*sic*] years old now). I mean, the moment I feel I have got nothing more to give musically, I will not be around on this planet anymore, unless I have a wife and children, otherwise I have got nothing to live for."

Not LSD

While he continues to talk about mystical things, he says that he doesn't like LSD, "because it is naked. I need oxygen," he says and takes a deep breath.

Hendrix talks about his close friend Arthur Lee, the leader of the group Love: "I'm very fond of him. We are like brothers. We could start a new human race with our music. I would very much like to do more things with him. We have just recorded an album together. We think and feel the same way, so it would be wonderful if we could work out something together. We're a kind of spiritual Gypsies traveling around getting our message out through our music.

"I love reading fairy tales, H. C. Andersen and Winnie the Pooh. Fairy tales are full of fantasy and like music they appeal to your sense of imagination. I never play a song the same way twice. I cannot play something that I do not feel for and that I can't put my soul into."

Witch Doctor

Concerning his plans for the future, Jimi Hendrix says he intends to keep this band at least till the tour is over. With this lineup they have recorded about 150 tracks [*sic*], 15 out of which they will be able to use on their next album.

As for the bootleg album, which was supposedly recorded after the Woodstock festival, Jimi says he doesn't care.

"People have many weird ideas about me," he continues, "the ones that label me don't know me, or only know one part. Like I said before, I hate labels and the one with witchdoctor on it doesn't stick."

Immediately prior to the concert, Jimi Hendrix said: "I am the bus driver and you are my passengers."

As a matter of fact this remark summarizes all of his music—he is the captain of the spaceship, and he wants to take us the listeners along his space trip, out to where the sound waves are allowed to tickle you.

On stage he radiates electric energy, in private he is quiet and reflective . . . like a wolf in sheep's clothing, such is the nature of Jimi Hendrix.

---

1. The JHE began a third song, "Hey Baby (New Rising Sun)," but never finished it.

"JIMI HENDRIX: I AM A MAN LIKE MANY OTHERS, E.G., NAPOLEON"

SVEN WEZELENBURG | Originally titled "Jimi Hendrix: Jeg er en mand som mange andre, f.eks. Napoleon." From BERLINGSKE TIDENDE, September 3, 1970.

Another Århus reporter captured more peculiar statements from Hendrix on September 2, 1970.

Guitarist Jimi Hendrix will keep his present band till the end of the year, and plans not to give more than 20 concerts a year. He has recorded 150 tracks, but thinks that only 15 can be used for his next LP, which is not expected on the market at the moment. In the meantime he has released an LP with Otis Redding and Neil Young [sic], recorded at the Monterey festival in 1967. This should be very interesting.

—When I heard it, I noticed that I play "feelings" not music, says Jimi Hendrix. *I prefer to give concerts in Europe, where people listen to the music and not just sit and freak out. But I always play the best I can.*

Endless Sentences

Hendrix talks a lot about his music. About mystical, supernatural things. About euphoric drugs. About the audience. About peace. About war.

About his musicians: —*We feel good together. Mitch Mitchell is an artist on his drums.* Hendrix though calls himself an idiot because he signed a long-term contract with Capitol Records. This explains why he released the LP *Band of Gypsys.*

Otherwise he talks very hazy.

From his endless sentences can be cited:

—*I would die yesterday or tomorrow. We all go this way.*

—*We all come from somewhere, whether white, black or Indian.*

—*I don't get any pleasure from cocaine.*

—*You have to give up the word "religion."*

—*We all have a God in ourselves.*

—*I hate to perform outdoors at night, because I can't see the audience.*

—*LSD is naked.*

—*I am just a man like everybody else, Alexander the Great or Napoleon.*

"PLOP! FAREWELL JIMI!"

HASSE BOE | Originally titled, "Plop! Farvel Jimi!" From the DEMOKRATEN, September 3, 1970.

Copenhagen fans were warned about the disastrous and aborted concert in Århus, Denmark. Hendrix was asked for an explanation when he arrived in Copenhagen on September 3.

"I am so tired and have not slept for three days," said the world's best guitarist, Jimi Hendrix, before his concert in Vejlby-Risskov Hallen yesterday night. That is why he should have cancelled his performance, which only lasted eight minutes [*sic*]. [Four thousand] people who had paid more than 150,000 crowns in tickets sales can get their money back today.

INTERVIEW WITH JIMI HENDRIX

CHRIS ROMBERG AND SERGEANT KEITH ROBERTS | From a broadcast heard on Armed Forces Radio Network in Germany in late September 1970.

After Copenhagen, Hendrix's group flew to Berlin on September 4 for the Super Concert 70 at the Deutschlandhalle. Chris Romberg for British Forces Broadcasting Service TV and Sergeant Keith Roberts of American Forces Network interviewed Hendrix in his dressing room prior to the performance.

Chris Romberg: How about an introduction?

Jimi Hendrix: An introduction?

CR: Yeah . . . that will be nice.

JH: All right. [*Hendrix sings and the whole room laughs.*]

CR: That's not the right kind of introduction. We have to be serious. We're backstage at the Deutschlandhalle, speaking with guitarist Jimi Hendrix, and Jimi, I'd like to know, first of all, what you thought of your appearance in the film *Woodstock*, especially the scene at the end with the national anthem?

JH: I guess they could have showed other songs, probably. They came on at a little shot at the end of it. I wish they could have caught more of the musical side of it, really, you know.

CR: Did they try to make a political issue out it?

JH: Well, I really don't know. I don't know. Not really. [*Laughs.*] It's the way it is.

CR: What about festivals, like Woodstock? Do you think there will be another gathering of people that large that'll have the same kind of vibes?

JH: Well, I don't know, because it's pretty hard for the sound to get to all those people, in such a big crowd. Like, if they had smaller crowds, we really could get next to them more. It's just too big, you know.

CR: Now how do you feel about playing before, say, four hundred thousand people?

JH: Well, that's what I mean—it's just too big, you know? You know you're not gettin' through to them, all of them. And the idea to play to them is to try to turn them on or something.

CR: Do you think that large music festivals are actually just an extension of the commercialism angle? Is it too commercial?

JH: Oh, I don't think we'll play too many more of those, anyway, so there's really not too much to talk about really. It's just too much, there's just too many things going on, and not enough love or concentration on one certain thing.

CR: Prophetic words perhaps, because the last gig that Jimi Hendrix played was the night after [*sic*] he did this concert in Berlin, on the Isle of Fehmarn. It was another one of the large festival gatherings. It would be very hard to characterize Jimi Hendrix in words. You had to meet him. You had to talk to him. You just had to watch him. The night that he played the concert here in Berlin, he seemed very tired. I wouldn't say that he was strung out, but he just seemed tired and sort of uninterested. Let's go on with the interview; this is Chris Romberg of BFBS.

[Following is a backstage interview conducted by Sergeant Keith Roberts.]

Keith Roberts: Jimi, you've just come from the Isle of Wight, which is another of these large festivals. Did you enjoy that?

JH: Well, you know, I enjoy playing anywhere. But, like it was dark, you know, we was playin' at nighttime. I couldn't see [*laughs*] everybody. You know, if I could see the people instead of just lines of bonfires up there . . . That's the only way I could tell that those were hills back up there. [*Laughs.*] Oh well, that's all right. [*Laughs.*]

KR: Do you prefer playing at a concert like this one where the accent is more, is coming to listen to music, rather than gathering in a folk festival?

JH: Yeah, I guess so, you know.

KR: Do you think you're more appreciated here?

JH: Oh, I don't know. It's pretty hard to say. Sometimes it's easier playing in different places, at different times. Germany in the summertime is beautiful, you know.

KR: Do you enjoy playing in Germany?

JH: Yeah . . . yeah.

KR: Do you think German audiences differ from English audiences?

JH: I don't know. It' s pretty hard to say. We haven't played in England in a long time. We have to go out there and play again, and see. It's pretty hard to say.

KR: Is there really anyone in pop music say, or rock music that when you hear their stuff you go, "Wow! They really knocked me out"?

JH: Yeah.

KR: Who?

JH: Sly. [*Laughs.*]

KR: Sly Stone?

JH: Yeah, 'cause I like his beat, you know, I like his pulse, you know—"Music Lover," and "Dance to the Music," all those type of things. And Richie Havens, which is out of sight.

CR: And remembering past performances I've seen by Jimi Hendrix, I had seen him in concert three times. This time was the first in about a year and a half, and he had changed his style quite a bit. I think it probably had something to do with the Band of Gypsys album earlier this year, but he was much more melodic than he was in the past, in the past he was fire and brimstone and that sort of thing, and now his style had changed slightly. He had become more tuneful, more into being his creative guitarist. In other words, he was creative before, but now he was becoming creative in a different vein.

Later on in this interview you'll hear a question about the Monterey Pop Festival. That was the first time that I had been exposed to Jimi Hendrix, and that was probably his big national breakout, both in the States and around the world. At that time his act consisted of wild, you know, just dancing around the stage playing his guitar behind his neck and all the things that you've heard about Jimi Hendrix in his early days. At the end of the performance, he set his ax on fire and then he set his hair on fire [*sic*]. It was really something. The people were just really into Jimi Hendrix.

The night of the Deutschlandhalle, he was much more subdued, much quieter, and as we said, much more into the melody. His drummer Mitch Mitchell had slowed down quite bit too, but Bill Cox provided his much funkier bass line than Noel Redding was ever capable of. As Jimi says later on in the interview, Noel was more into playing melodies than he was into being a funky bass player. So let's go on with this unedited interview, again conducted the night of September fourth at the Super Concert in Berlin.

KR: I was wondering about the Experience that's appearing in Berlin tonight. There's only one man difference from the original Jimi Hendrix Experience, and that being your new bass player Bill Cox.

JH: Uh-uh.

KR: I was wondering how, eh . . .

JH: [*Interrupting*] We have a new road manager too, don't forget.

KR: Oh.

JH: Jimmy McFadden, besides Gerry [Stickells], and Eric Barrett.

KR: Well, we can't forget to plug . . . [*laughter*]

JH: [*Interrupting*] Well you can't forget it, because, like, those are the ones that keep it together, right?

KR: Yeah.

JH: Everybody forgets about that side of it, really.

KR: That's true. That's something I'd like to find out. . . . Behind the scenes people normally do a lot more than you or . . .

JH: It's like that beautiful airplane and everybody always forgets about the pilot sometimes, you know. Whatever kinda way you want to look at it.

KR: I was wondering about the, the group itself, however, and . . .

JH: Hmmm.

KR: . . . and the reason that the original Experience broke up, with Noel Redding and Mitch Mitchell, and now that you're back together with your old drummer Mitch, how Bill Cox came to you?

JH: Yeah, well, like, you know, him and I, we used to play together before, and, uh, like, we're doing like a lot of bass unison, bass and guitar unison things, which is nothing but a lot of rhythms. It's like, what do you call it? Patterns, like. Noel, he has his own thing. He has his own group. He's more of an individual himself, I guess . . . I wanted the bottom to be just a little solid. Noel's more of a melodic player, and Billy plays more of a solider space.

KR: Do you think that the Monterey festival, back in sixty-seven, was the original starting point for what we could say is now the fame of Jimi Hendrix?

JH: Oh, for our group, yeah, yeah, right.

KR: And as far as that Monterey festival goes, I was there and, I thought there were a lot of fantastic performances. Will there ever be anything in pop music like Monterey again?

JH: I'm not sure. I really don't know about pop music. No telling. It would be nice if it was, especially the next wave around though, the next time around. Oh well, that's too much [*laughs*].

KR: How do you feel when you're on tour? How do you feel at the moment?

JH: Right now you mean?

KR: Yeah.

JH: I'm just worried a little bit now, 'cause I sound a tiny bit like a frog. [*Laughs.*] You know, because of last night we was playing so loud. I was shouting on my tiptoes. It felt like my kneecaps were up in my chest.

KR: [*Laughs.*]

JH: Right now I just feel kind off nervous, but I think it'll be all right though. 'Cause now we're gonna go on and do our little gig, like, Mitch will be playin' drums and Billy's playing bass, and [*in a silly voice*] I'll be playing guitar . . . instead of up there screaming, you know.

KR: Do you get very worn out?

JH: Yeah, but certain things recharge me in an instant. I get worn out in an instant too. It all depends.

KR: Like interviews, maybe?

JH: Well, sometimes they're fun, you know.

KR: Yeah, okay. Sometimes they're fun to do too.

JH: Yeah, I wish you'd caught me at a more un-nervous time, because, like, right now we have to go on soon, like it or not.

KR: Oh, we understand that. . . . Good night.

CR: At this point, I think some personal business should come up perhaps in this interview. I've never been on film, and I've never been on television before, I've done strictly radio and had a very short career at that, and as we've said before, this interview was being filmed. Hendrix was nervous about being on film, I was rather nervous, in fact everybody that was in front of the camera was, and after we had wrapped what we thought was the end off the interview, there was some rather nervous goodnights exchanged.

Now, at this point we thought that the interview was concluded and the film crew started to shut down their camera, but just at that point the man from American Forces Television here in Berlin, Sergeant Keith Roberts, decided he was going to ask Hendrix what he thought of Mungo Jerry and their hit "In the Summertime." I already had my tape machine shut off, but I turned it on in time to catch the rest of these comments and this reaction from Hendrix and the crew that was in the room. [*Loud laughter is heard.*]

KR: Why does that name always spark laughter? When everyone hears Mungo Jerry . . . people bust up laughing.

JH: I think that's a happy song.

KR: It is; it's great song.

JH: It's goin' like this—[*sings*] "Well, in the summertime . . ." He said, "You got women, you got women on your mind." [*Laughs.*]

KR: What's your opinion of the song, and the group, of what you know of them?

JH: Oh, I think it's a beautiful summertime song [*laughs*] . . .

KR: Do you think they're gonna have a future in that group, with that group?

JH: Well, I don't know about the group, but the song is cute, nice and happy, and it's nice and light . . . and that kid who lays it down. I didn't know *they* was a group. I thought they just got together to make that one record? But, best of luck to anybody who wants to get it together. [*In a silly voice*] Mungo Jerry.

KR: Thanks!

"THE LAST HENDRIX INTERVIEW"

KEITH ALTHAM | From RECORD MIRROR, October 3, 1970.

After the Copenhagen gig, the group traveled to the Isle of Fehmarn to play the Love and Peace Festival. Due to many complications, the JHE's performance was rescheduled for September 6, 1970. Billy Cox—still suffering from the effects of a bad LSD experience from a few days earlier—returned home, and a gig in Rotterdam on the thirteenth was canceled because Hendrix now had no bass player.

Hendrix went to London and stayed at the Cumberland Hotel where RECORD MIRROR's Keith Altham interviewed him in his hotel suite on Friday evening, September 11. This article was published on October 3, not long after Hendrix's death.

Jimi Hendrix is dead. I knew him. I liked him. I am sorry that he is dead. Now that the eulogies, the euphemisms and the epitaphs are over it may be possible to put his existence into some kind of perspective for that was the most difficult thing for those who did not know him.

My first visit to the United States was with Jimi and the Experience for the Monterey Festival nearly four years ago and that revealed quite clearly the enormous contradiction between the person and the image he projected as a performer. On stage he was the demon savage—the brilliant wild man of the guitar to whom many of his public attributed a decadence and profanity which they suspected was the man himself.

In reality he was quietly spoken, sensitive and nervous to the extent that he would emphasise the fact by constantly fluttering his fingers to his face and mouth in mock alarm.

He smoked, drank, ate and made love. Sometimes he smoked, drank and ate the wrong things and made love to the wrong people. A bit like you or me.

The major problem in separating Hendrix the person from the performer was that he worked often in fantasy—his lyrics were usually the stuff that dreams were made of—and lived the fast, uneasy reality of a rock and roll star.

In three years he traveled further, lived harder and saw more than you or I might in ten. Those who do not understand the pressures of this business will moralize. Those who do will sympathize.

That is not to say or infer that I believe what happened to Jimi was the inevitable result of the tempo of his life or that he himself saw his end as some kind of destiny.

On the three occasions I saw him during the week before his death he was enjoying life and planning for the future. No one will ever convince me that what happened was anything more than a tragic accident.

Jam

Following Billy Cox's split back to the States, Jimi turned up at Mike Nesmith's party at the Inn on the Park at my suggestion and Mike's invitation.

Jimi asked me there what I thought he should do about a new band and I replied that McCartney's advice to "Get back to where you once belonged" was never a bad idea for a revival. Jimi laughed and said that was what he was going to do.

A few evenings later he was at the Ronnie Scott Club and sat in with Eric Burdon's band War when he did an incredible jam on "Tobacco Road." That was the last public performance that Jimi ever played.

A day later and just four days before his death, I went to the Cumberland Hotel and did this interview with him.

There were three girlfriends in the room and we watched Kenny Everett's TV show[1] which Jimi thought one of the funniest he had ever seen. We drank Mateus Rose and Jimi made plans to dine out that night.

Hendrix's last concert, September 6, 1970, Isle of Fehmarn, Germany. MICHAEL OCHS ARCHIVES/STRINGER

I feel the interview is important because it shows Jimi's frame of mind shortly before the accident. He was not despondent or morose about the future and the tone of his replies was often frivolous and marked with peculiar, wry smiles and shakes of the head.

People said he was a changed man both in appearance and manner. Was it true?

"Everyone goes through changes," said Jimi. "I look around at new groups like Cactus and Mountain and they're into those same things with the hair and the clothes—wearing all the jewelry and strangling themselves. I got out of that because I felt I was being too loud, visually.

Freaky

"I got the feeling maybe too many people were coming to look and not enough to listen. My nature just changed as well and I went and hid for a while.

"I started cutting my hair and losing jewelry, ring by ring, until I had none left. The freaky thing was never a publicity hype—that was just the way I was then. If I felt like dressing up, I did. If I felt like smashing a guitar, I worked up some anger and smashed. The anger has dissipated and I don't feel the need to dress up so much now I see others doing it.

"Billy Cox has split so I don't know what to do next. Direction is the thing I'm finding it hardest to find at present and I'm still interested in the big band concept, but right now I feel like it's better to go back to that small unit again. Maybe the problem is trying to do too many things at the same time—composing, playing and singing, but I hate to be put in one corner. I don't like to be just a guitarist or just a tap dancer!"

Among other things, Jimi has been called the source of psychedelic music?

"That's something that I've heard said but it's difficult to accept," said Jimi. "I listen to some of the things I've written and think 'damn.' I wonder where my head was at when I wrote that.

"Most of my writing was a clash between fantasy and reality and I felt you had to use fantasy to illuminate some aspects of reality. Even the Bible does that. You have to give people something to dream on.

"The day is coming when to make an album will be a really mind-blasting experience because you are going to have audio-visual and sensory facets combined."

Wealthy

How does Jimi feel about his responsibility to his public and what things does he hope to turn them on to?

"I really don't want to get too heavy. I've this saying that when things get too heavy 'just call me helium, the lightest gas known to man!' I don't want to change the world. I'd just like to see some more color in the streets!

"There are basically two kinds of music—the blues is a reflection of life and then there is sunshine music which may not have so much to say lyrically but has more meaning musically. You don't have to keep screaming 'love' in order to convince people it's necessary."

Even in consideration of his enormous expense, Jimi must be a very wealthy man by now and I asked him if he felt wealthy enough?

"Not the way I'd like to live, like I want to get up in the morning and roll over in my bed into a swimming pool and swim to the breakfast table and then swim into the bathroom for a shave . . ."

"You don't want to live just comfortably—you want to live luxuriously?"

"Luxuriously? I was thinking of a tent over a mountain stream!"

---

1. *The Kenny Everett Explosion* aired on ITV in the United Kingdom. The series was a mixture of short sketches and pop music.

EPILOGUE

Despite Hendrix's wish to be remembered by just a jam session, a formal funeral service was held in his hometown of Seattle. Among those who attended were Al Aronowitz, Eric Barrett, the Reverend Harold Blackburn, Miles Davis, Alan Douglas, Freddie Mae Gautier, Dolores Hall, Eddie Hall, John Hammond Jr., Ayako June Hendrix, James Allen Hendrix, Janie Hendrix, Leon Hendrix, Nora Hendrix, Tom Hullet, Abe Jacobs, Michael Jeffery, Eddie Kramer, Buddy Miles, Steve Paul, Noel Redding, Gerry Stickells, Chuck Wein, Devon Wilson, and Johnny Winter. Later, an informal jam session took place at the Seattle Center Arena with Noel Redding, Mitch Mitchell, Buddy Miles, and Johnny Winter.

Hendrix's estate was estimated to be worth $500,000 at the time of his death in 1970. Because he left no will, his father was named the sole beneficiary. Two years later, Diana Carpenter, a sixteen-year-old runaway Hendrix met while living in New York in 1966, lost a court case to have her daughter Tamika, born in 1967, recognized as his heir. A Swedish court in 1975, however, did find that James Henrik Daniel Sundquist, born in 1969, was Hendrix's son. The case failed in American courts because a blood test could not be conducted to determine paternity.

Hendrix's final record—a double LP with the working title *First Rays of the New Rising Sun*—was never completed. Instead, several nearly finished tracks turned up on the LPs *Cry of Love* (1971) and the soundtrack to *Rainbow Bridge* (1971). In 1997, *First Rays of the New Rising Sun* was released on CD. The track selection was a compilation based on Hendrix's notes and the tracks that were nearest completion.

After Hendrix's death, Michael Jeffery had come under much criticism for the way he'd managed Hendrix's affairs. On March 5, 1973, Jeffery died in a midair plane collision on his way to Britain. Producer Alan Douglas took over production of posthumously released Hendrix recordings in 1974. In 1995, Hendrix's father formed Experience Hendrix, LLC, which currently handles production of all Hendrix releases.

In 1991, several attempts were made to have Scotland Yard reopen an investigation into Hendrix's death after one of his former girlfriends and others announced they had solved the mystery of his final hours with new evidence they had uncovered. However, in 1994, Scotland Yard said it had found no evidence to pursue the case any further.

In recent years, several authors have challenged the concept that Hendrix died of a drug overdose, contending that he was a victim of foul play. A former Hendrix roadie's account alleged that, in a drunken confession, Michael Jeffery admitted to hiring thugs to kill Hendrix because the musician wanted out of his contract and had other money disputes with Jeffery. Another theory proposes a government plot by the FBI's Counter Intelligence Program (COINTELPRO) to eliminate Hendrix because he was a strong supporter of the antiwar and civil rights movements. Fans remain divided and continue to debate the circumstances of his death on the Internet.

A Hendrix tribute concert was held in Seattle in September 1995. It featured Noel Redding, Mitch Mitchell, Buddy Miles, and Billy Cox, and it marked the last time all four band members played together. Redding continued to perform until his death in 2003, as did Mitchell and Miles, who both died in 2008. Billy Cox, the only surviving member of the Band of Gypsys and the Jimi Hendrix Experience, performs annually with a touring all-star Hendrix tribute band.

QUOTABLE HENDRIX

Personal Ambition

"To be a movie and caress the screen with my shining light." —*New Musical Express*, March 11, 1967

Money

"Money to me is like if you're lost in the woods, and you have to go use the restroom, right? There's no restroom for a hundred miles, but there are leaves, so what you do is just bend over and, you know, make sure you don't fall on your, you know, and then you just use the leaves. You have to use the leaves if you don't have no tissue or whatever it is. And that's exactly what money is for me—something I might have to use . . . I have no feel for money whatsoever except what things I need, things that I want."

—Said at the launch party and reception for Track Records at the Speakeasy club in London on March 16, 1967

Playing Loud

"They said play as loud as you like, and we were really grooving when this little fairy comes running in and yells, 'Stop! Stop! Stop!—the ceiling in the studio below is falling down.' And it was, too—plaster and all."

—*New Musical Express*, April 15, 1967

Not Dumb Anymore

"Ha-ha, I'm not just that dumb Jimi now—but Mr. Hendrix." —*Bravo*, June 26, 1967

Gimmicks

"Gimmicks, here we go again, gimmicks, man. I'm tired of people sayin' we rely on gimmicks. The world's nothin' but a big gimmick—wars, napalm bombs and all that, people get burned up on TV and it's nothin' but a big gimmick. Yes, we do."
—From the film *Hear My Music Talking*, 1967

"One time I was rolling around the stage and I fell off into the crowd. I tried to get back but the crowd was pressing in so I threw the guitar back. I didn't mean to break it, but when you throw a guitar it breaks." —*Newsweek*, October 9, 1967

Freedom

"It gets tiring doing the same thing, coming out and saying, 'Now we'll play that song,' and 'Now we'll play that one.' People take us strange ways, but I don't care how they take us. Man, we'll be moving. 'Cause man, in this life you gotta do what you want, you gotta let your mind and fancy flow, flow, flow free."
—*New York Times*, February 25, 1968

Our Music

"Our music is like that jar of candy over there. Everything's all mixed up. Regardless of what the scene might be—you don't put yourself in categories or else you find yourself really unhappy because then you might want to do something else. The best way to accept some of the things we do—if it's all that important—is to take every song for what it has to offer itself instead of trying to put it all in one big thing." —*East Village Other*, March 8, 1968

First Influence

"The first guitarist I was aware of was Muddy Waters. I heard one of his old records when I was a little boy and it scared me to death, because I heard all of those sounds. Wow, what is that all about? It was great." —*Rolling Stone*, March 9, 1968

Musical Background

"I was schooled by radio and records. My teachers were common sense and imagination." —*Die Welt*, January 15, 1969

Sounds

"Just dig the sounds, it's all freedom." —The spoken intro to "Red House" during the October 1968 sessions at TTG studios, Los Angeles, California

"My own thing is in my head. I hear sounds and if I don't get them together nobody else will." —*Melody Maker*, February 22, 1969

Relationships

"You can't hold on to relationships when living a wandering life like I do. But I'm an adventurer, traveling around the world looking for excitement and maybe I'll find a girl to settle down with . . . maybe some time . . . now I'm so tired of everything . . . I get completely wrecked by all these press conferences, all unnecessary disturbing things. I have no time for my music. Soon I'll go back to England and just think about myself and my music for a while; relax, hear my beard grow." —*Vi I Tonåren*, January 10, 1969

Live Performances

"I always enjoy playing, whether it's before ten people—or 10,000. And I don't even care if they boo, as long as it isn't out of key." —*Melody Maker*, March 1, 1969

No Funeral

"I tell you, when I die I'm not going to have a funeral, I'm going to have a jam session. And, knowing me, I'll probably get busted at my own funeral. I shall have them playing everything I did musically—everything I enjoyed doing most. The music will be played loud and it will be our music. I won't have any Beatles songs, but I'll have a few of Eddie Cochran's things and a whole lot of blues. Roland Kirk will be there and I'll try to get Miles Davis along if he feels like making it. For that, it's almost worth dying, just for the funeral." —*Melody Maker*, March 8, 1969

Death

"It's funny the way most people love the dead. Once you are dead you are made for life. You have to die before they think you are worth anything."

—*Melody Maker*, March 8, 1969

Musical Messenger

"A musician, if he's a messenger, is like a child who hasn't been handled too many times by man, hasn't had too many fingerprints across his brain. That's why music is so much heavier than anything you ever felt." —*Life*, October 3, 1969

Uncaged

"I don't know, sometimes everything makes me uptight once in a while. What I hate is this thing of society these days trying to put everything and everybody into little tight cellophane compartments. I hate to be in any type of compartment unless I choose it myself. The world is getting to be a drag. I ain't gonna be any cellophane socialite. They don't get me in any cellophane cage. Nobody cages me." —*Hit Parader*, November 1969

Future Plans

"I've come to the end of one musical circle. It's now time to go into another . . . I want to be part of a big new musical expansion. The circle's completed—and I'm starting back already. This is the end of the beginning—the start of something else." —*Disc*, September 12, 1970

Good-bye

"The story of life is quicker than the wink of an eye. The story of love is hello and goodbye. Until we meet again."

—A line from Hendrix's last poem, "The Story of Life," September 17, 1970

APPENDIX

INTERVIEW WITH ERIC BURDON

STEVEN ROBY | From STRAIGHT AHEAD, October/November 1995.

I had the pleasure of interviewing Eric Burdon in 1995 for my Hendrix fanzine, STRAIGHT AHEAD. Burdon crossed paths with Hendrix many times during his career, including early on, when Hendrix worked for Little Richard as his lead guitarist in 1965 (although that detail gets overlooked here).

    Not only does Burdon have the distinction of performing with Hendrix during his last public jam, but he was also the first person Monika Dannemann called when she couldn't revive Hendrix on September 18, 1970.

Steven Roby: Tell us about the first time you met Jimi.

Eric Burdon: The first time I met Jimi was when I was rehearsing my new band at a club called the Telephone Booth. He had come down to look for players to be in the Experience. Chas [Chandler] knew I was putting a new band together and that I was looking for a guitar player. Noel Redding had come to audition. I was giving him the "don't call us, we'll call you" routine, when I noticed Jimi standing in the back of the room. As Noel was leaving, Jimi grabbed a hold of him and asked, "Do you want to play bass?" We did get a chance to jam before they all left.

SR: When was the next time you saw him—at Monterey Pop?

EB: No. You've got to understand, we were running with the same crowd—basically sharing the same ladies, so I got to see quite a lot of him. We'd all end up at Zoot Money's pad after a night on the town. On one level we had a lot in common. We were connected to the same stable.

SR: What was the scene like at Monterey?

EB: It was a religious experience; a harmonic convergence of the hippie era. A time when it all came together, in a better way than I've ever seen since. Sure Woodstock was *the event*, and history looks at it as the peak, but Monterey was the crown jewel of concerts. Monterey was Jimi's return back to the States. In Jimi's head, it was his first hometown gig. He was at his best showmanship.

SR: It certainly shows in the film that was made.

EB: I remember going out to the front few rows near the press box where I had my seat. These kids next to me were asking, "Who's going to following the Who?" The pressure was mounting, and it was very exciting. As soon as I heard it was going to be Jimi, I rushed to my seat to see the show. These kids then asked, "Who is this Jimi Hendrix?" and I replied, "You'll find out." Partway through Jimi's set, I looked over and noticed their big smiling faces giving me the thumbs up. The brightest moment for me was watching JH paint his guitars for that night. It was by sheer luck that I went by the motel where he was staying. You see, they didn't have any phones in the rooms, just one in the motel lobby. I had rented a motorcycle and swung by there to check it out. In the courtyard I saw him out there with a bucket of paint, a paint brush, and two of his axes . . . the one he was going to sacrifice that night. I thought this is like some Navajo chief . . . burning sage . . . getting ready to commit himself to the forces. It wasn't until later that I discovered that there was a lot of Indian blood in Jimi's family. This whole scene I was witness to was an indication to me that there was much more to this man than I could fathom out in just one night.

SR: Both the Animals and the Jimi Hendrix Experience had the services of Michael Jeffery as a manager. Much has been written about him and some of his questionable doings. Can you share with us some of your insight on the man?

EB: This interview is about Jimi Hendrix. I've lived that story. It hurt me a lot, but it hurt Jimi much more. It hurt all of us a lot because he's not around to tell the tale. I'd rather talk about JH.

SR: OK, what about 1968? Did your paths cross or any tours coincide?

EB: Yeah, quite a lot . . . East coast . . . West coast in America. We did a festival in Switzerland together. That concert ended in a riot and subsequently set off ten years of riots. I remember this concert because it was one of the very rare occasions I got to trash his ass musically. We had a hot band. We were on a roll and very tight. Jimi had dropped his acid at the wrong time and was losing his peak. By the time he went on he lost it completely. That disturbed him, but I guess in his own head he got back at me. When I left the Zurich airport he was standing with my wife in his arms, and that was about the last time I ever saw her . . . [*laughs*] . . . and that was perfectly acceptable to me then . . . it didn't faze me at all . . . it was like, "OK, motherfucker, I'll see you further down the line."

SR: Of all the times you saw Jimi perform, when do you think he was at his best?

EB: I think he was in prime at the Hollywood Bowl concert. He came up to my house after that show. We hung out and listened to some new unmixed material. That was one of the periods [during which] I felt we had a friendship going. He could have been anywhere doing anything, he was the toast of the town, and yet there we were . . . sitting up on a hill . . . smoking joints, listening to music . . . feeling like we was on top of the world . . . which I guess we were.

SR: You were also on the same bill with Jimi at the 1969 Newport Pop Festival. There are some great photos and footage of you and everybody else that showed up to jam that day. What can you tell us about that concert?

EB: Jimi had done such a bad show on Friday that he came back and did a second one on Sunday.

SR: After Newport Pop, were there any instances when you saw each other prior to September 1970?

EB: He came to our office sometime after Chas pulled out of the picture. I think he was considering what to do about his life and the future. This was when I just started with the band War and Gold & Goldstein. We tried as a company to help him because we were tied in with him businesswise. The company we had just shot a movie of him at the Royal Albert Hall in 1969. This is where the pain for me comes in because my deal with Jerry Goldstein was, "You find us several acts to build a company, and that movie will be yours." I was in effect going to be given executive directorship of this movie. At that time everything was hunky dory, and I didn't see that anything could go wrong, but it was just beginning to sour! My previous managerial situation had now become Jimi's situation, and I tried to warn him that it was the Animals' money that was used to get him off the ground. I told him, "I got fucked, and you're going to get fucked the same way if you don't wake up." And of course he just laughed and was too busy conquering the world. I expected this reaction. I didn't think he'd listen to me, but I thought it was worthwhile to tell him. I also talked to Noel and Mitch about the same thing on Derring Howe's boat, and they just phased me out as well. This was the beginning of me starting to move into the position of a guy who was trying to ride on Jimi's coattails after he was deceased . . . carry the mantle and all this bullshit. In effect, you might say it was true because I had this fucking movie. It was the best bit of film that Jimi was ever in or associated with . . . thirty-five millimeter, and a crystal-clear performance. This was what caused the walkout. Gold & Goldstein told me, "Just do another year's tour with War and make enough money so we can stop, and then we'll turn over the negative to you and you can get on with it." I had Saul Bass. He was one of the biggest and best cinema photographers in the world. He's the best title designer in the world. He's done specialist work for Stanley Kubrick. I had him sold on the idea, and we were just about ready to do the deal, and then Jimi died. Six months later I walked into a record store and there was a [film] clip used on a[n LP] cover from my fucking movie! I went, "*What's this!*" I went over to Gold & Goldstein and the story unfolded that they never intended to turn it over to me in the first place and this was just another story of me allowing myself to get fucked. I went out of the office and never went back. I then got back with War.

SR: Jimi may have been the world's greatest guitar innovator, but probably not the best at dealing with big business situations.

EB: Jimi was just as bad as any of us for signing anything that was stuck under our nose, and then trying to play clever by saying, "I didn't know about that, man." I know Chas had a hell of a time trying to straighten out his affairs before taking him on. I think that when he and Chas parted ways, it was the end of the magic spell. Chas can be a complete bastard to people, and that's why he was a manager. Of course he was the right kind of bastard for Jimi because he wouldn't take any of his shit. So, their two egos broke down, and flowed together, and came up with the apex of Hendrix's career . . . the three wonderful albums.

I am sure that Jimi was more than capable of producing, but being a producer is a phantom position. A producer should be like a midwife. If you look at the recording adventure, to me it's like giving birth . . . creating a child. The artist is the mother, and the baby is the recording. The midwife is the producer to assist the musicians to be able to do what they need, and assist the creation to come to fruition. So, Chas was kind of like a heavy mother. A real dominant mother, but nevertheless a mother figure for Jimi. So he felt really safe, and he did his best work under that situation. I am not saying that he wasn't capable of producing, he was, but a lot of being a producer is making sure that this is booked, and those amps can be arranged, blah, blah, blah. A producer does a lot of the work a musician doesn't want to do. That's where these guys come in, and either enhance the product, or totally fuck it up. So, in Jimi's case, when the producer left, he was bungling around from one idea to the next. Since Jimi didn't write music, the body of his work had to be captured on magnetic tape.

SR: That's probably why so many different jams exist on tape.

EB: I never saw him without his guitar except towards the end of his career . . . in fact around the time when I first met him, and he wasn't with his guitar at this party in London, I knew he was going to have problems. Without his guitar he was lost and insecure. He just wanted to play—*all the time*—and you can't do that. I had the same problems when I was with the Animals and we first came to America. I wanted to jam with everybody . . . Fats Waller . . . that's why I became a musician. So there's a place in time and space, particularly in music, where talent and commercial value, in light of what's to be exploited, that they lock horns and become enemies of each other . . . because he just wanted to jam, jam, jam . . . keep the flow going. The agent/manager [or] attorney/producer's position is always,

"Don't jam, man, you'll give it all away. If they see you tonight, they won't come tomorrow night."

SR: In other words, save a little?

EB: Yeah, and of course by that time Jimi had burned so many axes, and made so many psychedelic sacrifices, that's what the audience's chant became: "Burn the guitar! Bum the guitar!" And at this time Jimi was trying to reach Miles Davis, and become the jazz icon that he should have been. In fact he would have created a new jazz that we all need, and a kind that's missing today.

SR: During the last week of Jimi's life he had the opportunity to come and jam with you and War at Ronnie Scott's club. This was Jimi's last public appearance and it took place on Wednesday, September 16th. What can you tell us about this jam?

EB: I hadn't seen Jimi for about a year, but I'd hear about him and keep tabs on him through people like Alvina Bridges in New York, and Eric Barrett, his road manager. Anyway, I came into London with War, and Eric Barrett came to see me. He said, "You've got to go and see Jimi because he hasn't been across the door for six months." This was during the period when he met Monika, and he was doing his own private thing away from the road. My reaction to Eric was, "Hey, I've tried to reach that guy on several occasions; if he's in that kind of a mood, ain't nobody can bring him out of it until he's ready to come out of it. I ain't going to him. If he wants to come talk to me, I'm playing at Ronnie Scott's club tonight." So, one night later he came down.

SR: That had to be on the Tuesday the 15th.

EB: He came in with a string of ladies on his arm, including my Mrs., who I hadn't seen in awhile . . . "Hey Angie, how ya doin' babe?" It was all cool, and nobody said anything. We were just glad that the guy had come out of hiding and across the door, out in public. On the night that he jammed with us, he came up and played on the last few tunes in the set. It was a jazz audience . . . the

London jazz brain intellectual circuit. It's not unknown for them to boo people off the stage, especially if they are rock and rollers. When we went in there with War, it was a very adventurous thing to do. We were the first rock band to ever play there. It was an experiment, and to have Jimi come join in, it was great! We were on cloud nine, but the audience gave him a hard time and booed him off. So he left and went backstage. I went to go have a talk with him. I told him, "Don't give up, you've come across the door this far, don't stop now dude, get out there and play, motherfucker!" He went back out and there was a problem with a fight for control of the band between Howard Scott, our guitar player, and Jimi. Howard forced Jimi to the background and Jimi was playing rhythm guitar during "Tobacco Road." The fire was building, and I heard Howard play solos like I never heard him play before. He really forced Howard to shine that night. Then he came back and did a rip-roaring performance in grand Jimi Hendrix style. Afterwards, Jimi said, "I'll see you around." And that was it. I never saw him again.

SR: A couple of days later you received a call from Monika Dannemann about Jimi.

EB: Yeah, what can I tell you? I felt he was in good hands. I didn't know her, but in my opinion he could take care of himself. I had seen him in dreadful states before. Back then we were human enough to not even think twice about it. When she first called me I told her to get him some coffee and walk him around, and if there's a problem call me back.

SR: Was that pretty early in the morning?

EB: It was still dark, but that's not unusual for London. It was pouring rain. She called me back so I assumed there was a problem, and I told her to get an ambulance. She argued about it, saying that there were incriminating things in the flat . . . that I guess she took care of. I spent the next few hours after I had been over to the apartment looking around London for Mike Jeffery because I wanted to kill him. I definitely had malice in my heart at that point. The press came after Monica so I took her up to my mother's place so she could hide from the English press. And that was it. The world stopped.

SR: I recall hearing you in a radio interview talk about when you went over to the flat, and you had noticed he had written the word "love" with his finger on the back window of a car.

EB: It was written in the humidity, the mist on the window . . . on an Opel, a copy of a Corvette. I figured it must have been him coming in late at night from a party. I also found this note by his bed, which is now included in that book, *The Lost Writings of Jimi Hendrix*.

SR: What was your reaction to that final poem written by Jimi?

EB: I still stand by what I felt that day, looking at the onsite evidence after the body had just been moved and the bed was still warm. There was still an indentation on the bed where he had been lying . . . it was that fresh. So I found this note by the side of the bed, read it, and thought it was a suicide note. I'm not saying that he set out that night to deliberately commit suicide, but he had the will to die. He might [have] said . . . "Fuck it, I can't deal with this shit anymore. I want to play and they won't let me." I've been there too in that same state of mind. You get really depressed and real suicidal . . . only an artist can explain that.

SR: When you arrived at the flat, had the ambulance already taken him away?

EB: Yeah . . . in reflection, Monica has shown me these instructions for her to do all these paintings. I've taken them to be for real because I've seen Jimi's notebooks and sketchbooks before. It looked like his directive and his hand, knowing his interest in numerology and color healing in the relevance to the human spirit . . . I mean for a twenty-seven-year-old guy who grew up a black kid in the ghetto . . . he was fuckin' intelligent. He was bright. He was enlightened! I did a bit of detective work, and if you're going to commit suicide, you don't take nine pills . . . you swallow the whole fuckin' bottle! I could be nuts, but I took that as a message, especially when I saw the message that was written by him.

SR: Do you mean the poem he wrote, "The Story of Life"?

EB: Yeah, the guy had tripped out on LSD, and I have been inside the same hallucination where I saw Jesus or Buddha together or separate—or the devil . . .

many times. . . . After thinking about it, I think that he was doing too much dope to be in the public-eye situation he was in, and to be surrounded by all the "yes people" he was around by the time Jeffery had taken control. Everybody was saying things like, "Yes, Jimi . . . Have this one Jimi. . . ." I think that he was living a hallucination that he was Jesus, and he was inside a passion play, and that, in a way, he manufactured his own crucifixion.

SR: That's interesting. I've never heard that theory before.

EB: Well, if you do enough acid you start to think that. It is an awesome drug and he did do an incredible amount. LSD figures into Jimi just as much as the Stratocaster does. It was just as important to rock-and-roll music. We try to play that down in these sober times, but anybody who tries to push that aside is full of shit. The whole movement was pushed by *Sgt. Peppers Lonely Hearts Club Band*, which came out of a bottle of Sandoz.

SR: That's true. That album was a heavy influence on a lot of people and the times.

EB: If you go to Catholic school, you never forget the bleeding hands and the bleeding feet . . . those images are with you forever.

SR: I know what you mean. I went through twelve years of that.

EB: When I've tripped out with Jews and black people, they would see the lighter side of things . . . there'd always be a laugh. If you tripped out with an Irish Catholic . . . it was like . . . *dun-da-dun-dun* [*mimics the theme to the TV cop show* Dragnet].

SR: A serious religious experience.

EB: Absolutely. I think that was the root of Jimi's problems. For me, to see that final note . . . it's about as good an interpretation of struggling for the Christ head [as] can be.

SR: It's a very deep poem with a hint of that "rising sun" theme he was working on.

EB: The next time I saw it, it was [copyrighted] and belonged to certain people. I think that in Jimi's head; when he went out he felt he wrapped things up nicely. I don't know any artist in the recording business, [who] is out there on the rock-and-roll circuit, doing gigs every night, [who] has an idea how much material there is in the can. I had no idea. I'm still haunted by bootlegs, things I forgot about, and demos that come out as finished recorded material . . . and that's happened to Jimi big-time. I think he may have left this world thinking, "Hmmm, I've left three great albums, I'll be remembered for that . . . I'm going for immortality."

SR: It is amazing that for such a short career he left behind so much in the can, and that twenty-five years after his death new recordings are still being discovered.

EB: Yeah, I just heard *Voodoo Soup* for the first time this morning, and it was really fucking painful to listen to. The way I look at . . . it's just a string of demos that should have never reached the record-buying public.

SR: No matter how hard they try to enhance and overdub them.

EB: The music that he left us is real, and you can only judge an artist by his work. It's just like the actor James Dean . . . three magic movies . . . it's a pity that the act can't be left that way. Even your magazine for instance—I think there's enough in Jimi as a complete artist, the way he saw himself, for us to keep loving and praising him for a lifetime.

SR: In closing, do you have any final thoughts on Jimi?

EB: Perhaps I should better define what I said earlier about the possibility of Jimi wanting to commit suicide. That was my initial feeling coupled with seeing "The Story of Life" poem sitting by the side of the bed. Later on I found out that Jimi was still alive when they took him away in the ambulance. As the years went by my confusion grew even though I wanted to hold on to my feelings that he was simply suicidal at the time. I felt that in addition to that last poem, a lot of his lyrics could even be interpreted in that manner. Take the lyrics to "I Don't Live Today" for example. I just wanted to make that point clear that for me there was a swing of one theory to the next, except I always held onto the theory that it was just a bad case of mismanagement, confusion, and loneliness that would lead somebody to want to slip away.

The other point I would like to address is about the Black Panther Party. When he arrived back in New York, they were always pulling on him to see things their way. I know that caused a lot of confusion in Jimi. Sure he wanted to stand up and be counted with the brothers, but I don't feel he had that degree of black pride to pick up a gun to want to change things, like the Panthers did. I think he probably had second thoughts about it. That led to a lot of confusion further on down the line [as] to where his heart was at.

CREDITS

I gratefully acknowledge everyone who gave permission for material to appear in this book. I have made every reasonable effort to contact copyright holders. If an error or omission has been made, please bring it to the attention of the publisher.

"Jimi Hendrix Talks to Steve Barker (January 1967)," by Steve Barker. First published by the Jas Obrecht Music Archives (www.jasobrecht.com) from original interviews by Steve Barker BBC/www.otwradio.blogspot.com and *Wire* magazine /www.thewire.co.uk.

"Come to a Soul Revival with Jimi Hendrix, a Rebel from Mars via Cuba," by Keith Keller, reprinted by permission of *BT*.

"Spanish Galleons Off Jersey Coast or 'We Live Off Excess Volume,'" by Bill Kerby and David Thompson, reprinted by permission of the *Los Angeles Free Press* and www.lafpmusic.com.

"Jimi Hendrix Talks to Steve Barker (November 1967)," by Steve Barker. First published by the Jas Obrecht Music Archives (www.jasobrecht.com) from original interviews by Steve Barker BBC/www.otwradio.blogspot.com and *Wire* magazine /www.thewire.co.uk.

"An Experience with Hendrix," by Liam and Roisin McAuley, reprinted by permission of Liam and Roisin McAuley.

Interview with Jimi Hendrix, by Meatball Fulton, reprinted by permission of Meatball Fulton.

Interview with Jimi Hendrix, by Jay Ruby, reprinted by permission of Jay Ruby.

"The Persecution & Assignation of Rock and Roll, as Performed by the Jimi Hendrix Experience . . . Under the Direction of Jumping Jimi Himself, the Cassius Clay of Pop," by Michael Thomas, reprinted by permission of Hearst Communications, Inc.

"I Felt We Were Becoming the U.S. Dave Dee," by Alan Walsh, copyright © IPC + Syndication.

"Experience," by Don Speicher, reprinted by permission of the *Great Speckled Bird*, published by the Atlanta Cooperative News Project.

Interview with Jimi Hendrix and "Jimi Hendrix, Black Power, and Money," by Jacoba Atlas, reprinted by permission of Jacoba Atlas.

"A Jimi Hendrix Doubleheader" and "Hendrix," by Tony Glover, reprinted by permission of Tony Glover.

"Hendrix: As Experienced by Jane de Mendelssohn," by Jane de Mendelssohn, courtesy of www.international-times.org.uk.

"The Jimi Hendrix Experience: Slowing Down and Growing Up," by John Lombardi, copyright © 1999, Distant Drummer.

"The Gypsy Sun Jimi Hendrix," by Ritchie Yorke, reprinted by permission of Ritchie Yorke.

The Dick Cavett Show Interviews (July and September 1969), courtesy of *The Dick Cavett Show*.

The Tonight Show Interview by Flip Wilson, courtesy of Carson Entertainment Group.

"Jimi Hendrix: I Don't Want to Be a Clown Any More," by Sheila Weller, article provided by Rock's Backpages, www.rocksbackpages.com.

"Hendrix and His Band of Gipsies," by Bob Dawbarn, copyright © IPC + Syndication.

Interview with Jimi Hendrix, by Sue Cassidy Clark, from *The Superstars: In Their Own Words*, reprinted by permission of Sue Cassidy Clark and the Estate of Douglas Kent Hall.

"Spaceman Jimi Is Landing," by Alfred G. Aronowitz, courtesy of the *New York Post*.

"The End of a Big Long Fairy Tale," by John Burks, copyright © 2011, New Bay Media, LLC, 78385-1x:0611AS.

"Hendrix: I'd Like a Hit Single . . . ," by Keith Altham, copyright © IPC + Syndication.

"Hendrix—He's a Beautiful Person," by Gillian Saich, copyright © IPC + Syndication.

"Hendrix Today," by Roy Hollingworth, copyright © IPC + Syndication.

"Man, Myth or Magic? Jimi Hendrix Is Back, and Talking, and Happy," by Norman Jopling, article provided by Rock's Backpages, www.rocksbackpages.com.

Interview with Jimi Hendrix, by Chris Romberg and Sergeant Keith Roberts, courtesy of the Armed Forces Radio Network.

"The Last Hendrix Interview," by Keith Altham, reprinted by permission of Keith Altham.

INDEX

All song and album titles were played or written by Hendrix unless otherwise attributed. Page numbers in *italics* refer to photographs. References to notes are indicated by an italic *n*.